PRINCIPLES OF NATURAL LAW

FREDERICK VAN FLETEREN

Kendall Hunt
publishing company

Cover image © Shutterstock.com

Kendall Hunt
publishing company

www.kendallhunt.com
Send all inquiries to:
4050 Westmark Drive
Dubuque, IA 52004-1840

ISBN: 978-1-5249-2287-0

Published in the United States of America

Contents

B. SOCIAL ETHICS

Preface

Over the past fifty-five years, the nature and mission of Catholic universities in the United States have changed remarkably. The causes of this change are only partially evident. Partly the change has occurred as an aftermath to the Second World War. Money was easily available from the United States government in the form of grants or low-interest student loans to attend universities of one's choice. Money was made available to universities, and especially Catholic universities, to expand. At nearly the same time, the founding religious orders of these universities were in retreat. A lack of numbers no longer permitted these religious congregations to occupy a central role on campus as they once did: the Catholic university had outgrown its parent institution. Partly, the change has come in response to a certain understanding of the Second Vatican Council. To some extent, the Council was a Catholic response to the Enlightenment. An Enlightenment spirit began to affect the Catholic campus, much as the Enlightenment had affected Protestantism and Judaism in the nineteenth century. A secular *Zeitgeist,* at times even openly hostile to the mission of a Catholic university, appeared on Catholic campuses. Partly, expectations of Catholic universities changed. No longer was John Henry Cardinal Newman's *Idea of a University* the ideal of a Catholic university. University education became oriented to vocational training. Preparation for a profession or job was expected of a Catholic University by the Catholic populace.

As a result of these and many other factors, both known and unknown, the role of philosophy and theology departments at Catholic universities also changed. Rigorous philosophy and theology requirements did not fit into a curriculum, suited for technical training. No longer was *philosophia perennis* taught as a matter of course. No longer were Christian philosophy and Catholic theology perceived as being at the heart of the university's mission. No longer were opinions of philosopher and theologians on matters central to the university sought. The number of mandatory courses in philosophy and theology dropped precipitously because the matter of the courses was no longer thought to be central to the institution. Many times in fact it was not. In particular, ethics courses which once drew their subject matter from natural law—historically and to the present day the Catholic Church is the great defender of natural law—became readings in various philosophers and ethical systems, even sometimes at odds with Catholic teaching. The situation has reached such a point that today no good natural law ethics text in philosophy exists, at least to my knowledge. This book is a direct response to the present crisis.

During the better part of the last half of the twentieth century, perhaps the most influential Catholic ethicist was the late Rev. Charles McFadden, OSA (the Order of Saint Augustine). Many a preparatory school pupil, university student, or student nurse sat at his feet, either directly or indirectly. Ten years ago, my colleague, Joseph Schnaubelt, OSA and I decided to present a natural law ethics text in the spirit of MacFadden to a new generation. We are particularly qualified to present such a text: we had "sat at MacFadden's feet," were his university and monastic colleagues, and in my case had served as an adviser in presenting various texts.

We began the task of supplementing MacFadden's ethics. We consulted Austin Fagothey's *Right and Reason*; the moral theology manual of Joseph Noldin, the renowned Innsbruck theologian; the moral philosophy manual of Francis Hickey; writings of contemporary ethicists; and various other works. I have incorporated several personal texts, written over thirty years of experience in teaching natural law ethics to university students. The text here presented is surely in the spirit of Charles MacFadden, but in fact in no way represents a final text of his.

In contemporary America, a word need be said about gender-specific language. Natural law ethics finds its roots in ancient Greece and Rome. Latin speakers, following the Greeks, had two words *homo* and *uir* which have been traditionally translated into English by "man." Likewise, the German *Mensch* and *Man.* In each case, the former word signifies man as *homo sapiens,* the latter man as gender male. Feminist sentiments and the inadequacy of the English language present any contemporary writer with an intractable syntactical problem in English. Especially to the philosopher, no one English word can satisfy. English style must be maintained. This writer has solved this dilemma on an *ad hoc* basis. When "human being" or "person" could be used to designate man as *homo sapiens,* I have done so. But when these terms were either stylistically awkward or philosophically inaccurate, I have used the word English word "man."

A word of caution to the user: This text is meant to be used in conjunction with a reader presenting primary texts. Various such readers are available. No one of them is particularly satisfactory. Preparation of such a text awaits another time.

I would like to thank Joseph Schnaubelt, OSA and John Farrell, OSA for their advice in formulating the text. I would also like to thank my many students over the years for their advice in how to explain my ideas in a coherent fashion and for their encouragement in preparation of such a text. Finally, my thanks go to Gerhilt Terraneo who, by giving me the use of her apartment in the summers in Vienna, Austria, has facilitated the production of this text more than she can ever know. To many others who helped in one way or another, but whose effort goes unremembered and therefore unmentioned, I also express my gratitude.

Frederick Van Fleteren
LaSalle University

I

GENERAL ETHICS

CHAPTER 1

Ethics as Science

The nature of philosophy is itself a philosophical question. Traditionally, philosophy is a study of reality in its ultimate causes by reason alone. Such studies have traditionally been considered sciences. Obviously, considering philosophy as a science turns on the meaning of the word science. For the past few centuries, and especially since the late nineteenth, the meaning of science has narrowed somewhat from its traditional meaning. Science has come to mean experimental or empirical science. Any study following the method of observation, collection of data, hypothesis, experiment, and conclusion, or some variant of that method, has been termed a science. On the other hand, a study which does not follow such a method is not considered a science. Need we narrow the meaning of science in this manner? The ancient tradition takes a much broader view. According to Aristotle, science is "knowledge of things through their causes." Aristotle identified four causes as essential for understanding the ultimate nature of reality: Efficient cause, the producer; formal cause, what a thing is; material cause, the material out of which a thing is made; final cause, the purpose. Systematization is another aspect of science. It is an organized body of knowledge leading to certitude. Not all sciences issue in the same degree of certitude. According to these more ancient and broader traditions, philosophy is a science, that is, a rational enterprise. Philosophy is a science in the Aristotelian, though not in the experimental sense of the term.

Ethics or moral philosophy is a part of philosophy. According to Aristotle's definition, ethics is a science. In ethics, man studies causes of human action, especially final causes. Ethics is a rational enterprise, not a mere discussion of arbitrary subjective opinion. Traditionally, ethics and moral philosophy are interchangeable terms. Ethics stems from the Greek word *ethos*; morality from the Latin word *mos, moris,* both of which mean "habit," "custom," or "way of acting." Ethics is a study directing acts of the human will according to ultimate principles of reason. It is a practical normative science, studying the rightness or wrongness of human behavior by reason alone. In moral philosophy man endeavors to discover the ultimate reason for morality in human actions through human reason, unaided by divine revelation. Ethics is a systematized body of moral truths. It is a practical science, that is, its principles are studied in order to direct human behavior. A person should mold his life according to ethical ideals. In contrast, other sciences, except for logic, are speculative, not practical in nature. Speculative sciences are studied purely for the sake of knowledge. Sciences, such as physics, chemistry, or mathematics are for this reason speculative sciences. Knowledge so acquired need not influence human activity. Obviously, engineers, for example, apply mathematics to construct machines or other instruments. Physicians must know biology to heal human illness. Mathematics and biology can be applied. But the purpose of mathematics in itself is specifically the study of number. The purpose of biology is the study of the constitution of living things. Unlike these sciences, ethics is practical, not speculative.

Every science has general subject-matter which it treats, sometimes termed its material object, and a specific point of view from which it studies that subject-matter, sometimes termed its formal object. The material object of ethics is human behavior. History, psychology, sociology, anthropology, law, and moral theology are also interested in human behavior. All these studies have the same material object. However, each studies human behavior from a its own respective point of view. What distinguishes them from each other is the point of view from which each studies human activity. They have different formal objects. History studies chronological and causative relations between important human actions. Psychology studies human behavior largely from the point of motivation. Sociology studies human behavior from the point of view of man as part of a larger social unit. Anthropology studies human behavior from the point of view of its origins and development. All these sciences study the way man in fact acts, not the way he ought to act. They study the "is," not the "ought." When scientists in these fields attempt to deal with the "ought," they go beyond their fields into ethics. Law and moral theology, however, deal with principle, deal with the "ought." Law deals with an external standard by which to judge rightness and wrongness in human activity. Problems of conscience are normally not within the purview of civil law. Moral theology deals with internal moral principles, but from the point of view of both reason and divine revelation. Ethics is distinguished from all these sciences. Moral philosophy is interested in the rightness or wrongness of human actions using human reason alone. Herein we find the formal object of ethics, the morality of human activity, the point of view from which the moralist studies human behavior.

No matter the definition, science expects to achieve certitude. Certitude is the maintenance of a conclusion without reasonable fear of error. Metaphysical certitude concerns the principles of being, for example a whole is greater than its part or a thing is what it is. Short of faith, no stronger certitude exists for the human intellect. Physical certitude concerns laws of nature: "A gas expands when heated;" "nature is ultimately composed of atoms." Moral certitude concerns truths which involve human freedom. "Mothers love their children." We might find a mother who does not love her child. But this lack of love is against nature; such a mother is defective. Philosophy deals with all kinds of certitude, but moral philosophy itself deals specifically in moral certitude, that is truths which depend upon the free will of man. Over two thousand years ago, at the beginning of his study of ethics, Aristotle warned not to expect more certitude from a study than the particular study can deliver. It is the mark of an educated man to understand this principle. The mathematician and the ethicist are held to different standards because of the nature of their respective sciences.

Ethics is divided into general ethics and special ethics. General ethics establishes the nature of a moral act and universal principles of morality. Special ethics is applied ethics; employing principles of general ethics to the manifold circumstances of individual and social life.

ASSUMPTIONS

As propedeutic to its own study, every science assumes certain truths or principles proved by other sciences. A course in a specialized branch of physics assumes, for example, many principles proved in mathematics, geometry, and general physics. These truths are proved, but do not lie within the purview of the specialized study. Ethics uses this same procedure. Accordingly, ethics assumes certain truths which can be proved, but are not under its purview.

For example, from natural theology ethics presupposes God's existence. By God, the ethicist means a infinitely perfect, supreme being upon whom the universe in its entirety, and man in particular, depends for its continued existence. The existence of God can be demonstrated in various ways. The clearest demonstration of God's existence is probably based on order and design in the universe. Order and design indicates purpose. Purpose is the product of intelligence; the more order and design, the greater the intelligence behind them. The human mind always attributes order to an intellect. For example, a watch's intricate mechanism indicates the mind of a designer. The order and design in an automobile indicates a designer. Human intelligence is sufficient to explain the order and design of these machines. But every being in the universe, and the universe as a whole, possesses order and design. Almost daily, man discovers new order and design, for example DNA and RNA. Hence there must be an intelligent being, a designer, outside the universe. The human mind must acknowledge existence of an intelligence outside this orderly universe, an intelligence upon whom this order continuously depends.

In any Christian philosophy of the human person, several truths have already been established. Ethics assumes that man has a soul different in character from plant or animal souls. Since the time of the ancient Greeks, man has speculated concerning the nature of the human soul. The activities of a being betray its essence or nature. The operations or activities of the rational soul are immaterial, spiritual activities.

Man possesses an intellect. Unlike the higher animals, man knows abstract universal ideas. Man knows not only Fido, Rin-Tin-Tin, or Lassie, he knows dogness. Man knows not only individuals, but universals. Higher animals give no sign of such knowledge. Secondly, man makes universal judgements, knows universal principles. Mathematical statements are universal. $7 + 3 = 10$ is valid for all times and places. Moral statements are universal: "Genocide is immoral" applies to all men, at all times, in all places. Man reasons to conclusions. He reflects upon himself, upon who he is. Higher animals show no indication of performing such activities. Thus man has an intellect.

Man possesses a free will, that is, he makes free choices. The testimony of individual consciousness is that man is free to choose courses of action. Consciousness of freedom to choose is the strongest, most convincing demonstration for the freedom of the will. Over and above this personal demonstration, the structure of society indicates that all men accept the freedom of the will. The entire social structure assumes that men can and do act freely. Laws are made to direct men in society and punishments are established for those who violate laws. Rewards are offered to those who act nobly. Parents correct children. God is thought to reward good actions and punish evil ones. None of these actions make any sense if man is not free. There are no examples known to man of matter being free. Augustine of Hippo was the first philosopher to establish freedom of the will in great detail.

These operations of intellect and will have no direct relation to matter. Hence the principle from which these activities spring must be immaterial and spiritual. By definition, a spiritual reality is simple and immaterial, not composed of physical parts and hence not subject to physical laws, such as death. The first philosopher to study the spiritual nature of the soul in depth was Plotinus. In fact, Augustine of Hippo had difficulty conceiving spirit until he read Plotinus and his student Porphyry. The notion of spirituality removed the last great obstacle to his conversion. Through Augustine, the spirituality and immortality of the human soul entered definitively into the Western Christian philosophical tradition. The functions of intellect and free will differentiate man from other animals in the same genus and are the very reason that the science of ethics exists.

From logic and epistemology or philosophy of mind, ethics assumes that man's intellect arrives at truth and holds such truth with certitude. Ethics assumes certain rules of right reasoning necessary for the exploration of truth. Since the time of Descartes (1596-1650) the basic question in western philosophy has been the ability of man's mind to come to truth and the conditions under which man knows. The human intellect makes a spontaneous natural intuitive judgement that reality exists outside of it. In his day to day activities, man makes a judgement that he knows outside reality as it is, and that he exists. Man also knows several truths merely by analysis of the terms. Therefore, man's intellect attains truth. On the contrary, skepticism maintains that the human intellect is never in full and certain possession of truth. Since ancient Greece until the present day, skepticism has had many guises. But ultimately, skepticism is untenable. Every science assumes man's ability to attain truth. Every scientist assumes that reality exists outside his mind: the chemist assumes that elements exist in reality; the physicist assumes the real existence of atoms; the biologist assumes that human organs really exist. Study of science is idle if the human intellect can not come to truth. Man is certain of many truths, that a thing is what it is or that a whole is greater than its part. Various truths of logic are similarly certain. Ethics uses reason, man's intellect in action, to prove the morality of various human acts. Ethics, like every other science, necessarily assumes the ability of the human mind to come to truth..

FAITH AND REASON

The relation between what man knows from reason and what he takes from faith merely on the authority of God revealing exercises an enormous influence over a person's ethics.. For many, ethics is a purely a subject of religion, not a matter of reason, Since many of these same people believe religion to be an exclusively private matter, for them principles of ethics are not discussible. For others, tension may exist between what reason teaches and what faith maintains. Still others insist that ethics is a matter of pure reason, devoid of faith, Finally the traditional Catholic position has posited an ultimate harmony between truths know by faith and those known by reason. Here we take reason to be the human power to know reality, faith to be an assent to a given truth solely on the authority of God revealing. The question of the relation between faith and reason therefore should be taken up prior to a study of ethics.

Truth must be one; there must be unity in truth. A principle can not be true in physics, but false in mathematics. Were such apparently to occur, an error must have taken place in one or both of the sciences. Unity in truth must exist between all sciences, and therefore between philosophy and theology. What man knows by reason should harmonize with, or at least not contradict, what he knows from faith. Historically, four classic positions have arisen, and still exist today, concerning the relationship between faith and reason: Mitigated rationalism, rationalism, fideism, and the double standard of truth.

Mitigated rationalism has been the mainstream Catholic position. Both faith and reason play a part in the human attainment of knowledge. Faith and reason ultimately harmonize. Justin Martyr (circa 165) was the first Christian to take up the relationship between ancient secular wisdom and the Bible. But it was Augustine of Hippo (354–430) who treated the subject in more detail. He held that faith sets the agenda for philosophy. *Credo ut intelligam.* "I believe in order that I might understand." The biblical text underlying Augustine's thought was Is 7:9, the Septuagint version: "Unless you believe, you will not understand." The task of philosophy is to bring understanding to the tenets of faith (*intellectus fidei*). Faith is temporally and logically prior to reason. Augustine's position is anthropological: ordinarily, man believes, on the grounds of authority, some tenet before he comprehends the same tenet. Man believes before he comprehends. Ancient Greco-Roman philosophy sought a way to happiness—Christianity is the fulfilment of that search. Platonists especially had seen man's destiny, happiness, but not the means of attaining it. In fact, Augustine never uses the term theology to describe his thought. Varro was a theologian, not Augustine. Augustine was interested in Christianity as the truest philosophy (*philosophia uerissima*). Nevertheless, Augustine believed that the dictum "faith precedes reason" is itself a reasonable proposition.

Thomas Aquinas (1225–1274), a Dominican friar and professor of Christian thought in Paris, followed Augustine in maintaining the unity of faith and reason. But for Thomas, reason precedes faith. Man's reason is finite, but can bring him toward faith. Man can come to certain truths by reason; others are left to faith, without contradicting reason. Certain truths are preambles to faith (*praeambula fidei*). Revelation also serves as a confirmation of truths known by reason. Thomas approaches the problem from a logical point of view. The difference between the Augustine and Thomas can be illustrated in their respective positions concerning a rational demonstration of God's existence. Augustine first asks for faith in God's existence. To the believer, Augustine then demonstrates the existence of an eternal truth. Since this truth is immutable, it is either equivalent to God or what is beyond it is God. The human mind can know God's nature only through distant and obscure images. On the other hand, Thomas maintains that human reason, faith aside, can prove God's existence. But man can know only a few divine attributes by reason alone. Ultimately man knows God's nature from revelation. Thomas and Augustine agree on several points. Both believe in the unity of truth. "Truth, wherever it is, is God's." Both believe in an ultimate harmony of faith and reason. Both believe in the necessity of divine revelation either to confirm what man knows from reason or to indicate truths beyond man's ken. But they approach the problem from different, though harmonious, points of view. In his encyclical on this subject, *Fides et Ratio,* Pope John Paul II presented an Augustinian view of man as a God-directed being. He accepted the position of *credo ut intelligam.* But the pope also maintained that reason can lead to faith, a Thomistic position. Interestingly Augustine experienced in his own life that reason can lead to faith: Augustine's read certain Platonist books which led him to Christianity. In our treatment of ethics, we take the position of mitigated rationalism.

The position directly opposed to mitigated rationalism is the double standard of truth. Whether this position was actually held by some Arab philosophers is a matter of dispute among historians of philosophy. Arab philosophers knew Aristotle's speculative writings which inexplicably had been lost to the West. Averroës (1126–1198), an Arabian commentator on Aristotle, maintained two ways to truth, faith and reason. Some have seen in his writings the doctrine that a tenet could be true by reason, but false by faith, or contrariwise, false by reason but true by faith. Whether or not the historical Averroes ever held this position, or it is derived from his works, is disputed. From the Crusades, the west became familiar with Arabic thought. Siger of Brabant was a representative of the double standard of truth in the Christian West. For the reasons outlined above, this position has been termed Averroism. Even today, some thinkers maintain a similar position. Nevertheless, truth must be one; there can be no contradiction in the truth. The double standard denies this obvious truth.

Rationalism has at least two distinct, but interrelated meanings. In the wider sense, rationalism maintains that all truth is open to reason, there is no need for faith. In a narrower sense, rationalism means a philosophical system which has as its primary goal, not an understanding of reality, but construction of an internally consistent system by which the world can be interpreted. For rationalism in the narrow sense, geometry stands as the paradigm. Euclidean geometry, for example, is an internally consistent mathematical system. But Euclidean geometry has nothing to do with reality directly since material reality is three dimensional, while Euclidean geometry is two dimensional. But such a gap is not the rationalist's concern. The ancient Greeks were rationalists in the wider sense. Religion and philosophy had little to do with one another, though many Greek philosophers maintained some kind of relationship with a religious tradition. Manicheans were gnostics of the third and fourth century who appealed to the aristocrats of North Africa in the time of Augustine of Hippo. Manicheans were rationalists. On the surface, it is difficult to harmonize gnosticism with rationalism. But Manicheans probably maintained that, once revelation was given to the elect, reality could be understood without need of belief. Manicheanism has had several revivals: in the tenth century Balkans with the Bogomils and in the thirteenth-century Spain and France with the Albigensians. Gnosticism is experiencing a revival in some late twentieth-century theologians who maintain that Christianity arose out of gnosticism or in contradistinction to it. Many modern cults are gnostic. Augustine of Hippo developed his thought on faith and reason against Manichean rationalism.

In the modern period, Descartes (1596–1650) stands as the outstanding example of rationalism. Though Descartes was a believer, he intentionally attempted to construct a philosophical system based on reason alone. He died before he could elucidate the moral implications of his rationalism. Immanuel Kant is best classified as an idealist, but his moral system is rationalistic in the sense that it derives solely from rational principles, internal to the human mind. Likewise, present day science and British and American philosophies such as logical positivism and some versions of linguistic analysis may be classified as rationalistic since they allow no place for faith. Rationalism ultimately stumbles against the finitude of the human intellect. According to classical philosophy going back to Parmenides, all reality is potentially understandable, but not necessarily to the human mind or to this human mind. To God, all things are known perfectly, even himself, Rationalism holds that all reality here and now is actually understandable by the finite human intellect. Such a doctrine contravenes human experience.

Fideism is precisely contrary to rationalism. All knowledge stems from faith, man has no need for reason. Coming at the end of the second century, Tertullian (166-circa 230) stands as the first fideist, "What does, Jerusalem have to do with Athens?" he queried. What does faith have to do with reason? Tertullian's answer was "absolutely nothing." Christians study at the "porch of Solomon." Ultimately, Tertullian became a gnostic. Reformation theologians were also fideists. Fideism was among the tenets over which the Reformation was fought. Luther (1483–1546) taught and preached salvation by "faith alone." He had no time for the "whore reason." Luther's distrust of reason remains current in the German theological-philosophical psyche even to the present day. The Danish Lutheran theologian Søren Kierkegaard (1813–1855) was a nineteenth-century fideist. Man is saved by a "leap of faith." The highest human existence stems from this religious stance. The more irrational the leap is, the better. Biblical fundamentalists are in the final analysis fideists. Fideism ultimately falters on the complete distrust of human reason. That human reason is at times weak and blinded by emotion is certainly true. That man *in statu uiatoris,* in his pilgrim state, can not know all truth directly is apparent. But that man can know no truth whatsoever, especially truths which lead to human happiness, directly contradicts human experience.

CHAPTER

2

Human Behavior

THE MORAL ACT

The first consideration in the study of ethics must be to determine what acts have morality. Traditionally, acts which have a moral dimension to them have been called human acts. A human act is as an act which proceeds from man as man, that is, from man as a rational being. What differentiates man from the animals is his intellect and will. Human acts proceed from these powers. Human acts involve knowledge, voluntariness (consent), and freedom. To perform a human act, man must know what he is doing, be internally free to do it, and consent to the action. Since in every human act man has knowledge, consent, and freedom, man is responsible. In fact, they are the only acts for which man is responsible. Human acts are imputable to the agent who does them, that is they belong to him and no one else. Responsibility is an attribute of a person, imputability an attribute of an act.

Acts of man are distinguished from human acts. An act of man is an act which man performs, but not insofar as he is man. What distinguishes man from animals is intellect and will. Man performs an act of man, but the act does not proceed from intellect and will. At least one of the constituents (knowledge, voluntariness, or freedom) for a human act is missing. For example, the beating of the heart or a yawn is an act of man.. If a sleep-walker were to steal or injure someone during his sleep, or if a person were to blaspheme while under the influence of ether, these acts would be acts of man, not human acts. In such cases, these acts do not proceed from man as a rational being and hence do not in any way involve morality.

The term freedom can be used in various ways. Man can be free from passion or addiction. For example, a drug addict or an alcoholic in the true sense of the term is not free. Such addictions can usually be overcome with a reasonably diligent effort. Likewise, man is not free from obligation. Though he may disobey traffic laws, man is not free from the obligation to obey them. He must pay the penalty. Or, man is free not raise his children. But he has an obligation to do so. Man is not free from obligation. Nor is man free from external necessity. For example, man is not free from the law of gravity. When the term freedom is mentioned in regard to man's will, it is used in none of the above senses. Rather freedom of the will denotes freedom from internal constraint. In this sense, man is free to act as he wills. But even here, a distinction must be made. The human will is so constituted that it can only seek good. In coming to class for example, a student is doing so because he is seeking some good, whether it be to pursue truth, to obtain credits, or even to get some sleep. Likewise, when a student misses class, he does so only to seek some good, whatever that may be. Man may err about the good and at times seek apparent rather than real goods. But man is necessitated toward good. Plato (428–348) was the first philosopher to write of this necessity explicitly. Augustine followed him. Within that context however, man is free. He is free to act or not act, free to perform this act or that act, free to perform an act well or badly. When we speak of freedom of the will, it is in this fourth sense that we use the term.

TYPES OF HUMAN ACTS

Human acts may be classified in several ways. Human acts are perfect, when done with full knowledge, full freedom, and full consent of the will; they are imperfect, when done with imperfect knowledge or imperfect freedom or imperfect consent, or with both imperfect knowledge and imperfect freedom and/or imperfect consent.

Human acts are good, when in conformity with the moral order; bad, when in opposition to the moral order; indifferent, when they involve no moral law. Throughout the centuries, philosophers have debated the existence of indifferent acts in concrete situations. In the concrete, only good or bad acts exist.

Human acts are positive, when they involve the actual doing of an act, either in conformity or in opposition to the moral order; negative, when they involve the omission of some act which man is morally obliged to do either in order to live up to, or not fail in, some obligation.

Human acts are simply voluntary, when an individual knows and wills an act in itself, that is, knowing the nature of the proposed action, it, in itself, appears to the agent desirable for its own sake; conditionally voluntary, when the act is done with both knowledge and freedom but also with regret. In this second case, a deliberate and free act is done, but the individual does the act only because the present conditions make it the only wise thing to do.

Human acts are directly voluntary, when the object of the act of the will and its external effects are willed immediately, that is, willed in themselves. Human acts are indirectly voluntary, when an act is not immediately willed in itself but another act is willed which man could and should foresee may bring about this second effect. A thorough understanding of this distinction aids in the solution of many moral quandaries.

Human acts are actually voluntary, when an intention is made and never retracted, has influence over the performance of an act, and the person is conscious of the act at the time. Human acts are virtually voluntary, when an intention is made and never retracted, the intention influences the performance of the act, but is not adverted to at the time of the action. A human act is habitually voluntary, when an intention is made and never retracted, but has no formal influence over the performance of the act. A human act is interpretively voluntary, when, in the judgement of prudence and common sense, a deliberate and free act would here and now have been done if the ability and opportunity to do so were present.

Each of the above divisions is complete; every moral act will find classification in each of the above divisions. Thus the same moral act may be (1) perfect, (2) good, (3) positive, (4) simply voluntary, (5) directly voluntary, (6) actually voluntary.

CHAPTER 3

Modifiers of Responsibility

In practice, responsibility for human acts varies. Man's knowledge, consent, or freedom may be restricted or completely taken away. The following are the classical modifiers of responsibility

IGNORANCE

Ignorance in general is simply a lack of knowledge. Ignorance is privative if one ought to possess the knowledge, negative if one has no obligation to possess it. The only kind of ignorance which has moral significance is privative. Various types of privative ignorance have moral relevance. According to its object, ignorance is either ignorance of law, that is ignorance of an existing law, ignorance of fact, that is ignorance of a given fact which involves some law, or ignorance of penalty, that is ignorance of a penalty attached to a given act. According to its subject, ignorance is either invincible, when the person can not obtain the requisite knowledge with a reasonably diligent effort, or vincible, when the agent can obtain the knowledge with a reasonably diligent effort. "Reasonably diligent effort" is a term of art and may be defined as the effort which the ordinary prudent person would make to attain knowledge. Vincible ignorance can be further subdivided into simple ignorance, where some effort, but insufficient and ineffectual, is made to obtain the relevant knowledge, crass, when no effort whatever is made, and affected when deliberate steps are taken not to obtain the knowledge. From a moral perspective, the three types of vincible ignorance are most important.

Ignorance affects moral responsibility in various ways. Invincible ignorance takes away responsibility totally. When invincible ignorance is present, no knowledge, one of the three constituents of a human act, is present and therefore there is no human act. Vincible ignorance does not take away responsibility, but lessens it. Responsibility is directly proportional to the amount of negligence involved in not obtaining the knowledge. In a sense, affected ignorance lessens consent and therefore responsibility for a given act, since the act is done without proper knowledge. Affected ignorance in some sence diminishes responsibility since it is ignorance. But affected ignorance also involves greater responsibility than acts done from either simple or crass ignorance, since affected ignorance is deliberate, usually with the idea of building up a pretext for lack of responsibility.

PASSION

Passion is a strong emotion. Emotion is a movement of the sensitive appetite, that is, the pursuit of or aversion to an object once it has been apprehended by the senses. Under passion, psychology includes all emotions such as love, hate, joy, grief, desire, aversion, horror, hope, despair, courage, and anger. This list is not complete. The morally relevant distinction is between antecedent and consequent passion. Antecedent passion precedes an act of the will and causes it. Consequent passion is excited or created by the will itself. Passion may be either strong or weak. Since antecedent passion by definition precedes and at least partially causes an act of the will, the freedom with which an agent performs an act is obviously at least partially taken away. Since freedom is diminished, moral responsibility is lessened. At times, antecedent passion may be so strong as to take away moral responsibility completely. Normally however antecedent passion only lessens moral responsibility. Consequent passion does not enter into the formation of the will-act and hence it neither increases nor decreases moral responsibility. Even though antecedent passion lessens moral responsibility, every time such passion is present does not entail that only a slight moral offense is committed. When the preceding passion is quite strong and has a notable influence on freedom, frequently only a slight moral offense is committed, Many times, however, such preceding emotion does not notably impair freedom.

FEAR

Fear is mental anxiety arising from some imminent evil. Fear is mental anxiety, not physical constraint. Fear can be grave or slight depending upon the influence it has on the person in question. In order to ascertain an individual's responsibility under the influence of fear, the impact which the threatened evil has upon him must be evaluated. It is not the case that certain objective things constitute grave fear, while others amount only to slight fear. Rather, what constitutes grave fear for one individual may constitute only slight fear for another. Similarly, what constitutes slight fear for one person may be truly grave for another. The responsibility for a given individual's acts is judged by the influence that the particular imminent evil has upon him or her. Fear is intrinsic or extrinsic, depending upon the source of the fear. Fear is intrinsic when it proceeds from the mind of the person himself, extrinsic when it proceeds from outside the person and constrains him to act. Some acts are done "with fear," others "from fear." The morality of an act is in no way lessened because it is done "with fear." For example, an individual may steal "with fear" of being caught; but he would, in such a case, steal all the more readily if no possibility of being caught existed. It is only acts motivated "from fear" that have a lessened moral guilt, since these acts would not be done if the constraining fear were not present.

Fear lessens moral responsibility in direct proportion to its intensity and its constraining influence. Of itself, mental fear never takes away responsibility completely. If fear were so grave as to destroy freedom totally, then all morality in the act would vanish. In this case, however, the principles concerning passion would then take precedence. In cases of complete panic, for example, all responsibility may be destroyed. But panic arises from emotional and mental anxiety. It is not merely mental. When fear is purely mental constraint, no instance can be found in which all freedom is destroyed. The mind acts freely but with reluctance when under the influence of fear. Moral responsibility is proportional to the amount of freedom present in the act.

VIOLENCE

Violence is external physical restraint placed upon a free agent, to force that agent to perform an act against his will. Perfect violence is use of external physical force on a free agent, sufficient to force him to perform a given act, despite the fact that this person resists the physical restraint, insofar as the agent is able to do so. Imperfect violence is use of physical restraint on a person who partially resists, that is, does not resist to the full extent of his powers, or in any event does not perform the act against his will; the violence is not itself sufficient to force the person to perform the act. The presence of external physical force distinguishes violence from fear.

Perfect violence totally destroys freedom and therefore takes away moral responsibility. A person may be forced to perform an external physical act, but a persons's internal consent can not be subject to force. Therefore, a person acting under perfect violence is not responsible for the action. There is no human act. Imperfect violence only partially destroys freedom. Either the violence is insufficient to force the agent to do the act or the moral agent consents to perform the act. In either case, moral responsibility may be lessened, but not taken away. Moral responsibility in such cases is in proportion to the amount of freedom in the action. Moral responsibility is lessened because the act partially proceeds from physical constraint; but moral responsibility is not totally destroyed because the act proceeds partially from a free will. Resistance is called for even in cases where it would be no avail, if, without such resistance, consent would be likely.

HABIT

Habit is the effect of repeated acts and an aptitude to reproduce them. Habit is a quality, difficult to change, whereby an agent, whose nature it is to work one way or another at choice, is disposed easily and readily at will to follow this or that particular line of action. Ethically, habits are classified as good or bad, that is, as virtues or vices, according as they lead to actions in conformity with or against the moral order. The majority of human acts are done under the influence of good or bad habits, vices or virtues, frequently without reflection. By lessening freedom, habit also lessens the actual responsibility of an agent, because actions are less perfectly attended to, and in varying degrees escape control of the will. A distinction exists between habits acquired and retained knowingly, voluntarily, and with some foresight of the consequences likely to result, and habits acquired unconsciously, without noticing, and therefore without thought of the possible consequences. If a habit is knowingly and willingly retained, effects of that habit are indirectly willed, even though the person does not advert to the moral character of the act at its execution. If a person has not been responsible for acquiring a habit and retaining it, actions proceeding from it are not voluntary. But, as soon as the existence and dangers of a habit are noticed, efforts to uproot it become morally obligatory. If a person realizes that he has a bad habit, takes firm and proportionate steps to overcome it and, despite his efforts, occasionally acts without advertence and in accordance with the tendency of the habit, no moral responsibility is involved in the act. It is an act of man. If a vice is knowingly retained without a due attempt to eradicate it, the immoral acts which follow from it are imputed to the individual. There is, however, a lessened moral responsibility when such acts are done without deliberation.

PERSONAL INFLUENCES

Other factors may influence human act and affect responsibility. Age is one such factor. Perfection of knowledge and strength of will are greatly affected by age. A child's mind is undeveloped in many respects; he can not abstract moral principle easily, if at all. A child is inclined to obstinacy, and yet has a ready submission to God and parents. A child can have adequate knowledge of morality in many regards, but some moral problems are too advanced for his understanding. Adolescence is marked by a struggle between liberty and control. Man's sensual, and especially sexual, nature can create difficult problems for the human being during this period. The adolescent is inclined to waver between optimism and pessimism, hope and despair. He has the faculty and inclination to labor, to cultivate tender sentiments, and to seek noble ideals. A great deal depends upon the direction given these tendencies by proper education. Adulthood is a period of maturity, marked by fixity of character, stable control of one's physical and intellectual efforts. Pride, vain-glory, and heartlessness are the most common faults during this period. Old age is characterized by weakening of faculties. Each age has its own peculiar nature and its own tendencies toward good and evil. All these tendencies are factors entering into analysis of moral responsibility.

Temperament is another factor. Temperament is the peculiar physical and mental character of an individual. In most persons, a varied blend of "sanguine," "choleric," "melancholy," and "phlegmatic" temperaments exists; in each person, one or other of these "temperaments" ordinarily predominates. A person's temperament is modified by physical and moral environment, such as climate, home-life, education, and friends. Temperaments undoubtedly influence the will, but ordinarily not in an irresistible manner. In many instances, temperament lessens moral responsibility since it influences the will.

Natural talent is also a contributing factor in moral responsibility. Talent is a special aptitude or faculty for effective action along certain lines. The presence or absence of special aptitudes necessarily influences man's intellectual and moral development. Strictly speaking, moral sense of obligation should develop in proportion to acquisition of knowledge, which is greatly dependent on intellectual ability. However, a greater possibility of over-estimating the effect of natural intellectual talent on morality exists than of failing to recognize it. There is no rigid relationship between intellectual ability and morality.

SOCIAL INFLUENCES

Gender can also exercise influence on human responsibility and moral character. Gender is the sum total of peculiarities of structure and function distinguishing male from female. The influence of gender is not limited to the body but extends to intellect and will. In the contemporary world, the tendency to blur distinction between genders has come to the fore. Yet such distinction is real. In a general sense, the male gender possesses more energy and strength than the female; these advantages are counter-balanced by lack of modesty and sentiment. Also generally speaking, the female gender possesses a sense of modesty, religious sentiment, and patience to a greater degree than males. The countervailing tendencies include an lesser capacity to resist evil. At best, these are general characterizations: Each gender possesses good and bad qualities and good or bad tendencies, all of which influence formation of a moral act. If any of these tendencies at any given time lessens free will (and this frequently happens), moral responsibility is lessened, but never destroyed.

Education is another contributing factor in moral responsibility. Education at home and in school certainly creates predispositions toward good or evil. As Plato realized some twenty-five hundred years ago, good moral education lies at the basis of moral behavior. Lack of moral education is felt in contemporary American society at all levels, witness the violence in our schools and on the streets. An immoral education can be overcome, but with great effort. One can lead an immoral life, even after good moral education. Nevertheless, education inclines a person to act in accordance with ideals of that system. Education is an influential factor in the formation of a moral act. If a person has, through no fault of his own, received a poor moral education, moral responsibility for his acts is certainly not as great as in the person who has had the opportunity of good moral training.

Society as a whole is another factor in moral responsibility. Every person is influenced to some degree by the *Zeitgeist*. His times, his nation, and his country influence his actions. The physical elements of soil, climate, national type, and language have an impact. *Zeitgeist* influences the individual intellectually and ethically, in his view of right and wrong. The relationship existing between character and environment has been studied over centuries and is still debated at great length. The extent and degree of each influence may be questioned, but environment is certainly a factor. An individual can overcome a bad environment—hence social influence never totally takes away moral responsibility attached to an act. But a great effort is often required to overcome a bad social background—therefore moral responsibility may well be lessened to some extent.

Heredity is another influential factor on moral responsibility: No doubt the influence of heredity on character was greatly over-emphasized in past times. Nevertheless, the importance of genetic research in our own time can not be overestimated. Certain physical and mental traits are inherited. Inheritance of certain traits may make it difficult for a person to deliberate properly or choose freely. Such heredity would lessen moral responsibility attached to acts done under its influence.

Despite the factors mentioned above, grave evils for which man is responsible exist all too frequently in both society and individuals. Normally, a person has due knowledge of the immorality of possible actions, that is no moral ignorance exists. Normally, a person is not mentally or physically coerced. Normally, man is in calm possession of his faculties when he acts. His age, environment, education, and heredity figure in, but do not determine, his activity. The average human being has knowledge, freedom, and consent enough to be responsible fully for his actions. Evil is unfortunately not hard to accomplish; but rather difficult to avoid. A life of virtue is the product of serious ardent effort. The effect of salvation by God's grace must be left to theology.

MENTAL ILLNESS

In the past fifty years, man's knowledge of mental illness has increased several-fold. Science knows much more about depression, mania, obsession, and schizophrenia. Methods of psychological and psychiatric treatment of mental illness have advanced. True professionals, however, admit that much more is to be learned. From an ethical standpoint, many factors mentioned above enter in. Only human acts have morality about them. A person is responsible for what he knows and is free to do. Therefore, the mentally ill person is responsible for what he knows, is free to do, and consents to do. He is not responsible for what he does not know or is not free to do. He is not responsible when his consent is internally or externally compelled. There are obviously grades of knowledge, freedom, and consent. Thus, diminished responsibility often exists. Once a mentally ill person realizes his illness, a moral obligation to pursue treatment insofar as it might be helpful exists under the principles of habit.

ACTIONS WITH TWO-FOLD EFFECTS

Principles of the Double Effect

Often one act produces two or more effects, some good, some bad. Such actions may give rise to serious moral problems. Man may hesitate to perform an act which produces evil, even though good will also be achieved. Over centuries certain principles have been developed to solve such moral problems. These principles are derived from St. Thomas' discussion of the right of self-defense in *Summa Theologiae.* They are four in number. All four principles must be simultaneously verified for an act to be morally allowable. These principles have become known as the "principles of the double effect" and are always referred to in the following order:

(1) The proposed action from which the two effects follow must be morally good in itself or at least indifferent. Later in the text, the basis for terming an act to be good or bad will be discussed at length. For the moment, that some acts are good and others bad is presupposed. Whether in practice an indifferent act exists will also be left aside. The first principle states that an act must be good in itself, no matter the consequences. The morality of acts is not determined merely by consequences.

(2) The good effect must not come about from the evil effect. The good effect must proceed immediately from the act. Evil can not be directly done so that good comes about. The evil effect can only be allowed. But, because one act follows another chronologically does not entail that the first act causes the second. This principle deals with causality. The evil effect may not cause the good effect. This principle makes explicit an implicit aspect of the first principle.

(3) The evil effect may not be directly intended. The evil effect can be only indirectly voluntary. This distinction was encountered in describing various kinds of human acts. The motive prompting the action must be a desire to bring about a good effect. The agent must not be prompted by a desire to bring about an evil effect. Of course, the person sees that the evil effect follows from his act, but he does not desire it. The motive behind his act is not a desire to achieve an evil. When the entire motive of an act is evil, the act becomes evil itself. In actuality, this principle is also a specification of principle one.

(4) A proportion, a proper balance, between the good and evil effects must exist. A fitting and proper proportion exists only when the good to be achieved either outweighs or at least is equivalent to the resulting evil. To allow great evils for the sake of small goods is unreasonable. Over the past century, theories have arisen concerning the morality of an act, that it is to be judged only by consequences. Utilitarianism and consequentialism are examples of such theories. The theory of the double effect clearly shows that the moral value of an act is not be judged merely by its results. An act possesses morality in itself, apart from its consequences. Man must take consequences into consideration, but consequences alone are not a final determinant. In *Veritatis splendor,* a recent encyclical on morality, John Paul II indicated clearly the evils of consequentialism.

A case in point may be helpful: May an officer of the law shoot after a fleeing drug dealer? Two effects follow from the action. The good effect is the capture, imprisonment, and punishment of the culprit. The bad effect is the resulting damage to innocent persons or the property of innocent persons from stray bullets. The solution to the case may be found in the principles of the double-effect. The first principle is verified. For an officer to shoot a fleeing criminal if it is the only or best chance to apprehend him is morally good or, at the very least, indifferent. The second principle is verified. The good effect of capturing and punishing a criminal results from the shooting. His capture and imprisonment is not effected through and because of injury to innocent people or destruction of their property The third principle is verified. The officer's act is prompted by a desire to apprehend the criminal, not by a desire to destroy innocent life or property. His motive is proper. The fourth principle is in all probability verified. The criminal has broken grave laws, drugs are a constant danger to society. A proportion exists between good effect of apprehending the criminal and possibility of harm to an innocent third party. Thus the officer's action is justified.

If the principles of the double effect are verified, one may risk his life for others. For example, to save another from certain death, we may expose ourselves to grave danger. Health care professionals, soldiers, police officers, fireman often do this. Ordinarily, one is not obliged to expose oneself to danger of death to save others. However, members of the above professions implicitly contract to do so in most cases. In dangerous jobs, sufficient reasons must be present to pursue such work. Acrobats and daredevils may practice their professions since the danger is remote because of their expertise. Body contact sports may be justified on the same grounds. The same may not be said, however, for auto and hydroplane racing. Prizefighting presents a special case and will be treated later.

The principles of the double effect must be taken as guidelines in the discussion of acts with two effects. Men of good will may differ in their application. However, the principles indicate the proper questions to ask: Is the act moral in itself. Is the good brought about by the evil? What is the motive? Is there a proportion between the good and evil? Only by asking these questions may answers to perplexing cases come about.

COOPERATION IN EVIL

A special case of the principles of the double effect exists with regard to cooperation in evil. Many times a human being knows that an evil is to be committed and that he is involved with it to some degree. Such are cases of the double effect. According to the first principle, the act done must be good in itself or at least indifferent. According to the third principle, one may never concur in an evil intention. In either case, that is when an evil act is either done or intended, formal cooperation exists and the act would be evil. However, many times the act itself is not evil and there is no intention to join in the evil intention. Such is termed material cooperation. In these cases, the fourth principle of the double effect should be employed. The proportion between good and evil must be weighed. Ordinarily, the closer to the evil, the greater the reason must be to sustain the evil; the more remote from the direct act, the fewer grounds necessary to justify one's act. Participation in an unjustified war would come under these principles. The planner of the battles and those directly engaged arc formal cooperators. A general who is directly engaged would have greater responsibility than an ordinary soldier. A soldier participating in battle would have greater moral responsibility than one at home not so participating. A doctor participating in an abortion is a formal cooperator. So is a nurse. Others such as nurses' aides or janitors have much less responsiblity.

READINGS

1. Plato, Lesser Hippias
2. Thomas Aquinas, *Summa Theolgiae*, I-II, questions 6,76-78. II-II, q. 64, art. 7.
3. E. Gilson, The Christian Philosophy of St. Thomas Aquinas, 282-86
4. C. Grisez,
5. Pojman.

CHAPTER 4

Natural Law Theory

Aristotle referred to purpose as final cause. Finality or purpose is apparent everywhere in the universe. Every being, animate or inanimate, has a final goal, an ultimate objective for its existence. The inanimate world of the sun, the moon and the stars has its objective, whether it be the beauty and intracacies of their own existence or the production of light and darkness to constitute days and night or seasonal changes. An acorn, from the first moment of its living existence, has the goal of becoming an oak tree; an animal embryo, from the first moment of its living existence, is destined to develop into a full grown member of its species. The same holds for a human zygot. If the entire universe has an objective, a goal of existence, it is reasonable to assume that man has a final goal and ultimate destiny.

Every being in the universe attains the objective of its existence by observance of law. Physical laws govern movement of the sun, moon and stars, and growth of each member of the vegetative and animal species. Each being in the universe has its own specific nature which it shares with every other being in the same class. The nature or essence of a thing determines the acts a thing can perform, a doctrine which goes back at least as far as Cicero, if not to Aristotle. Each nature has a vast number of requirements which it must obtain in order that it may develop and finally reach the goal of its existence. The sum total of these requirements which any given nature must obtain in order to develop is called the law which that nature must observe in order to reach its final goal. Similarly, man has laws which will result in development of his nature and attainment of his final destiny. The sole difference between human nature and other natures is that man is free to accept or reject the laws of his nature. The possibility of rejection does not mean that laws do not exist. It merely means that man can suffer consequences when he rejects the laws of his nature. For example, man is free to drink whatever he will. The natural law suggests that he not do so. But man is free to drink. He must however suffer the consequences of acting against natural law.

Every being in the universe is directed to its objective by a law which is in harmony with its nature. All natures below man have one thing in common: they are totally material. Hence inanimate, vegetative, and animal beings are governed by physical laws. Physical laws are, of course, absolutely determining laws, driving these beings toward their goals. But man's soul is spiritual—hence man will have to be directed toward his final destiny by a spiritual, not material, law. This law will be in harmony with his nature which possesses an intellect and will. Hence the spiritual law which man must obey will be a law which he will know by means of his intellect and obey by an act of his will. Man freely chooses whether to obey the law which must be observed if he is to reach his final destiny. In this sense, man is truly the molder of his own destiny.

By his intellect man can ascertain a body of moral ideals. Without any notable intellectual effort, he arrives at the principle that "good must done and evil avoided." This principle is called the "primary principle of the natural law." This principle is know by intuition in the first moral act a human being performs. Some philosophers, such as Augustine of Hippo, think that the golden rule "do unto other as you would have them do unto you" or negatively "do not do unto others as you would not have them do unto you." is intuited in this manner. This principle or a variant is found in practically all civilizations. Nevertheless, it is not as basic as "do good and avoid evil" since the golden rule is valid only in societies or persons which are fundamentally moral. In any event, these principles are know by everyone in the commission of his first human act. Realizing the existence of God, the spirituality of his own soul and its immortal destiny, man reasons that certain acts are obviously good—adoration of God, proper care of his health, respect for the person and property of his fellow-man—and hence that such acts should be done. Similarly, he reasons that blasphemy, murder, and stealing are evil and should be avoided. Such principles are called "secondary precepts of the natural law" because they are relatively easily deduced from the primary principle and common experience of human nature. Such principles are almost immediately known. With greater difficulty men reason to the moral goodness or badness of difficult moral problems, such as the validity of contracts, or contraception. Such principles are "tertiary precepts of the natural law." They are known with difficulty and by a longer reasoning process. They are not immediate deductions from human nature. Disputes may arise concerning which principles belong in what category. Similarly, principles of categories two and three may shift according to a particular society. For example, the morality of abortion appears to be a greater problem in our society than in many others. From the time of Aristotle until America of the eighteenth and nineteenth century and even in many parts of the world today, the morality of slavery has been difficult to ascertain. The sum total of these primary, immediate, and remote moral truths constitutes natural law, which man must observe to bring his spiritual nature to its final destiny.

Many philosophers of the Enlightenment, for example John Locke and Thomas Jefferson, held to the existence of a natural law, albeit not as consistently as Thomas Aquinas. John Locke was a nominalist, that is he did not believe in natures. He thought that only individuals existed and were grouped together arbitrarily by the human intellect. Though he did not believe in natures, somewhat inconsistently Locke thought that man could reason to principles of the natural law rather easily, for example the existence of private property. Indeed, Locke's disciple Thomas Jefferson thought many principles to be "self-evident." The perspicacity and moderation of Thomas Aquinas in this matter becomes more evident when viewed against this background. Contemporary philosophers are not as sanguine as Enlightenment thinkers concerning man's ability to know outside reality. Indeed, many contemporary philosophers are complete skeptics. Because some modern thinkers doubt man's ability to know natures or evern doubt that antures exist, they doubt man's ability to know a natural law. Many scientists who believe quite easily in universal empirically verifiable laws of physical nature doubt the existence of universal moral laws. Thomas Aquinas' nuanced position speaks clearly to this difficulty. He thought that knowledge of the natural law differed much in the manner of principles of mathematics. Some principles are immediately known—two things equal to a third thing are equal to each other; some are known with ease—two plus two equals four (from the base ten); some are known only with difficulty—the fourth derivative.

The history of natural law theory is long and complex. Socrates tried to ascertain universally valid definitions of moral virtues. His student Plato certainly believed in a natural morality. Man should live according to noble ideals which really exist. Socratic definitions become universally valid moral ideals. Nevertheless in some of his works law (*nomos*) and nature (*physis*) are opposed. This opposition occurs because law is viewed as conventional—Plato had civil or religious law in mind. Aristotle presents a view of nature which underlies later natural law theory. Acts are in conformity or not in conformity with man's nature. Aristotle's ethical works primarily have to do with virtue which later becomes a major factor in natural law theory. Nevertheless, the term natural law is not found in Aristotle. The first use of the term is found in Stoic philosophy. Stoics believed in seeds of reason (*Logoi spermatikoi, rationes seminales*) present in the universe. These seeds determine activity, even human activity, according to law. Since much of Stoicism was fatalistic, the term later fell into disfavor among Christian thinkers. Cicero was a great defender of natural law, especially in his orations against enemies of the state. A great many of the precepts of *ius gentium* generated by the ancient Romans were directly related to natural law principles. We find the idea, and the term, natural law in Augustine of Hippo. Even the thief does not abide theft of his own property. There exists a law which extends to all mankind. Many precepts of natural law are found in the early canons of Church law and the decretals of Gratian. Thomas Aquinas had a strong influence on the development of natural law. His theory in its main outlines has been presented above. In the late Middle Ages, when an Aristotelian notion of nature fell out of favor and nominalism ruled the day, natural law fell into disfavor. The Protestant Reformation confirmed this decline. Individual conscience, unrestrained by universal moral principle, became the final arbiter of morality. During the Enlightenment, such figures as John Locke in England and Thomas Jefferson in America held to the natural law. In the case of John Locke, his nominalism did not support his natural law theory, but he does not appear to have recognized the contradiction. Locke thought that one could argue from reason to precepts of natural law, especially concerning private property. For Thomas Jefferson however, many principles of natural law are directly intuited. The American Declaration of Independence and the American Constitution stand as outstanding documents witnessing the revival of natural law in the eighteenth century. Today, in many quarters we are witnessing a revival of natural law. The weakness of legal positivism is all too evident. Civil law can not be the director of morality. In history, the great defender of natural law has been the Catholic Church. The church's position of mitigated rationalism allows it to defend reason while holding to the necessity of faith.

LAW

In many law schools today, law unfortunately goes undefined or its nature is thought to be immediately intuited. Several etymologies for the word law (*lex* or *ius* in Latin) have been suggested. The usual derivation is from *"ligo, ligare"* (to bind). Other derivations proposd are *eligere* (to choose) or *legere* (to read). *Ius, iuris* can be translaed into English either as "law" or "right," according to context. The etymological connection of *ius* with the word justice is obvious. Many English legal words derive from it, such as juridical and jurisprudence.

In his treatise on law in *Summa Theologiae,* Thomas Aquinas defines law: "an ordinance of reason for the common good, made by an authority and promulgated." Law is a command, not a mere suggestion or good idea—it is an order. The command must be based in reason, not merely the whim of the legislator. The medieval Franciscan theologian-philosopher John Duns Scotus (1266-1308) denied the basis of law primarily in reason. According to Scotus, law was based primarily on the legislator's will. Even unto today, philosophers debate whether law belongs to the intellect or to the will. Legal positivists, for example, argue that law is based solely in the will of the legislator. But Thomas argues that law is based in reason, that a law not based in reason is really no law at all. In fact, society acts in this manner. There are literally thousands of laws on the books in every city of the United States to which no one pays one whit of attention, for example, spitting on the sidewalk. Such laws are outmoded, that is the reason for their existence no longer remains. Likewise, there are certain times, cases of necessity, when a law does not bind because it is unreasonable. A policeman will not enforce a traffic regulation in the case of a pregnant woman about to deliver her baby. Rather, he will abrogate the law in this specific case because it is not reasonable at this time.

Law is always made for the common, not the private good. Unfortunately, essentially due to the rise of utilitarianism, contemporary society has lost a proper notion of the common good. Utilitarianism maintains that the common good is merely the sum total of individual goods. The goal of society is to produce the greatest good for the greatest number, understood as individuals. Special interest group utilitarianism is a contemporary version. Such a philosophy of society is of course false. There are goods for the whole which do not necessarily redound to individual benefit. Payment of taxes might be an example. In regard to the common good, utilitarianism commits the logical error of composition, arguing that, because individuals have a characteristic, the whole must have the same characteristic. The founders of the United States constitution had a relatively clear idea of what constituted the common good. Classical ideas were not foreign to them. Today, politicians and some courts in the United States are trying to harmonize a philosophy of utilitarianism with a natural law document, the constitution of the United States. This effort must be in vain. This attempt has had the unfortunate effect of burdening courts with all sorts of cases which would surprise, if not shock, the founding fathers. Starting with Augustine of Hippo, Christian philosophy has had an accurate idea of the common good. Augustine himself advised his monks that, in proportion as they seek the common good over the individual good, they are advancing in charity. He further thought there could no true republic without justice. Thomas well understood that the common good existed over and above individual goods and was not the sum total of them. The United States must return to a proper notion of the common good of earlier ages if the rule of law is to be maintained.

Law is made by a public authority. Private authority may give precepts, but can never make laws. The father or mother of a family gives precepts, not laws. The proper authority is determined by locale.

Finally, a law must be promulgated, that is, it must be made public. Persons can not be held to a course of action that has not been clearly and adequately pointed out to them. The legal dictum "ignorance of the law is no excuse" is in general true, but implies that a law has been sufficiently promulgated. Ignorance means ignorance on the part of the subject of the law through their own negligence. According to Thomas Aquinas, promulgation belongs to the essence of law. During the Middle Ages, a dispute arose as to whether promulgation belonged to the essence of law or was merely an essential condition. Duns Scotus held that promulgation was a necessary condition, but not an essential part of law. The dispute was largely speculative, since both parties demanded promulgation for a law take effect.

The natural law of course corresponds to this definition of law. The natural law is a command of reason for the common good. "Murder is immoral," for example, is certainly a reasonable command for the common good. The author of natural law, both Thomas and Augustine suggest, is God. In order to maintain natural law theory, one must realize the existence of natures. Given natures, it follows as night the day that certain laws govern those natures. Historically, every philosopher or theologian who concurs in the existence of natures also maintains a maker of those natures. Finally, natural law is promulgated through the use of human reason. Every man has an intellect by which he may observe and reason about human nature. Thomas argues that this very situation is the promulgation of natural law.

Every law must have a sanction, otherwise there would be nothing to compel observance of the law. Sanctions are natural when they are intrinsically related to law. For example, gluttony begets sickness and ultimately loss of health. The natural law has natural sanctions. Sanctions are positive when a proper authority arbitrarily lays down a particular punishment for a given offense, for example a fine for speeding in an automobile.

Law is a much broader concept than legal positivists admit: various kinds of law exist. God is the supreme law-giver insofar as the universe in general and man in particular depends upon him. God gives natural tendencies by which all things are inclined toward their proper ends. According to author, law is either divine or human. Divine law consists of eternal law, natural law, and positive law, which is further subdivided into primitive, Old Testament, and New Testament law. Human law consists in ecclesiastical, civil, and international law, and the *ius gentium* (the Law of Nations).

Eternal law is "God's plan for all creation, existing eternally in his own mind." Eternal law directs all things to their proper ends. If there were no eternal law, then events would occur without reason. Eternal law appears in Cicero and Plotinus, and enters the Christian tradition through Augustine. Every being in the universe has an end given it by God and tendencies within that nature impelling it toward that proper end. The sum total of all these laws governing nature is called eternal law. Eternal law is much wider than merely moral action and takes in more beings than man. All beings in the universe, and therefore all laws both physical and moral, fall under eternal law. God was not necessitated to create any particular being or the universe as a whole. Such necessity would limit divine freedom. Once he did, however, eternal law arises. Once created, all beings have ends and tendencies toward those ends. In the realm of physics, laws are irresistible. Even physical evils, such as earthquakes and volcanoes, represent the accurate fulfillment of physical laws. Miracles are not violations of the physical laws, merely suspensions of their effects. Moral laws can be broken, but violation of such laws is nonetheless unnatural. Man is endowed with free will. Of all material creation, he is the only being who can reject laws of his own nature. But man rejects the laws of his nature at his own peril.

Natural law is the human participation in the eternal law which inclines all things toward their proper ends. As eternal law, so natural law is divine in origin. But natural law is proximately based in human nature and promulgated through the use of man's intellect. Natural law is universal because, based on human nature itself, it refers to all men, Natural law is immutable, insofar as human nature does not change substantially. It is not subject to abrogation or dispensation. If human nature were to change substantially, so would natural law. In this case, however, no human natural law would exist, but rather some other natural law which applies to that species of being. Objectively immutable, the natural law is subjectively mutable in the sense that more remote precepts are not universally known and are only gradually realized by man.

The primary precept of the natural law is the precept known by all men intuitively in their first moral act. Thomas Aquinas states it as "do good and avoid evil." Augustine of Hippo maintains that the golden rule, "Do not do unto others as you would not have them do to you," is a primary precept of morality. The golden rule however is useful only in societies which are themselves moral. Secondary precepts of the natural law are immediate deductions from human nature, such as the morality of murder. Tertiary principles of the natural are remote conclusions drawn from human nature and difficult to know. In our own society, the morality of contraception might be an example. Man can not be ignorant of the primary precept of the natural law. With regard to the secondary precepts, individual vices and corrupt environment may cause distorted concepts of immediate conclusions of natural law. Cannibalism in primitive society and abortion, or even infanticide, in our own may be examples. Sincere men may err in regard to remote conclusions of natural law. Such difficulty indicates need for revelation. Not even God can dispense from precepts of natural law. However, at times God who possess supreme dominion over all creation could suspend certain moral laws for a just cause.

Natural law should be the basis of positive law. Civil law should merely mirror, amplify, or clarify natural law. Civil law which violates natural law is immoral and invalid. In our own time, Martin Luther King justified his breaking of the civil code when it was in violation of natural law. In his letter from a Birmingham jail, Martin Luther King refers to Thomas Aquinas, stating that an unjust law is no law at all. In this matter, Thomas but echoes Augustine of Hippo. The principal sanction of the natural law is loss of man's final end. There are, however, some natural temporal sanctions.

HUMAN POSITIVE LAW

The term positive stems from Latin, the past participle of *ponere* meaning "to place." A law promulgated by a tangible sign such as writing has come to be called positive law. Positive law is a dictate of reason, in harmony with natural law, making specific and clear what is left indeterminate by natural law. Like all law it must be promulgated by the proper authorities of the community for the common good. Though the ten commandments follow natural law, in the sense that they are written down by God they are divine positive law. State law is human positive law. Human beings are by nature social beings. For man to live fruitfully and happily, in the normal course he must live in society. Authority is necessary in society, if this authority is to bring proper benefits to its members. Thus authority is necessary for man in his present state. Civil law must be made by proper authorities. Civil law must be reasonable, properly promulgated, and in harmony with natural law. It must promote the common good.

Anarchists aside, no one denies the need for positive law in human society. Authority is a necessary element in every society, at least with man in his present state. Without authority order is impossible. Anarchists deny the necessity of positive law, be it divine or human. They believe in individual human self-sufficiency. According to anarchism, God could not endow man with freedom and then destroy that freedom by imposing specific courses of action. As was pointed out above, freedom has several interrelated meanings. Human beings retain their internal freedom from necessity even though they are not free from obligation. Positive law is both necessary and consistent with internal human freedom of choice. Human beings must do those things which perfect their natures and avoid those things which harm their natures, if they are to reach their final destiny. In this sense, there is no inconsistency between law and freedom. Human beings remain physically free to do what they will; they are not morally free. Human geings have the power to obey the law or violate it.

In general, laws bind in conscience. The legislator wills all means to accomplish the end of the law. One such means is that law bind in conscience. Over the centuries, philosophers have debated the existence of purely penal law. A penal law is one which does not bind in conscience, but b inds to the sanction. The sanction attached to it is sufficient that the law be observed. One must pay the penalty if he is caught disobeying the law. Such laws exist. One need think only of traffic regulations and particular taxes. These laws are obeyed because the penalty attached to non-observance is sufficient that they be obeyed. If every law were to bind in conscience, life would be intolerable and moral rigorism would reign supreme.

DIVINE POSITIVE LAW

Divine positive law is superimposed on natural law. God has explicitly and formally promulgated divine positive law and its existence is known to man through revelation. Divine positive laws is found in Mosaic Old Testament Law and in some New Testament Law. The former law has, of course, been superseded by the latter. Old Testament Law embodied moral, judicial, and ceremonial precepts. The exact time of the abrogation is not known. Some theologians place it at the death of Christ, others at the first solemn propagation of the new law on the first Pentecost.

New Testament law embodies three types of precepts. Dogmatic precepts concern those tenets which man must believe. Moral precepts are concerned with what man must do or avoid. Spiritual counsels concern the ideals of spiritual perfection. This new law will remain until the end of time. Many precepts of divine positive law are also precepts of natural law, for example "Thou shalt not steal." Others are purely positive laws, for example "Keep holy the Sabbath." Since God is author of divine positive law, he can dispense from it.

Some philosophers have held that all morality is based solely on divine will in such a way that there is only divine positive law, no natural law. William of Ockham (?1285-1347), for example, held that all morality was based on divine will. There is no natural law, only divine positive law. Ockham was forced into such a position by his nominalist metaphsics—he denied the existence of natures. Divine moral precepts were xfor Ockham arbitrary. God could have made adultery good, but decided against it. Divine positive law was contained in Scripture. Man could not reason to its precepts, but was in absolute need of revelation. The existence of natural law precludes this position. Natural law follows from the existence of natures. Nevertheless revelation is necessary in the present human condition for human beings to obtain a clear idea of various precepts of natural law.

CIVIL LAW

The state has the right and indeed the duty to make civil laws for the common good. With regard to property, the civil law should perfect and make more precise the right to private property. The civil law in general does two things. It can constitute and determine rights. It can also prescribe formalities which must be observed, especially in contracts, so that they be valid or licit. Civil law can affect juridical acts in several ways. (1) A civil law can neither prohibit nor affirm nor even assist an act, but only allow it to exist. (2) A civil law can make an act illicit, but not invalid. (3) A civil law can rescind an act. (4) A civil law is able to render an act invalid in the external forum (that is for the purposes of society, though such may not bind in conscience). (5) A civil law may render an act invalid in both the external and internal fora. Civil laws can bind in conscience. (6) Civil laws can render an act invalid. (7) Some civil laws do not bind in conscience. But when a formal judicial decision is made, civil law does bind in conscience.

IUS GENTIUM OR WORLD LAW

Ius Gentium or World Law is formally neither natural law, divine positive law, nor civil positive law enacted by states to regulate their relations with one another. *Ius gentium* is based on the will of humankind, on universal custom. It can be found in the laws of most countries. *Ius gentium* gradually but tacitly evolved by human agreement when independent states were formed. Many tenets go back to the ancient Romans. In surveying their vast empire, the Romans looked at laws and customs common to all or most of the peoples they governed. A code based upon these laws and customs was developed. The development of this code is a tribute to Roman genius for governing. There is some overlap between natural law and *ius gentium.* Laws of prescription with regard to property, the inviolability of ambassadors, the freedom of the high seas, dominion over certain waters surrounding a nation, and respect paid a flag of truce are examples of *ius gentium. Ius gentium* is neither necessary nor unchangeable—it is based upon human agreement. Total agreement does not exist concerning precepts of *ius gentium.* For example, Thomas Aquinas holds that property rights are not part of natural law, but arise from *ius gentium.*

Ius gentium is not the same as international law, though they may be similar in some regards. International law is derived principally from congresses between states and nations. It is formal written legislation. The Geneva Accords with regard to war or the Helsinki Accords with regard to human rights are examples of international law in our own time.

Cicero, Oration against Cataline, Pro Milone
Augustine, De libero arbitrio I.
Gatian's Decretals
Thomas Aquina, Summa Theolgiae, Treatise on Law
Grotius
Germain Grisez

CHAPTER

5

Conscience

Conscience is the last judgement of the practical intellect concerning the morality of an action, that is whether or not an action is in conformity with or in opposition to a moral law Conscience is the intellect in its practical function of judging the morality of an act, declaring a given act to be good and to be done, or to be evil and thus to be avoided. Conscience is the act whereby the human intellect applies universal principles of moral law to specific situations in daily life. Conscience is an act whereby a human intellect takes a particular situation, matches it up against principles of natural law, and declares a proposed action either to be in conformity with natural law (a good act) or in opposition to natural law (a bad act). Conscience ordinarily operates by deduction, reasoning from a universal principle to a particular conclusion. Nevertheless, moral principles are garnered by induction in the first instance. Man looks at individual cases to form moral principles. The moral principle once derived is then applied to individual cases. Aristotle opines that the application of universal principles to a particular situations is difficult.

In free human conduct, human beings know from experience that they are conscious of acts they perform. They pass judgement on them, considering whether they may or may not do a particular act or whether they should have done or omitted another act. This judgement is moral conscience and is the subjective proximate general rule or standard of right action. It presumes that the obligation imposed by law is known. Conscience imposes upon human beings an obligation to act in accord with law. Conscience tells us that a particular act is in conformity with, or in opposition to, a particular law.. Conscience is an act of the practical intellect, that is, conscience is the intellect in its function of judging morality. The judgement of conscience differs from other judgement only in that it concerns exclusively moral matters.

There are several kinds of conscience. A conscience may be antecedent, concomitant, or consequent according as it judges before, during, or after an act. A conscience is certain when it holds its conclusions without reasonable fear of error, that is it hold its conclusions with conviction and assurance that the judgement has a solid basis. A certain conscience could be erroneous. Conscience is doubtful either when no moral judgement is reached or, if a judgement is reached, it is maintained with reasonable fear of error. A conscience may be either correct or erroneous. A correct conscience judges in accord with the moral norm. It bases its judgement on the objective and actual moral order. An erroneous or false conscience does not judge in accord with the moral norm. It bases its judgement on what is objectively false. An erroneous conscience is vincibly erroneous if an individual could have and should have made his intellectual moral inferences more carefully. A conscience is invincibly erroneous if an individual could not have arrived at the objective truth through normal diligent effort, that is the effort of a prudent person. A probable conscience holds a conclusion based on reasons which are probably true, but may just as well be more probably false. An improbable conscience holds a conclusion based on an opinion which is not well founded. A perplexed conscience is one that believes it will do moral evil regardless of which of two alternatives it chooses. A scrupulous conscience is troubled for frivoulous reasons. It may attach moral gravity to acts which are only slightly immoral and may attach moral character to acts which have no morality. A lax conscience deems acts morally allowable for trivial reasons. It grasps the slightest reasons to classify an objectively grave evil as only slightly immoral and unhesitatingly classifies slightly immoral acts as possessing no moral character whatsoever. If passion, ignorance and other modifiers of responsibility never interfered with the human being's intellectual operation, only true consciences would exist. But these modifiers obviously exist and therefore different types of conscience follow.

Various moral principles guide the use of conscience. One may always follow a certain conscience. That man may follow a certain correct conscience is apparent. Man must follow a right conscience, if certain, in both its commands and prohibitions. That one may follow a certain erroneous conscience follows from the fact that conscience applies a universal moral precept to a particular case. If one makes an erroneous, but certain judgement, he must in fact follow that conscience. Otherwise, he would be willing to do an act which he thought wrong. Thus one may follow an invincibly erroneous conscience, but may not follow a vincibly erroneous conscience. In the latter case, the conscience by definition can not be certain.

Human beings may never act against a certain conscience. However, they may never follow a doubtful conscience÷÷but have a moral obligation to strive to make it certain. One may never act in doubt. Moralists customarily distinguish between doubts of law and doubts of fact. In cases of a doubt of law, a doubtful law does not bind. But an individual must have made a valid effort to determine the existence or correct interpretation of the law. In cases of doubt of fact, one may never act, but must strive to resolve the doubt. One may follow the morally safer course, which is usually not to act, but is not obliged to do so. One must seek to find the relevant information. One may also consult prudent, well-informed persons concerning a course of action.

When a doubt of fact can not be resolved by any of the methods mentioned above, certain reflex principles come into play which may aid in the solution of many cases. In cases of doubt, the condition of the possessor is to be preferred. Facts are not be presumed, but are to be proved. Acts are presumed to be valid until proved otherwise. What is first in time is ordinarily taken to be first in right. The presumption is in favor of the right of the superior over the inferior. All of these reflex principles can help resolve doubts of fact.

During the past few centuries, disputes have arisen concerning the degree of probability needed to resolve a doubtful conscience when consulting a moralist regarding a course of action. Some moralists held that only the more probable opinion could be followed. This position became known as probabiliorism or tutiorism. Other moralists thought that there must be at least equal weight on both sides before an act may be considered moral. This opinion was termed equiprobabilism. A third theory held that an act could be performed if there were a solidly probable, though minority opinion in its favor. After much discussion, the theory of probabilism won the day. As long as an opinion is solidly probable, it may be followed. An opinion, however, must be solidly probable, not held by only a few extremists. Probabilism guards against extremism in morality.

Human beings who have and invincibly perplexed conscience one must choose the lesser of the two evils. If both evils appear equal, one may choose either alternative. One may not follow either a lax or a scrupulous conscience, but must strive to rectify it.

READINGS

1. Thoms Aquinas, *Summa Theologiae* I, q 79, articles 12-13; I-II, articles 5 and 6; De Veritate II, 16 and 17.
2. John Henry Cardinal Newman, Grammar of Assent, pp. 105-13.
3. Germain Grisez, Morality.

CHAPTER 6

Sources of Morality

An act is morally good when it conforms to right order, that is natural law; otherwise it is morally bad. There are three elements in every moral act, of which, sometimes one, other times another, still other times all together, contribute to make an action conformable or not conformable to natural law: the object, the motive, and the circumstances.

The object of an act is that which the will primarily and directly intends when a specific action is performed, that towards which the very nature of an act itself tends. Thus the object of the act of prayer is the payment of due reverence to God. All acts, or at least a great majority of them, have inherent morality. If the object of an act be morally bad (blasphemy or stealing, for example), no motive on the part of the agent can possibly turn it into a good act.

The motive of an action is the reason which induces an agent to perform an action. An act derives its essential morality from its object, but a motive or purpose which an agent has in doing an action plays a role in determining its total morality. If a motive or purpose of the agent is totally and gravely evil, an act becomes wholly bad, even though it had a good object. This apparent change in morality occurs because the object of the act is not really what it seems to be. For example, money may be given a poor man, but if the sole and total motive is to bribe him, then the act is actually bribery, not giving alms to the poor, If the motive is only partially evil, the moral goodness is lessened but not totally destroyed. For example, if money is given to the poor, but pride is a partial motive, the act remains good, though its goodness is lessened. Even though a motive be totally good, it can not justify an evil act, bad by its object. One may not commit murder, even if the motive be good. An act that is morally indifferent (if there be such) becomes good or bad by the intention of the agent.

Circumstances of an action are conditions attached to an act which determine and distinguish it from other acts of the same type. Circumstances have only an accidental influence on the morality of an act; they slightly increase or decrease the moral responsibility or moral goodness or badness of an act. Circumstances do not make a good act bad nor a bad act good. The circumstances are who, what, when, where, why, by what means, and how. How: an action may be carried out in one of several manners: half-heartedly or intensely, with fear or hate. When: the quantity or quality of time consumed in an action may affect its morality, for example an act hastily done or done over a long period of time. Where: the place in which an act is done may affect its morality, for example public or private, sacred or profane. Why: a special motive may prompt an action. Who: a special condition or position of an agent may affect the morality, for example, a public official or a minister of the church. By what means: the special character of a means used to perform an act may affect its morality, for example expression of anger by secular or sacred words. What: a special quality or quantity of an object may affect the morality of an action, for example, stealing a watch or a sacred object, stealing a dollar or ten thousand dollars. Circumstances heighten the morality of an act when the circumstances bring about a transgression of another moral precept, for example to kill one's parents or to have intercourse with a married person. Circumstance may cause a bad act to be the source of injury to others, for example scandal. Circumstances related to quantity may create a grave moral offense because of an increase in quantity, for example, the circumstance of how much one steals (five cents or five million dollars). Circumstances relative to the physical completion of an internal act alter its essential morality. Thus, one might firmly resolve to take the life of a neighbor (an internal act of murder); one might then change one's mind or it might become impossible to commit the murder. The circumstance that an internal desire and resolution were never externalized certainly lessens moral responsibility in an essential way; a mere desire is an essentially different type of moral offense than an externally completed act. The circumstance that an evil action was committed many times against one person furnishes a possibility, not a certainty, that malice or hatred against the person may be involved, for example repeated theft or calumny.

For an act to be wholly good, the object, the motive, and the circumstances must be good.

CHAPTER

7 Effects of Morality

Imputability is that quality by which a free act is attributed to a person, as an effect is attributed to a cause. There are two types of imputability. Physical imputability occurs when an act is attributed to a person as a physical cause of an act. Moral imputability occurs when an act is attributed to a person as its moral cause, that is, the act is done with knowledge, consent and freedom. In itself, there is no implication of morality in mere physical imputability. Moral responsibility is the obligation to account for an act and to suffer its consequences. Moral responsibility follows from moral imputability of an action.

Merit and demerit are consequences of moral imputability. A good moral act produces merit for its agent. Likewise, a bad moral act produces demerit. Merit is defined as a right to reward because of a good rendered to someone else. Merit is either condign or congruous. Condign merit is demanded in strict justice; there is a moral obligation to bestow it. For example, a general is bound to give his soldiers adequate food, clothing, and shelter. Soldiers condignly merit these. Congruous merit is the bestowal of merit which is not morally obligatory, but is fittingly bestowed. A soldier who bravely carries out a perilous mission congruously merits a medal of honor. Before one can condignly merit recompense, the act must be free, morally good, and bring some good to another; the bestower must not be already bound, for some other reason, to confer this good on another person; and the merit must be desired and acceptable to the one receiving it. That one be liable to demerit for an act, the act must be free; a morally bad act; and bring harm to another, that is, in some way involve the violation of obligations to someone, for example not giving what should be given, as adoration to God. Does man condignly or congruously merit eternal happiness upon the completion of a good life. God is not obliged in justice to give eternal happiness to anyone. Such an obligation would place external constraint upon God. But a good life, we believe, produces happiness. God would not fail to give this reward. Therefore, strictly speaking, the bestowal of eternal happiness is congruous, but, in a broad sense, man condignly merits eternal happiness, since God, infinite truth, has promised it.

Reward is that which is rendered an agent for a good act, what an agent has merited. Punishment is an evil which an agent must suffer for performing a bad act. Reward is primarily a good given to an individual for a good act. Punishment is primarily an evil visited upon an individual for performing a bad act. Reward and punishment primarily look backward toward an act, not forward. Therefore punishment is primarily retributive in character; an evil visited upon a person for an evil he has done. Retribution can correct a harm done and restore the moral order, for example, $5000.00 awarded to a person for damaged property. However, punishment may have secondary objectives: correction, that is, correction of a fault; deterrence, to keep others from performing evil acts or to direct them toward doing good ones. Civil law follows principles laid own by natural law. If an act is free, bad, and harmful to another, an agent is punished. If an act is not free or is done without knowledge, civil law does not punish an agent, for example, an insane person may be put in a home for treatment, but is not jailed.

READINGS

CHAPTER

8

Ultimate Basis of Morality

THE ULTIMATE BASIS OF MORALITY

Morality is the quality of human acts by which some are called good and others evil. Right moral order is the disposition of human acts to lead man to his final destiny. Acts are good or bad in relation to this final end. If an act leads toward man's final destiny it is good; otherwise it is evil. Acts take on value in relation to man's final end. In this sense, morality is relative, that is, relative to man's final end. However, relative more often than not has taken on another meaning when referring to moral acts. Some philosophers have believed that all morality is relative, that is relative to time, place, environment, custom, and habit, to mention but a few factors. Acts regarded as good or bad in one culture may well be regarded as having the opposite morality under changed circumstances of age and place. According to this thesis, no absolute basis for morality exists. All moral principle is human conventional agreement, in one way or another. Natural law theorists will insist, on the other hand, that the essential morality of an act does not change with changed circumstances, that moral absolutes exist. For example, genocide is immoral, no matter what the circumstances. Acts of charity are good no matter the time or place. An act is good or bad because of its essential intrinsic nature, not because of accidental extrinsic factors.

Positivistic theories of morality contend that morality is extrinsic to an act. Thomas Hobbes (1588–1679) lived during the English civil war. Dujring that time there was real doubt if society could rule itself. Hobbes' experience led him to believe that the value of an act is determined merely by a legislator's will. Thomas Hobbes held that an essentially corrupt human nature could be constrained only by law. Morality exists only in so far as civil law exists. Acts are good or bad according to human decree. Many modern and contemporary legal theorists hold essentially the same position.

Divine positivists, such as William of Ockham, hold that an act is good or bad because of divine decree. Murder, blasphemy, adultery, or idolatry could have been decreed good acts by God, but in fact were not. Contrariwise, God could have decreed acts of charity, adoration of God, or telling the truth bad, but in fact did not.

CUSTOM

Some theorists have soughto,place the basis of morality in custom. Many social scientists hold this theory. Levi-Strauss held to cultural relativism. The most influential moral relativist of the last two centuries was Friedrich Nietzsche. He thought there to be no intrinsic morality, merely various kinds of people. Some were born leaders, aggressive, proud, and ambitious. Others are born followers, humble, passive, charitable. The former Nietzschean termed *Übermenschen,* supermen; the others *Sklaven,* slaves. Since the majority of men are slaves in the Nietzschean sense, they enshrined their own way of acting as moral. The historical movement which had the most influence on morality was the Judaeo-Christian tradition. Christians, and Jews since the time of the prophets, supported slave morality. The last real Christian was Christ. He was an *Übermensch.* One goal of Nietzschean philosophy was to produce more *Übermenschen.* The enormous influence of Nietzsche on twentieth-century thought and political activity can hardly be overestimated. German National Socialism took Nietzsche as its philosophical founder. Various political and social movements which seek power or empowerment are variations on Nietzschean themes. In our own time, attempts have been made to resurrect Nietzschean philosophy. These attempts regard Nietzshe as misinterpreted. They say that Nietzsche intended merely that man take responsibility for his activity, as an *Übermensch* does.

But acts have an intrinsic morality and do not take their morality merely from divine or human decree. Each and every man has a nature with the same specific destiny. Human nature itself has a destiny and is essentially unchangeable. Plato was a man in the same sense that Franklin Delano Roosevelt was a man. What differences exist are not essential. Evolution is a very likely scientific hypothesis. But this theory explains how man evolved, not what his essential nature is. Certainly, if the universe evolves in such a way that the species *homo sapiens* no longer exists, then there will be no human morality, as we now know it. There will be morality, but not a *homo sapiens* morality. Essential human nature is unchangeable. Certain moral acts perfect human nature and thus lead it to its end. Because some acts serve this purpose, they are morally good. Other acts are harmful to human nature and hinder it from attaining its destiny. Because these acts are destructive, they are morally evil. Acts are good or bad insofar as they are perfective or destructive of human nature, that is insofar as they lead or do not lead human beings to their final destiny. Morality is based on human nature and its destiny. Acts are good or bad by nature, not by divine or human fiat.

Nietzsche is subject to the same criticism as legal positivism. That custom exists there is no doubt. But to reduce all morality to custom is absurd. There are acts which every culture has viewed as good, others as bad. Rape for example is abhorred in every culture. Local custom can be criticized in light of natural law. If this were not true, man could never criticize his culture. Accordingly, if slavery were customary in a land, it would be good. If the custom of another land were genocide, that act would also be good. The morality of the Ku Kux Klan or Mafia could not be criticized from outside that culture.

Jean Jacques Rousseau also believed that morality was based on convention. Similarly to other Enlightenment figures, he thought that human beings were originally in a state of nature, that is, some state prior to entering society. According to Rousseau, in this state humans were naturally good, that is, they took no more from nature than they needed. However humans found it advantageous to enter society. This movement into society, convenient as it was, produced bad effects. Society corrupted man. Rousseau must be viewed against the customs of the corrupt French court at the time. His social doctrine is called the theory of the "noble savage." Rousseau's solution was that human beings should return to nature. Many environmentalists today are fundamentally Rousseauean. Man in society corrupts nature and himself. Rousseau prepared the way for the French revolution much in the manner that John Locke prepared the way for both the English and American Revolutions.

Divine will is of course the ultimate basis of all creation and in this sense the ultimate basis of reality. God was free to create or not. Nothing could force the divine will. But once God created human nature, certain ways of acting followed from that nature, that is certain acts were in accord with that nature and certain acts were not. But morality does not depend merely upon a capricious divine whim.

The proximate basis for morality is that an act fulfills or does not fulfill a moral obligation which rests upon human nature. An act is morally good when it fulfills an obligation which rests upon human nature, morally bad when it violates such a moral obligation. There can, however, be acts of supererogation which human beings can perform and which lead them to their final destiny. Such acts are good, but not obligatory. Humans can reason to moral obligation by considering human nature, in both body and soul, and in all its relationships, that is to God, to fellowman, to society, to himself and to all creation below him. If an act fulfills a moral obligation, that act is good. If it does not, that act is bad, that is, it involves a violation or omission of moral obligation. Therefore, the proximate basis for morality is right human reason considering human nature in its totality.

SENTIMENTALISM

Throughout history philosophers have searched for the ultimate basis of morality. Natural law in its various forms has been the theory which historically has attracted most attention. It is the conclusion of *philosophia perennis.* But there have been attempts to find a basis for morality elsewhere.

Sentimentalism is one such attempt. This theory maintains that human have a special sense within them, distinct from other faculties, which determines whether an act is good or bad. Some of these philosophers think that man has an aesthetic power by which he judges things to be beautiful. When this power is pleased, man calls that object beautiful, otherwise he calls it ugly. When this power is turned toward morality, the same applies. When the sense is pleased. an act is termed good, when displeased, the act is called bad. Moral judgements are immediate and intuitive. The ultimate arbiter of morality is this moral sense. Thomas Reid (1710–1796), Francis Hutcheson (1694–1746), Adam Smith (1723–1790), and Johann Herbart (1776–1841) are classic theorists of sentimentalism. Martin Luther (1483–1546) held that the ultimate arbiter of morality was individual conscience, a variation on the same theme. In Great Britain, Bishop Joseph Butler (1692–1752) maintained that the final objective arbiter of morality is conscience. He identified the moral sense with conscience. Adherents to sentimentalism were many times Protestant.

According to sentimentalism morality becomes completely subjective. The criterion of morality is the moral sense of each person. Moral principle has no truth in itself. Rather the principle "genocide is immoral" could be true for one person and false for another. However, the ultimate basis for morality must be unchangeable, absolute, objective, and certain. An act must be by its very nature good or bad. Whether acts are good or bad depends upon their intrinsic nature, whether they lead human beings to their final end or not, not upon subjective opinion. Opinions of individual persons, while important in deciding action, are not the ultimate arbiter of morality.

At first glance, moral sense theory appears close to the classic teaching on conscience. Indeed Joseph Butler identified moral sense and conscience. In reality, conscience is the intellect in its function of judging morality, not some separate faculty. Further, conscience tells man whether an act is right or wrong, but does not determine its morality. Conscience is therefore the proximate subjective norm of morality. By it man applies general moral principles to individual acts. Sentimentalism, on the other hand, teaches that the moral sense is the ultimate norm of morality. For a sentimentalist, there can be no appeal beyond conscience. By such a subjective criterion, grave moral evils could be and in fact have been justified.

RATIONALISM

Moral rationalism holds that the ultimate basis of morality lies within human reason itself. Reason is the final judge, the ultimate foundation of morality. Kant is often classified as an idealist because of his philosophy of mind, that causality, universality, or necessity, among other natural categories, are in actuality categories of the mind, not reality. However, in ethics Immanual Kant (1724–1804) should be classified as a rationalist. In his epistemology, Kant thought that natures were unknowable. A human being could not know natures of things from what he sensed. Natures were unknowable x's. As a result, natural law could not be sustained as a basis for morality. Kant therefore sought a basis for morality elsewhere, and decide upon reason itself. In establishing morality, Kant thought the human will to be autonomous. The intention of a moral agent determines the morality of any act. Kant thought that only acts done from the motive of duty were morally good. Acts done from inclination had at best no morality whatever. For example, if a student came to class out of a moral obligation to do so, the act would be good. If, however, he came to class because he liked it, out of inclination, the act would have no morality about it at all. Kant gave two criteria by which to judge duty. The first Kantian moral principle is to "universalize the act." In any given situation, an agent must ask himself what would be the outcome if everyone involved in this kind of situation were to act in a certain way. If the outcome would be good, then the act is good. If the outcome were bad, the act would be bad. For example, a professor does not feel like lecturing at the end of term because he is fatigued. According to Kant, the professor should ask himself the following question. What would the consequences be if every professor, or perhaps every person, did not come to work when he felt fatigued? Of course, society in general would disintegrate. Therefore, according to Kant's first principle, the professor has a moral obligation to lecture. In effect, by this first principle Kant attempts to reintroduce a kind of universal natural law which his epistemology would not afford. Kant's second principle of morality is "persons should be treated as ends in themselves, not as means to the agent's end." What Kant has in mind is apparent. Other people should not be used for one's own ends, as for example sometimes occurs in American business. This principle sounds good in theory, but in practice lacks cogency. A student uses a professor or a librarian as a means toward knowledge. These are morally good acts. The professor buys a newspaper form a newsagent and on both parts this is a morally good act. Nevertheless, Kant's second principle is taken as a moral aphorism in many strata of contemporary philosophy and theology. Kant calls his system the "categorical imperative," categorical meaning absolute, not hypothetical, on the side of the moral agent and imperative indicating obligation. Human beings must act this way as a rational being, if they are to act morally, that is in accord with their rational nature.

At the end of his moral discussion, Kant states three postulates necessary for the moral life. According to Kant, these tenets can not be proved, but must be accepted if there is to be morality. The first is the freedom of the will. Without freedom there is no morality. By freedom Kant means internal freedom of choice. Secondly, Kant postulated the existence of God. Earlier Kant had denied that man could prove the existence of God by reason. His epistemology left no possibility of proving God by an existential inference from effect to cause, since man could not know outside reality. And he thought the ontological argument, proving the existence of God from the idea of God, to be equally invalid. It treats existence as a predicate, like beautiful or intelligent or industrious. Such is obvioisly not the case—Thomas Aquinas would agree. However Kant postulates the existence of God as the one who metes out ultimate justice as necessary for the moral life. Finally, Kant postulates the immortality of the soul. There must be a time when justice is meted out; experience teaches that it is certainly not in this life. Therefore, the soul must be immortal. In all three instances, Kant tries to reintroduce into his philosophy what he could not accept from an epistemological standpoint in his speculative philosophy.

Despite Kant's best efforts toward a rational system, morality still becomes subjective, that is dependent upon an individual person's judgement. Each man's individual judgement according to the principles of the categorical imperative is the norm of morality. Kant's moral categories have no specific content beyond what an individual gives them. Kant only apparently makes reason the norm of morality. The basis for morality is not absolute and unchangeable. For Kant, an act is good when it brings about benefit to society, that is a universal custom, bad when it does not. But on what basis is the human being to judge benefit to society? Natural law theorists maintain that the answer to this question goes beyond man's reason to the appreciation of duty to God, fellow man, society, and himself. Kant's two maxims actually take him to a kind of natural law, wherein he admits that acts are good or bad in themselves because they contravene certain obligations, but his epistemology does not allow him to admit natural law. Further, because of his conception of duty as the basis for morality, Kant totally destroys the distinction between what must be done and what may be done. There is a difference between respecting one's neighbor's property and giving alms to the poor. One is obliged to the former in justice, to the latter in charity. According to the Kantian standard, both must be equally rooted in justice, in universal custom. If a man were not to perform acts of charity, he would be acting unjustly. True, Christ gave us a new commandment, to love one another. But the exegesis of this biblical passage must accord with the objective distinction between justice and charity. There must be a distinction between what must be done and what may done. Otherwise, we are in a system of extreme moral rigorism. Thirdly, Kant's attempts to save freedom of choice, God's existence, and immortality of the soul fail. These postulates actually belittle human reason. God does not exist because we need him. Indeed much of German philosophy of the eighteenth and nineteenth century is influenced by Martin Luther's notion of the complete deprivation of the powers of the human intellect.

EMOTIVISM

During the twentieth century, the most influential philosophical school of ethics among Anglo-Saxon moralists has been logical positivism and its intellectual twin grammatical analysis. Both schools analyze human statements, and only human statements, to ascertain their real meaning. Their theory of ethics is called emotivism. In 1936, A.J. Ayer published the groundwork of logical positivism, entitled *Language, Truth, and Logic.* In this work, Ayer divided all propositions—and he dealt only in propositions—into analytic and synthetic. Analytic propositions take the form of "X is X." They are true by analysis. They are tautologies, and therefore always true. However, these propositions say nothing about existing reality. Synthetic propositions are of the form "S is P," that is some predicate (P) exists in some subject (S). In these propositions, the predicate adds to the idea of the subject. Such propositions have meaning if and only if they fulfill the principle of verification. The principle of verification states that only those synthetic propositions have meaning which can be verified by sense contents, that is the five senses. Ayer then went on to apply this principle to, among other things, moral principle. A moral statement, for example "genocide is immoral," is not analytic because the idea of the predicate, in this case "immoral," is not contained in the idea of the subject, in this case genocide. At first the proposition appears synthetic; however, in actuality the statement is not synthetic either since no sense content exists by which it might be verified. Therefore, moral statements have no meaning and are purely statements of emotion. "Genocide is immoral" is a statement of one's attitude toward genocide, such as "genocide—yuk," or "genocide—phooey," but no more. The author of these statements may wish tht you agree with them, but nothing more. Attempts have been made to improve upon the principle of verification. The principle of falsification was introduced whereby a statement has meaning if and only if there exists a conceivable sense content which would prove that statement false. The effect of this principle on moral propositions is negligible from a positivist perspective, and thus its effects on the emotive theory of ethics is insignificant.

Emotivism is open to the obvious objection that the principles of verification or falsification are not themselves verifiable or falsifiable in the positivist's narrow sense of the term. Thus, emotivism falls on idts own sword and does not fulfill its own criterion. It too is dependent upon first principles. That criticism aside, the question remains whether acts are moral or immoral in themselves and whether statements about such acts could be true or false. Wars have been fought over the principle "genocide is immoral." To reduce such wars to battles over emotion or semantics would trivialize them beyond common sense. Acts have intrinsic value. An act of rape is by nature intrinsically bad. Our emotional reaction to it follows from its intrinsic immorality. According to Ayer, the statements "genocide is moral" and "genocide is immoral" could both be true at the same time and in the same respect, depending merely upon the attitude of the one saying them.

HEDONISM

Hedonism, from the Greek word *hedone* meaning pleasure, was first introduced by ancient Greeks. Hedonism is sometimes called egotistical utilitarianism. There are two kinds of hedonism. Psychological hedonism maintains that human beings are forced by their very nature to pursue pleasure or to avoid pain. In this matter, human beings have no choice. They are so constituted. Ethical hedonism goes farther and maintains that what brings pleasure is good and what brings pain is bad. Acts are good or bad according as they bring pleasure or avoid pain. The strict hedonist must hold that only quantities of pleasure exist, that is all pleasure is somehow material. Otherwise, pleasure would not be ultimate, but the principle by which man judged pleasure would be ultimate. Many hedonists realize that this theory is crude and have therefore tried to modify it. Epicurus himself an ancient Greek thinker, realized that there must be a difference between intellectual and sensual pleasures. John Stuart Mill held the same position. "Better to be a man dissatisfied than a pig satisfied," proclaims Mill. But these two men correct hedonism illogically. If pleasure is to be the chief good, then there could be no criterion beyond pleasure by which to judge goods. As a result, there could not be different kinds of pleasures, only differences in amount. In its crudest form, hedonism holds: Do all to attain the greatest amount of self-satisfaction.

Aristippus of Cyrene was the first Greek to hold this doctrine. Epicurus preferred social and intellectual pleasures to sensual ones and even conferred a value on pain as a form of enhanced pleasure, or at least a means of obtaining greater pleasure. Man might take salt for example to enhance the pleasure of drinking. Among modern philosophers, Thomas Hobbes is perhaps the only true hedonist. But Jeremy Bentham, better known as a social utilitarian, provides a kind of mathematical calculus by which humans can judge one pleasure to be better than another. The late B.F. Skinner and the scool of behaviorism which folllwed him, in general should also be classified as hedonistic because of the various theories of gratification. Various utilitarian jurists could also be classified as hedonists.

In general, hedonism proceeds on the false assumption that complete human happiness is to be found in various material goods. Acts are good which bring pleasure or at least avoid pain, and bad when they bring pain. That man seeks only pleasure is contradicted by individual conscience and human experience. Human beings do certain noble acts which do not bring material goods, for example, dying for one's country, and other ignoble acts which lead to the possession of material goods, for example stealing. All men at all times have regarded dying for one's country as good and stealing as bad. Hedonism makes the human being the sole and ultimate judge of what is morally good or bad. It divorces human beings from social obligation as well as obligation to God.

UTILITARIANISM

Hedonism is too selfish a philosophy to abide in its purest form. Philosophers have therefore attempted to correct its most disastrous social effects. Hedonism's philosophical twin, however, is social utilitarianism. Social utilitarians accept hedonism as their basis, but set the goal of philosophy as "the greatest good for the greatest number." According to utilitarianism, acts derive their morality solely from their usefulness to individuals or society. Utilitarianism is hedonism for the masses. In general, utilitarianism emphasizes that morality derives from the usefulness of human activity in attaining goods of this life. According to social utilitarians, society is only the sum total of individuals. Society itself is a fiction. Corporations are legal fictions. Therefore, the goal of society must be to promote the greatest amount of pleasure for the greatest number understood as individuals. Social well-being and prosperity in this sense are the norm of conduct.

Social utilitarianism finds its origins in nineteenth-century England. Its founder was Jeremy Bentham (1748–1832) and its greatest promoter John Stuart Mill (1806–1873). They enuntiated "the greatest felicity principle" that the only goal for an individual or for society is promotion of the greatest good for the greatest number. This greatest good is understood in terms of pleasure. In France, Auguste Comte (1798–1857) promoted a variation on the same theme, as did Rudolf Lotze (1817–1881) in Germany. Herbert Spencer (1820–1903) held that an act is morally good only if it confers good on both an individual and society. Any act which injures either an individual or the community would be a morally bad act. Wilhelm Wundt (1832–1920), the German psychologist, called his own theory Progressive Social Utilitarianism. He maintained that acts are good which advance mankind to higher levels, that is in art, science, and culture. Among contemporary American philosophers, John Rawls classifies himself as a contractarian, but hiswethicakdtherhy contains elements akin to social utilitarian. He holds that social benefit should be decided by disinterested groups of citizens. In this way, he thinks the evils of hedonism can be avoided. Many a contemporary politician in the Western world is in reality a social utilitarian, consciously or unconsciously. Social utilitarianism survives today in its modified British form in most European parliamentary democracies.

Social utilitarianism in its various forms is subject to the same criticism as materialistic hedonism. Social utilitarianism is "hedonism for the masses." It gives no criterion for the morality of acts which have neutral social consequences, which neither help nor hinder social prosperity. The judgement of what acts are beneficial to society and what acts are not is left to individual conscience so that morality once again becomes subjective. Many evil acts, for example abortion or some types of genetic research, are approved simply because they bring material goods. Further, utilitarianism has a false philosophy of community: the common good is the sum total of individual goods. In this opinion, utilitarianism commits the logical error of composition, that is because individuals have a certain characteristic, the whole has the same characteristic. A basketball coach, for example, would be quite surprised to learn that his team has no existence beyond the individuals who comprise it. The best basketball team is not necessarily the one with five best players, but rather the one with the five best players who work together. Likewise, the common good for society is not necessarily the good for the most individuals.

In essence, Wundt's theory of progressive social utilitarianism is not a moral theory at all. It seeks to improve art and culture without offering a moral standard for acts in no way connected with the arts. No moral criterion is offered to men whose lives are not concerned with cultural and artistic matters.

READINGS

1. Kant,
2. Nietsche,
3. Hobbes,
4. Rousseau,
5. Bentham,
6. Mill

CHAPTER

9 Virtue

Every being has an end. *Omnis agens agit propter finem.* Qualities exist which enable each being to perform its function well. For example, a knife's function is to cut. Sharpness is that quality which allows a knife to perform its proper function well. The Greek word for this quality was *arete,* which translates as "excellence" and hence "virtue" in English. The Latin word *uirtus,* from which the English word virtue is derived, in turn stems from the Latin word *uir* for man (the opposite of which is *femina* or woman). The word means "manliness" or "strength." Gradually, virtue came to mean that which allows a human capacity to perform its function well. Since the ancient Greeks thought that only intellect distinguished man from animals (the Greeks had no precise conception of will), *arete* or excellence or virtue belonged only to the intellect. According to Aristotle, the intellect performs two functions, speculative and practical. The speculative intellect pursues truth for its own sake. The practical intellect seeks knowledge to direct human activity. In Aristotle's *Nichomachean Ethics,* virtues of the speculative intellect, those habits which allow it to perform its function well, are wisdom, understanding, good counsel, and reasoning among others. Many of the virtues of the practical intellect Aristotle borrowed directly from Plato, *Republic* IV. Plato may have taken them from Athenian society. These virtues numbered four: prudence (practical wisdom), fortitude (courage), temperance (moderation), and justice. With the Christian dispensation came gradually specific notions concerning free will. Augustine's notions of free will were developed in light of chapter seven of Paul's Epistle to the Romans. Augustine developed more fully free will and its relation to salvation by God's freely given grace. The virtues of the practical intellect became virtues which modified the will. For this reason, they were later termed moral virtues. The term cardinal virtue (from the Latin *cardo, cardinis,* in English "hinge") was later applied to them.

Moral acts leave a mark upon the human person. Like other acts, when moral acts of the same type are frequently repeated, they build habit. The habit of doing one specific type of morally good acts is called virtue. Moral virtue is therefore defined as a good habit, inclining a rational creature to perform its functions well, that is to operate in a good manner. Virtue is an operative habit, that is, it is characterized by activity and resides in some but not all members of the human species. An operative habit contrasts with an "entitative" habit which is passive in character and resides in all the members of a given species, such as hearing and sight. Virtue can never be the source of an evil act. Virtue resides in the rational powers of man. Hence, in the strict sense no being lower than the human in the scale of being can possess virtue. A dog is loyal for example only by analogy to human beings. A given virtue is present when a morally good act is done with constancy and frequency, when promptness and ease characterize the individual's action, and when the individual derives a certain enjoyment from this activity. Virtue is operative and active by nature. Virtue is further divided into infused and acquired. Infused virtue is given man by God freely to perfect his human powers of intellect and will. Faith, hope, and charity are examples. Acquired virtue comes about through activity. A person becomes honest by being honest. *Faber fit fabricando* (a man becomes a carpenter by being a carpenter).

Socrates and his student Plato held that virtue and knowledge were identical. If one knew what was good, he would do it. Evil stemmed from ignorance. The solution to evil in the world was education.. From Pythagoras, Plato justified the liberal arts as "training of the mind to see the good." Augustine allowed as how Plato was the closest of all ancient philosophers to Christianity because he knew the importance of seeing the Good. Despite Socratres' and Plato's best efforts to prove otherwise, virtue and knowledge are not identical. The possession of knowledge does not necessarily imply virtue. "If to do were as easy as to know what were good, chapels had been churches, and poor men's cottages princes' palaces (*Merchant of Venice,* Act 1, Scene 2)." Knowledge is essential to virtue; one must know what is good. But this moral knowledge must be put into practice. Man has both intellect and will. The operation of both intellect and will lies at the basis of virtue.

Aristotle characterizes virtue as a golden mean between two extremes, excess and defect. Man can offend against virtue by either excess or defect. According to Aristotle, man offends against virtue by excess when he goes beyond the standard demanded by it. Man offends against virtue by defect when he fails to meet the standard. *In medio stat uirtus,* said the medievals. For example, man may offend against the virtue of fortitude by excess, by rash activity such as the acts of a daredevil, or by defect, that is by timidity. There are objective and subjective standards to virtue. For example, one may offend against the virtue of temperance objectively by drinking too much or subjectively by drinking in an unnatural manner.

CARDINAL VIRTUES

Prudence is the practical moral virtue by which humans are inclined to choose the proper ends and the proper means to attain those ends. For example, a prudent person knows the proper amount of work to put into a given job. He also knows how to go about changing working conditions without upsetting the entire operation. Man offends against prudence by excess when he thinks too much and consequently does not act or acts too late. He offends against prudence by defect when he does not consider at all. Ancient philosophers asked whether, if a man had one virtue, did he have them all? The apparent answer to this question is no, since one could be honest for example, without being temperate. Yet, if a man had prudence, always choosing the proper goals and the proper means to attain those goals, he would have all virtue. In the Christian dispensation, love occupies much the same position. If one has love, he has every virtue. Augustine writes in *De ciuitate dei:* "Whence it occurs to me that the best short definition of virtue is the order of love (cf. Song of Songs 2:4)." Again, "love and do what you will" (*Tractatus in epistulam ad Parthos*: *Dilige et quod uis fac*).

Fortitude (courage) is the moral virtue by which man is inclined to be strong in the face of danger, especially danger of death. Man offends against fortitude by excess when he goes beyond the prudential mean by risking life or health unnecessarily. Man offends against fortitude by defect when he is too timid to act in light of only small or no risk. A daredevil may offend against the virtue of fortitude by excess. A timid person offends by defect. In recent years whether to tell a patient that he or she is dying has come to the fore. The topic is far too wide for an introduction such as this. But the virtue of fortitude can only be practiced in light of such knowledge.

Temperance is the moral virtue by which man is inclined to moderate pleasures of the sensitive appetite, especially pleasures involved with food, drink, and sex. The sensitive appetite, which man possesses in common with irrational animals, is the desire or aversion for the object after it has been apprehended by the senses. Man offends against temperance by excess when he indulges in too much pleasure. In accord with his theory of virtue as the golden mean, Aristotle held that man offends against temperance by defect when he is able to seek no pleasure whatsoever. Aristotle comments that such apathy toward pleasure is seldom found, so seldom in fact that Aristotle coined a word for it which translates into English as "insensibility." We may all agree with Aristotle's sentiments.

Justice is the moral virtue by which man is inclined to give others their due. Aristotle himself recognized that his theory of the golden mean did not apply to justice. Justice is of three kinds: commutative, distributive, and legal. Commutative justice is the moral virtue by which man is inclined to give another person his due. This type of justice reigns between individuals. Commutative justice is always based on a contract. The contract need not be written and in fact could be unilateral. Commutative justice also rules over contracts between corporate persons, that is groups of persons gathered together for particular goals, or between a corporate person and an individual. Corporate persons really exist and are not merely legal fictions. Distributive justice is the moral virtue by which society is inclined to render an individual his due. Distributive justice would incline society to insure food, clothing, and shelter for all its citizens. How this situation would come about is not prescribed by distributive justice. In our own time, questions of health-care have become a focus of distributive justice. By this virtue, society owes an individual reasonable health-care. What this may mean changes as medicine and society change. In the ordinary case, offenses against distributive justice do not oblige to restitution, since we know neither who has perpetrated the evil nor who has been offended. When both are known, restitution is obligatory. Legal justice is the virtue by which individuals are inclined to give society its due. Ordinarily, man learns his obligations to society through the law. But legal justice goes beyond civil law. In contemporary society, obligations of distributive justice have taken precedence over obligations of legal justice. But obligations of legal justice are not to be overlooked. Social justice is a term commonly found today and is a combination of the three types of justice. Justice is not the only source of obligation. Many obligations arise from other virtues, for example charity. Every man has obligations to support the poor. This obligation is rooted in the virtue of charity, not justice.

READINGS

1. Plato,
2. Aristotle,
3. Augustine,
4. Aquinas,
5. MacIntyre.

CHAPTER 10

Man's Final End

MAN'S TRUE FINAL END

As we pointed out at the beginning of the last chapter, every agent acts for an end. *Omnis agens agit propter finem.* Wherever there is activity, there must be direction. Activity without purpose is inconceivable. All being below the human in the scale of being acts for a purpose. These beings follow physical laws of the universe. The more man knows about the physical universe, the more order and design and purpose he discovers. Often, physical scientists explain various laws of the physical world, but they fail to see purpose. They often answer the question how, but fail even to ask the question why. Humans are endowed with intellect and will. In accordance with these natural endowments, they follow directions freely chosen by themselves. This does not mean that God has failed to set a goal for them. Human destiny is set for humans by God. But human beings have in some sense the ability to choose whether they will reach it. Obviously human choice is proper only when it harmonizes with God's designs. Human beings may freely choose a course of action, but they exercise this gift of freedom properly only when they choose to act in accord with those things perfective of their naturea and, thus, beneficial to them in the sense that they bring their nature to the proper goal, the destiny set for it in its nature by God.

From observation and reflection humans know that every time they act, they act for some purpose. If there were no final purpose, there would be no action. For example, students come to a university to obtain a degree. If this final cause were not present, the intermediate causes would also pass away. No one would come to philosophy class if there were no final purpose of obtaining the degree, or, if they did come, they would come for some other purpose, for example to learn philosophy. By the same logic, human beings must have some final cause, some purpose. From the time of Aristotle, if not before, philosophers have thought that all human beings desire happiness. In his *Hortensius,* Cicero again and again asserts that man seeks happiness. Through the enormous influence of this work on Augustine, eudaemonism, the theory that all human beings seek happiness, entered into the Christian tradition. Happiness is a universal craving of the human heart. All human beings in all times and places have desired it. The desire for happiness is a natural desire of the human being, essential to its nature. Even when a human being does evil, he does it because he sees it to be good, albeit mistakenly; he believes it will make him happy. Humans seek an objective evil because they erroneously believe it to be good, helpful, and productive of happiness. Plato was the first one to see that humans can act only for the good. His mistake was to think that, if man knew what was good, he would do it. Plato was correct that many human beings are ignorant of what produces true happiness. It was left to Augustine of Hippo to see that human beings always seek the good, but at times will an apparent instead of a real good.

A human natural desire implanted in him must be somehow attainable. If it were not, then God would have placed an unattainable desire within man and life would be intrinsically frustrating, Some modern philosophers have held exactly that opinion, that life is futile. But, if a good God exists, life can not be intrinsically frustrating. Indeed all other beings attain their purpose given them by God. There is a distinction between objective happiness, that is what, in itself, produces true happiness, and subjective happiness, that is what an individual seeks because he believes it will produce happiness. Human beings can only be happy when they possess what they want and are unhappy when they can not possess what they desire. But they must desire what is proper. Happiness is a desire satisfied by possession of a good. Augustine of Hippo writes in *De ciuitate dei*: "Man is happy when he possesses what he wants, provided he desires the right things." Happiness consists in degrees. Greater satisfaction and more lasting contentment result from possession of some things rather than others. No human being is perfectly happy in this pilgrim state (*in statu perigrinationis*) since no human beings has ever possessed anything capable of fully and permanently satisfying his desires. Ultimate human happiness must exist in the fulfillment of what differentiates human beings from animals, that is intellect and will.

What good is there which, when attained, will bring man full, perfect, and absolutely permanent happiness? This end or objective or good must possess certain characteristics if it is to produce complete happiness. It must be an objective reality outside of the human being. The cravings of human heart and mind seek something beyond itself. God has implanted natural cravings in the human heart; hence there must be some means of satisfying them. Full happiness comes with the subjective possession of what objectively constitutes perfect happiness. Human nature is the same in all human beings in the sense of what constitutes them as different from irrational animals. Therefore, the final end of all human beingcs must be the same. There must be that one, objective being which, when possessed, fully satisfies the human heart in such a way that it desires nothing more, and which will bring full and permanent happiness to all. The final end must be truly "final," subordinate to no other end. Plato was the first philosopher to see that the human final end must be the ultimate reality which humans seek in all their acts, the reality which, when possessed, fully satisfies the human being in such a way that he desires nothing more. No measure of evil, however small, must be associated with the ultimate end. Such an imperfection would inevitably destroy the completeness and absoluteness of the satisfaction. The final end must be "all sufficing" in its perfection; otherwise, additional satisfaction would be required for its completeness and its "ultimate" character would be destroyed. The possession of the final end must be permanent. If the possibility of losing it were present, the satisfaction would necessarily be imperfect. This argument is used by Augustine in *De ciutate dei* against reincarnation and eternally recurring cycles found in Plato's *Republic.* Augustine of Hippo was evidently the first thinker to see that, if a human being could lose what made him happy, such could not bring ultimate happiness. A human being is not expressly and formally striving for his final end in all his actions. Rather such striving is tacit and virtual. Here and now, human beings do not formally avert to the reason they desire given objects. Nevertheless, the quest for happiness pulls human beings constantly, even though they do not formally perceive it.

FALSE THEORIES ON MAN'S FINAL END

Many false theories have existed and still do exist on the final end of man, concerning what will bring him ultimate happiness. Among the ancients, there was general agreement that human beings had a final purpose, but they argued about what it was. Plato believed that human destiny lay in the intellectual apprehension of the good. He did not conceive of this good as a person. Furthermore, he thought that education in the liberal arts ending in philosophy could bring an elite few to intellectual sight of this good. Plato thought this end to be attainable in this life. His student Aristotle thought two things about ultimate happiness. In *Nichomachean Ethics,* he wrote that happiness consisted in cultivation of virtue and in philosophical leisure to contemplate good. He was not sure that man could attain such a state fully in this life. In *Eudaemean Ethics,* Aristotle opined that the great spirited man, the civic philanthropist or ruler, was the happy man. So far as we know, he never attempted to reconcile these views. It is the view of the *Nichomachean Ethics,* severely modified, which perdured in the West through Thomas Aquinas and his followers. Epicureans placed man's final end in the possession of pleasure. The Stoics placed man's final good in the virtuous life by which man strictly controlled his emotions. The Stoic ideal was *apatheia,* complete lack of emotion.

In modern America, philosophical pragmatism of William James (1842-1910) and especially John Dewey (1859-1952) has denied the very existence of a human final cause. Life is simply a continual and unending series of solving practical problems. The method by which these problems are solved is trial and error. The purpose of education is to learn the trial and error method of problem solving. As a result, moral law does not exist, merely a method by which problems are solved. Such pragmatism is ultimately insufficient. That a final end for human beings exists is shown by the fact that, if no final cause exists, all other intermediate causes disappear. *Omnis agens agit propter finem.*

Ultimate happiness can not be found in perfection of the body. Physical health, physical beauty, or sense pleasure can not produce ultimate happiness. These goods are sought only as means to a further end. They satisfy only one part of man and his lower part at that. These goods involve many defects, such as poverty, ignorance, and other vices which accompany them. The continuing possession of these goods depends upon external factors, that is, they can be subject to the whims of fortune (Augustine, *De beata uita* I, 1-4). Ultimate happiness can not consist in perfection of the mind by study and attainment of knowledge, Certainly perfection of the speculative intellect by virtue is a worthy goal. But study of the arts and sciences is sought for truth, beauty, and goodness. Such knowledge is acquired only by great labor and retained only through continuous effort. Perfection of mind can be lost—the incidence of disease of the mind indicates this imperfection. Most important of all, knowledge of the arts and sciences can be attained by only a few. If ultimate happiness consisted in perfection of the intellect through the arts and sciences, only a select few could attain it. This end would not be available to all human beings. Plato and his later followers thought that ultimate happiness was attainable through study of he liberal arts. Both he and his later disciples believed that only an elite few could attain this happiness. Porphyry (240-300) was looking for an universal way salvation. He realized the problem of attainment of the final end by only a few. Augustine of Hippo saw Christianity as the fulfillment of this desire for salvation of mankind. Though the attainment of knowledge in and of itself must be rejected as the ultimate end for man, Plato and his later disciples Porphyry and Plotinus saw clearly that ultimate human happiness must somehow consist in fulfillment of the human search for beauty and truth. Augustine held with them that ultimate happiness must somehow perfect the human intellect. Through Augustine, this doctrine definitively entered into the Christian tradition. Perfect happiness can not be found in external goods. Riches, honor, prestige, or friendship can not produce perfect happiness. These are acquired with difficulty, preserved only with great care, and with constant fear of loss. Most human beings can not attain them. Continuing possession of them depends upon external factors over which human beings have little or no control. They certainly lack permanence. In particular, wealth is sought for the sake of other things and thus can not be ultimate. Nor can ultimate happiness be found in all these goods taken collectively: A mere increase in quantity does not alter quality. All goods mentioned above lack qualities necessary to produce ultimate happiness. Possession of a number of these goods, or even all of them together, would not alter their imperfect character. Each of them is attained with difficulty and preserved only with great inconvenience and anxiety. Even taken together, they lack permanence. Death separates human beings from all these goods and never allows them to be satisfied fully with their possession.

Thus a desire for ultimate happiness is rooted in human nature. It was placed there by an intelligent and wise source. Such a desire must be capable of fulfillment; otherwise life would be intrinsically frustrating. Hence some objective reality exists which man can attain and which, when possessed, will bring man ultimate happiness. This objective reality which produces ultimate happiness can not consist in any bodily, mental, or external good.

MAN'S TRUE FINAL END: GOD

Divine goodness and wisdom demand that every desire of happiness, rooted in human nature, must have an object attainable by all human beings and which, when attained, will result in ultimate happiness for them. No partial good, no finite being, no good available in this life can fulfill these requirements. Hence the object of human desire for ultimate happiness must be the Infinite Being. Man has both an intellect and will. The human intellect seeks to know truth to which there is no limit. There is no truth which man does not seek to know. Likewise, the will seeks to possess good to which there is no limit. There is no good which the will does not seek. All truth and all goodness under another name are called God. Hence, the object of the human desire for ultimate happiness can be satisfied only by the possession of God. The final end must be sought solely for itself; and must totally satisfy the human desire once possessed. Only God is absolute goodness. Hence, if man is to possess total goodness, he must possess God. Augustine says of Plato that he is of all the ancient philosophers the closest to the Christians, because he located the final end of man in the possession of ultimate goodness (*De ciuitate dei*). Logically, we should expect that some finite truth could satisfy our finite intellect and some finite good could satisfy our will. The human intellect and will however are pointed toward the infinite. There is no limit to the truth and the good which humans seek. Only infinite truth, goodness, and beauty will satisfy it.

Boethius defined happiness as the "state which is perfect because of the possession of all goods." The precise nature of ultimate happiness, however, is beyond the power of human reason to fathom in detail. Certainly, ultimate happiness will consist in the fulfillment of the human intellect by truth and the human will by good. Ultimate happiness primarily consists in the activity of human intellect in the contemplation of infinite truth and beauty. This contemplation immediately results in the delight of the will in its conscious possession of the infinite good. The activity of highest human spiritual powers, intellect and will, should redound in some unknown way to the happiness of all lower human powers.

The distinction between two ends for man, a purely natural end and a supernatural one, has been debated since the Middle Ages. Followers of Thomas Aquinas usually make a distinction between a human supernatural end, attainable only by grace, and a natural end, attainable by man's own power. Such a distinction was made to preserve the gratuity of God's grace. Thomas himself appears not to have made this distinction. Augustine of Hippo saw Christianity as the fulfillment of the search of the ancient philosophers. As such he did not see two ends for man. Surely, pure nature (*natura pura*), untouched by sin and by God's grace, is a mental abstraction. Surely also in the actually existing order only one end for man exists. Medieval theologians speculated about obediential potency by which man could be receptive of God's grace, though this grace is not a part of nature. As such, man is a God-directed being. Modern theologians, such as Karl Rahner, speak of "supernatural existential" by which they mean to show that the human being is God-directed. Such theologians are in the tradition of Augustine of Hippo. "You have made us for yourself, O Lord, and our heart is restless until it rests in Thee" (*Confessiones* I,i,1). Further discussion of this topic must be left to a study of divine revelation.

READINGS

1. Plato (*Symposium*), Aristotle (*Nichomachean Ethics* X); Augustine of Hippo (*De beata uita* IV, 35; *De ordine* II, 45; *De ciuitate dei* VIII); Thomas Aquinas, *Summa Theologiae*; *De Veritate*

II

CURRENT ETHICAL ISSUES
A. INDIVIDUAL ETHICS

CHAPTER 1

Rights and Duties

"Right" translates into English the Latin word *ius.* As in Latin, so in English the word has various related meanings. The term "right" is used in a three-fold sense. In a legal sense, the word means "law" or a system or body of laws. For example, civil rights or Bill of Rights has this meaning. *Ius* in Latin is related to the word justice and legal terms which derive from it. Thus, "right" may be taken to mean just or equitable. This is the objective meaning of the word. For example, "it is right that a worker should receive his pay." "Right" may also be used subjectively. In this sense, "right" means a "moral power" in a person. For example, a person has "a right to life." In ethics, the third sense comes to the fore, that is right is used subjectively, as a moral power.

A "right" is "a moral, inviolable power of someone over something as his own." A right is termed a "moral" power because only a moral being, that is a being with intellect and will, can possess it. An infant, or even a fetus, possesses rights, since both possess intellect and will, albeit in as yet undeveloped state. Rational nature is present. According to this definition, animals do not possess rights. The reason that animals do not have rights follows from their nature. As we saw above, man has a purpose in life, to achieve happiness. This end may only be achieved by human acts, that is acts which follow from knowledge, voluntariness, and freedom. Since man is free, he must be able to achieve that which makes him happy. The possession of rights follows from this basis. Since animals can not perform acts which follow upon intellect and will, they do not strictly speaking have rights. This does not mean that animals can be treated impsroperly by human beings. Since he is a person, God has rights. One of God's rights is to have his creation treated respectfully. Animals are a part of his creation. Society or corporations are moral persons, that is a group of rational beings gathered together for a purpose. Comprised of rational beings, moral persons have rights. A right is "inviolable" as a moral power because no one may morally prevent one from exercising it. A right is not physically, but morally inviolable. One can be prevented physically, but not morally, from exercising a right.

The history of rights closely parallels the history of natural law. The traditional teaching on the nature of rights has drawn fire from various quarters over the past decades. To replace the traditional criteria of intellect and will, some have suggested a "not equivalent theory." According to this theory a separation between human nature and person exists (Dieter Birnbacher). Only those human beings are persons who have personal characteristics. A distinction is drawn between "mere human beings" and persons. Thus some human beings are not persons. Other theorists of non-equivalence are of the opinion that all human beings are persons, but wish to extend the concept of person to higher animals in order that they may possess rights (Peter Singer). Because higher animals have characteristics similar to persons, they would have rights. The basic contention is that only those beings which have interests have rights. This is extended particularly to the "right to life." The above-mentioned philosophers contradict the traditional teaching from Augustine to Kant that human beings and only human beings in so far as they are human beings with a rational nature must have freedom to act and thus have rights. God of course has rights, as do angels. A great social danger exists when philosophers decide who is a person on grounds of utilitarian worth.

Contemporary medical anthropology has indicated that human life begins with the coming together (*Verschmelzung*) of egg and sperm. Fertilization is the decisive source from which all later development continually comes. At that time at the latest, the genom of the new man is determined. Even before that human gender is determined. From the existence of the zygot on, the embryo is a functional, self-organized, and differentiated unit. As a dynamic and autonomous system, it fulfils all the conditions to be an individual in a biological sense. These conditions would also be fulfilled by an embryo *in vitro*. Biological research in itself can not determine conditions for personhood. But contemporary biological research does support the traditional doctrine of personhood and rights.

Rights are of many kinds. First of all, rights are either natural or positive. A natural right derives from the natural law, for example the right to life. Positive rights are based on positive law. Thus a positive right derives from either God or man. Divine right derives from divine positive law, for example the right of the church to teach the doctrine of Christ. Human positive rights are either ecclesiastical or civil. The church thus has a right to impose upon its members such obligations as it thinks necessary for their welfare. Civil right derives from civil law. The state has the right to impose such laws as are necessary or useful for the well-being of society. Rights are inalienable if they may not be morally ceded by the subject. Rights are alienable when they may be ceded. For example, the right to life is inalienable. The right to property is alienable. Rights are juridical or perfect when they are derived from legal rights, either from natural or positive law. For example, a worker has right to equitable wages. Rights are non-juridical or imperfect when they are based on a virtue other than justice. For example, a benefactor has a right to expect gratitude. This right is based in charity. A right to property is an exclusive right to the full and free possession, use, and disposition of a thing at will. It is a right in property when the object is actually possessed. It is a right to property when the object is owned, but not actually possessed. Right of jurisdiction is the lawful power of a duly constituted authority to make laws and to govern its subjects.

The subject of a right is the person in whom the right resides. The subject of a right must always be a person. The matter of a right is that with which the right is concerned. The matter of a right may never be a person. On this ground alone, slavery is immoral. The term of a right is the person who has an obligation to respect a right. The title of a right is the concrete fact by reason of which the person possesses the right. The title may be natural if derived from natural law or acquired if derived from some fact rather than from human nature, for example, a claim to property based on a will.

Coaction (or coertion) is the moral power which the possessor of a right has to secure the exercise of his legitimate rights and to remove all obstacles which prevent their exercise. As a property of a right, coaction is not the force itself, but the right to use force. The force need not be physical, it can for example be social.

Collision of rights is the apparent conflict of two or more rights in such a way that one person apparently can not exercise his right without violation of another's right. Such a conflict is only apparent because a true conflict of rights can not exist. When rights collide, certain guidelines prescribe the solution. The greater right prevails, the lesser right ceases to exist and in this instance ceases to be a right. The right which belongs to the more universal order prevails. A natural right prevails over a positive right. The more common good takes precedence over the private good. The right of the superior takes precedence over the right of the inferior. The closer relationship takes precedence over the more remote. Thus a soldier may place the welfare of his country above his own private right to life. The right of life is concerned with graver matter than a right to private property. Thus a landowner may not shoot a trespasser on his property. A claim on charity by poor relatives is greater than a claim on charity held by poor persons in general. These principles are guidelines and therefore admit of exceptions.

The limitation of a right is the boundary outside of which the right can not be exercised. A right may be limited by one ceding the right. Ceding of a right is often done through contract. The right may be limited by nature of the right, for example the right to worship. God may limit rights. A right may be limited by some other obligation which a possessor of the right is obliged to fulfill. Man has a right to go to the movies, but not at the risk of his life. A right ceases to be a right when it impinges injuriously on the rights of someone else.

A distinction arises between the possession of a right and its exercise. Monks, for example, voluntarily give up their right to ownership. Actual poverty may hinder the exercise of certain natural rights.

ORIGIN OF RIGHTS: FALSE THEORIES

Some philosophers even unto the present day believe that the state is the sole source of all rights. The classic example of this theory is Thomas Hobbes. He maintained that legality and morality were identical. Moreover, according to Hobbes there is no natural law. Contemporary legal positivists hold the same general theory, though they may disagree with Hobbes on anthropological questions. This theory is subject to the same critique as denial of natural law. The state is obviously the source of some rights, but not all. Some rights are proper to human nature. In nature, man is prior to the state. Therefore, man has rights independent of the state, rights which no state may rightfully take away.

Other philosophers have thought that all rights arise from contract. Here again some rights are based on contract, but by no means all. Contract is not the sole source of right. For example, man must have the right to enter into a contract; this right precedes any contract. Man has an obligation to keep contracts once made. This obligation arises prior to any contract. Certain inalienable rights can not be made the subject of a contract. For example, two people can not make a contract whereby one acquires the right to murder the other. The right to life and innumerable other rights obviously have a foundation far more basic than any contract into which man may enter. Thus a source of right and duty more basic than the contract into which man is entering must exist. This source of right and duty precedes any contract and lays down the moral principles which govern man's entrance into and maintenance of freely made contracts.

Still other philosophers have held that rights arise from custom. This theory is false, but contains a partial truth. Some rights, but by no means all, arise from custom. In fact, custom becomes law under certain conditions: The following principles apply to custom becoming a law. A proper authority must silently approve the practice. (Society must have a proper authority coercing a given number of people to act in a certain way.) The practice must be reasonable. The practice must be adopted by the entire community in good faith, that is not believing that it is forbidden by proper authority. The custom must continue without interruption or complaint over a long period of years. Subjects in bad faith continue to violate the law. However, when a proper authority over a long period of time says nothing, then the act becomes custom. In fact, only a few rights arise from custom. Custom indeed presupposes law, since by definition custom can only be a practice contrary to existing law. Custom can not touch natural law, since customs against nature would not fulfill requirements of a legitimate custom.

DUTY

Duty is correlative to right. When someone has a right, others have a duty to respect it. Duty is a moral obligation, that is, humans have a moral obligation to respect a right. Man is morally, not physically, forced to respect the rights of others. Objectively taken, a duty is that which must be done or omitted. Subjectively, a duty is the moral obligation to do or omit something. In ethics, duty is ordinarily taken in the subjective sense. There are various types of duty. According to the law upon which it is based, duty is either natural or positive. Positive duties are either divine or human, according to the author of the law which imposes the duty. Human duties are either ecclesiastical or civil. Affirmative duties impose an obligation to do something, in accordance with the primary precept of the natural law to do good. Negative duties impose a moral obligation to omit something, in accord with the primary precept to avoid evil. Duties are perfect if demanded in justice, that is when they relate to a juridical right. Violations of a perfect duty demand restitution. Duties are imperfect when they are demanded by some virtue other than justice, for example charity.

Apparent conflicts in duties often arise. As with collision of rights, guidelines exist to help solve problems. Duties based on the natural or divine law take precedence over all others. Duties to self come before duties to others. Duties to one's higher nature take precedence over duties to one's lower nature. Duties to one's immediate family take precedence over duties to those outside the family. Duties to one's country take precedence over obligation to other countries. Likewise duties to fellow citizens come before duties to allies.

EXEMPTION FROM DUTY

"Necessity knows no law." In this expression the word "necessity" refers to situations in which fulfillment of a duty involves danger or hardship. Three types of hardship are to be distinguished. Extreme hardship is present when the fulfillment of a duty involves death or a comparable evil for the person who has the duty. Grave hardship is present when fulfillment of a duty would involve a grave evil less than death. Serious loss of health, serious loss of reputation, loss of a great amount of money or property would all be grave losses. Ordinary hardship refers to usual difficulties involved in performing a duty.

Ordinary hardship never exempts from duty. Ordinary hardship is foreseen by the legislator; therefore it does not exempt from duty. Duty would lose all significance if a moral agent were to be free from it as soon as some ordinary hardship were involved. However, extreme or grave hardship exempts from natural affirmative duties, but not from negative natural duties, that is those arising from natural or divine law. Affirmative duties admit of exception for just reasons; but negative laws do not admit of exceptions. Affirmative duties exist *semper, sed non pro semper* (always, but not for always). Negative duties oblige *semper et pro semper* (always and for always). Man has an affirmative obligation to support the poor. However, he is not doing this at all times. Man has a negative duty never to murder. There is no instance when this duty does not bind. Extreme or grave hardship exempts from affirmative duty imposed by human law. For example, paying taxes is not obligatory when doing so would cause extreme or grave hardship.

Duty involves the necessity of doing or omitting something. The source of this necessity is obviously not physical compulsion. Certain means are necessary for the attainment of particular ends or objectives. For example, study is necessary if man is to attain knowledge. However, study is only hypothetically necessary, since man is not required to attain some kinds of knowledge. Study of astrophysics is necessary only if man desires to know that science. But there is no necessity of ever knowing astrophysics. In contrast, when a given end must be attained, an absolute necessity exists to use requisite means to attain that end. Man is destined for happiness necessarily. This happiness comes only from possession of God by the human intellect and will. To attain that end, a moral life is absolutely necessary. Moral obligation may therefore be defined as an "ought" resulting from the necessary connection of certain means with a necessary end. The source of moral obligation is the necessity of using definite means to attain a necessary end (man's final destiny).

CHAPTER 2

Religion: Human Obligations Toward God

The usual etymological derivation of the term "religion," found in Lactantius and Augustine, is *religare,* a Latin word meaning "to bind back." Cicero prefers *relegere,* "to gather together." Modern etymologists tend to agree with Augustine. Whatever the etymology, the intended meaning is that man comes from God and is bound to God through religion. According to John Henry Cardinal Newman, "religion is the golden chain which binds man to the throne of the Eternal." Objectively, the sum total of man's obligations toward God comprise "religion." Viewed subjectively, religion is the virtue by which man bestows on God the worship due him as supreme being. Religion therefore deals with theoretical and practical truths concerning God and our relation to him.

From a moral perspective, two types of religion exist. Natural religion necessarily arises from the relationship existing between man, as dependent upon God, and God, as the one who holds man in existence. Natural religion is known solely through human reason. Supernatural religion is based on divine revelation: man receives religious truth directly from God through communication of his word.

The attainment of his final destiny is essentially important to the human being. A provident God fittingly should see to it that man has at his disposal truths necessary for the development of his spiritual nature. These truths man should have in their purity, not mixed with error. Natural religion does not meet this criterion. Only with great difficulty can the human mind prove from reason alone that God exists. In itself, God's nature is almost totally obscure to human reason. The human mind can show that God is, but has great difficulty in showing what God is. Even the greatest theologians remain quite agnostic on God's nature. "God is known better by not knowing," says Augustine of Hippo, following the Platonic tradition and followed by many others. If human beings were solely dependent on reason, they would come to possess religious and moral truths at a comparatively late period in life, if at all; much of their earthly lives would be deprived of spiritual direction. Many would die before reaching an appropriate age to attain religious truth. Most human beings would never reason to an adequate body of religious and moral principles. Some would not have the needed intelligence. Most human beings would be too concerned with the other affairs of life to devote themselves to such a difficult task. Reason can arrive at truth, but is capable of error. Numerous errors and obscurities on more difficult religious and moral truths would occur, when derived solely from human reasoning. Human beings must devote their intelligent life primarily to the attainment of his final destiny. Only if human beings possess religious and moral truths necessary for attainment of their final destiny from their earliest years and in a pure state, not blurred by error and permeated with partial truth, can human beings attain their end. The only way in which man can come into the possession of such complete truth at an early age would be through divine revelation, that is, that God would see fit to use adequate means to bring required truth to humankind. Natural religion is inadequate for human beings; divine revelation is necessary on part of human beings and is fitting on God's part.

However, God is not bound to reveal himself. Man can only prove the fittingness of divine revelation, not its actual occurrence. Some theologians of the past, Anselm of Canterbury for example, have argued from the fittingness of divine revelation to its necessity and indeed to the necessity of God's incarnation. On part human beings, divine revelation is necessary because of the inadequacies of the human intellect. But God is under no restriction to act in the most fitting manner nor is he under any obligation to bring human beings to their final destiny. If he were so necessitated, his perfection in being would be thrown into question—he would not be supremely free. There can be no necessity with God.

NECESSITY OF RELIGION

Man has a duty to worship God. First of all, the human being is bound to internal acts of worship. Man has an immortal soul and a spiritual destiny. Man is morally obliged to strive for his final destiny. The pursuit of his final end necessitates performance of good acts and avoidance of evil ones. These acts proceed from man, as man, as a rational being, from intellect and will. Acts which proceed from intellect and will are internal acts. Hence, man is bound to internal worship.

But man is also bound to external acts of worship. Man is a nature composed of matter and spirit, body and soul. Both body and soul depend upon God. Therefore, man's entire nature should acknowledge its dependence upon God. Human physical nature paying tribute to God on whom it depends for continued existence is external worship. Human beings should exercise their higher faculties of intellect and will in such a manner as to bring their whole natures, material and spiritual, to acknowledge God upon whom they depend. In accord with their nature, humans should externalize their interior thoughts and sentiments. For example, man gives gifts to those he loves. Man has a natural tendency to externalize his thoughts. Hence, the externalization of internal worship springs from a natural tendency. External worship is many times necessary to preserve internal worship. Internal worship of God would not long endure when there is no external acknowledgment. Internal worship without phenomenal expression is inhuman. Mere internal fasting from food for example does not suffice. Man's end as union with God by intellect was clearly seen by the best of ancient philosophers. With Plotinus, man's final end as intellectual union with God reached its zenith among Hellenists. Augustine of Hippo acknowledged his debt to Plotinus and his student Porphyry in this regard. Plotinus and Porphyry are in partial harmony with the New Testament writings of Paul and John. The principle differences between the Christian and Neoplatonic view of salvation are that (1) in Christianity material creation, and especially man's body, is something to be saved, not something to be shunned and (2) man can not reach his final end without divine help. However, God is not necessitated to provide this aid.

Human beings are social by nature. They are born into society and develop within it. That human nature is social is more difficult for contemporary humans to realize since many philosophies of the day, from Hobbes to utilitarian socialism, are atomistic and mechanistic. Not only did God create human beings, but he holds them in existence and cares for them. This is termed divine providence. As a social being, man should pay tribute to God. Society should unite to honor God. This worship is public since it is done in a group. Thus human beings are bound to social worship

The necessity to worship God is opposed to the false theory of religious indifferentism. Various forms of indifferentism have occurred in history. Absolute indifferentism conveys the attitude that human beings are free to accept or reject religion in general. Accordingly, human beings are free to mold their lives life according to religious and moral ideals or on the contrary not to bother about them at all, willy nilly. Absolute indifferentism must be rejected. Human beings are morally obliged to strive for their final end by performing acts perfective of their nature and avoiding acts detrimental to it. The sum total of these duties to perform certain good acts and avoid certain bad acts is called religion. Human beings are therefore morally obliged to religion.

Practical indifferentism professes belief in God's existence, immortality of man's soul, and final destiny, but acts as if such truths are not essential. Practical indifferentists are theoretical believers, but practical atheists. Allied to practical indifferentism is relative indifferentism. Relative indifferentism conveys the attitude that human beings should direct their lives according to religious and moral ideals, but that all religions are equal—it makes no difference what religion human beings select. All religions serve the same purpose. Such a position is irrational. A person who professes this view would regard it as utter foolishness if carried over into other truths. Truth is objective, independent of what any one human being or group of huma beings may think. In mathematics, for example two plus two equals four, regardless of what anyone might believe. In geometry, the sum of the angles of a triangle equals one-hundred and eighty degrees, regardless of what some minds might believe. The same applies to all other geometrical truths. It is not a matter of indifference whether man regards two plus two as equal to four, five, or six. Nor is it a matter of indifference whether man regards the sum of these aforementioned angles of a triangle as equaling one hundred and twenty or one hundred and seventy, or one hundrd and eighty degrees. Two plus two equals one specific amount; the obligation of the mathematician is to discover what that amount is. The sum of the angles of a triangle equals one specific number of degrees, and it is the obligation of the geometrician to discover what that amount is. Similarly, in ethics every act is either morally perfective of human nature or morally detrimental to human nature (we shall abstract from the question of the existence of indifferent acts in practice). One act cannot be both morally good and morally evil at the same time, in the same place, and in the same respect. To adopt such an attitude is to commit "intellectual suicide." Since an act must be either good or bad (or perhaps indifferent), it is the obligation of man, as a moral being, to discover precisely which it is—and then to direct his life accordingly. Human beings are not justified in taking the attitude that for one person to regard an act as good and another to regard an act as bad are equally permissible. It does not matter in the least whether the act be murder, stealing, or divorce. Any given act must be either good or bad—we leave the question of indifferent acts aside for the moment.

One of the most pernicious distinctions in the history of philosophy was made by David Hume. He distinguished between matters of value and matters of fact. Only the latter could be true or false. According to such a distinction, the principle "genocide is immoral" is not subject to truth or falsity. Some contemporary philosophers, such as A.J. Ayer and the later Bertrand Russell, follow Hume's distinction in principle. When applied to religion, such a distinction leads to religious indifferentism. But such a distinction is false. Moral propositions have the quality of truth about them every bit as much as other statements. The Second World War was fought, at least partially, over the existence of moral truth. The same is true concerning the war with terroism today.

Relative indifferentism is no less a contradiction intellectually when carried over into revealed religion. The advocates of relative indifferentism take the stand that all religions are equally good. But all religions can not be equally good if they are not equally true. They can not be equally true since they teach contradictory tenets on essential matters. Man possesses a moral obligation to make a sincere intellectual investigation of religious matters and to discover the religion which might possess revelation, if there is one.

Relative indifferentism results from various causes. Lack of intellectual training or serious intellectual effort may be present. Some may concern themselves only with business or other occupations. Children may accept the religion into which they are born without investigating its intellectual and historical foundation. There may be intellectual laziness, often using the pretext that man can not discover with certitude historical religious truth. Finally, a false concept of tolerance may exist; because everyone has a right to his opinion, all opinions are equal. Sometimes, religious indifferentism is misunderstood to be essential to a democratic ideal.

Despite the enormous intellectual problems created by religious indifference in contemporary society, the right of each person to his own personal religious beliefs must be maintained. "Truth has rights; error has no rights" often was derived from arguments such as those above. But truth and error exist only in the abstract. Persons exist in the concrete. Individuals in all sincerity and good faith have a right to pursue honestly and sincerely the way to God, the eternal destiny of human beings. Such a right does not entail that all religions are equal nor that no religious or moral truth exists, as David Hume might say. But religious rights of individual persons do exist. The main protagonist of this form of religious liberty within the Catholic Church in the twentieth century was John Courtney Murray. Originally viewed as suspect if not heretical, Murray's work proved decisive before and during the Second Vatican Council. His doctrine of religious liberty is now the official doctrine of the Catholic Church.

ACTS OF AND AGAINST THE VIRTUE OF RELIGION

A vow is a special act of religion. A vow is a promise made to God concerning a good which is better than its opposite. Ordinarily human beings are held to vows which they knowingly and willingly make. Vows made from grave emotional fear are of course null and void. However vows made under light fear or under intellectual fear only still remain valid in and of themselves. Further, an oath calls upon God to witness a truth. In appropriate matter, making or taking an oath is moral.

Man offends against the virtue of religion by not giving to God the worship due him or by giving to others the worship due to God alone. Superstitious practices and practices of idolatry offend against the human obligation to worship one God. Divination, by which human beings seek special knowledge from demons, or magical practices to attain some other good also offend against the true worship of the one God. Human beings may tempt God by seeking whether they in fact have a certain perfection, for example does he really know the future. Human beings also offend against the virtue of religion by blasphemy, that is the use of insulting language in God's regard. Cursing, by which man calls upon God to produce an evil for someone, is also an offense against religion.

In matters of religion, special attention should be paid to perjury. Perjury is an oath, requesting God to witness a falsehood. It is an offense against the virtues of religion and justice. In itself, perjury is a grave evil, since it calls upon the supreme being to witness a statement which a human being knows in fact to be false. In contemporary society, where the virtue of veracity has been demeaned and the legal system is more and more seen as a game of morally irrelevant rules, perjury is often found. A legal system can not function without people speaking truth under oath. Attorneys, clients, witnesses, and judges are obliged to tell the truth. The widespread use of perjury to defend oneself or others has led to undermining the legal system in the United States. Morally speaking, the distinction between relevant and irrelevant matter does not exist. Perjury is always of itself a serious moral offense, no matter of its relevance to a particular case.

CHAPTER 3

Human Obligations to Themselves

HEALTH

Health is a broad term including chemical, material, biological, psychological, social, and spiritual well-being. Human beings are composed of spirit and matter, body and soul. Accordingly, man has duties to care for both his spiritual and physical nature. Such care is broadly speaking termed health. The philosophical argument for preservation of one's health is an extension of the argument against murder and suicide, given below. The argument is theistic in nature. Human life is God's gift. Only God has the absolute right over life. Human beings have the right of use and stewardship, but not absolute control over their lives. No one outside of God has absolute right over either body or soul. As a result, human beings are morally obliged to take measures to preserve their health. Not to do so is take unto oneself what is God's. This obligation is moral. Not to take care of one's health to a reasonable degree is not only irrational, but more importantly immoral.

Human beings have obligations to their intellects, their highest spiritual faculty. They are morally obliged to pursue religious truth and consequent obligations thereby entailed. Human beings are obliged to discover basic moral truths. They are also obliged to acquire knowledge of specific moral obligations which fall to them in thier state of life. This obligation extends to acquisition of truths not directly moral in character. For example, physicians and nurses are morally obliged to learn not only ethics of their professions, but also various sciences proper to their professional work. The same applies to professors, teachers, and lawyers.

Human beings have moral obligations to their wills, their other spiritual faculty. The will is the faculty of action. Human beings often know moral truth and their consequent moral obligations, but fail to act upon them. "If to do were as easy as to know what were good to do, chapels had been churches and poor man's cottages princes' palaces." (Shakespeare, *Merchant of Venice*, Nerissa, act 1, scene 2). Human beings must actually perform or avoid various acts. They have an obligation to mold their lives according to what they know to be true. Hence, human beings must strengthen their wills, principally by development of the cardinal virtues. They have an obligation to develop a will which possesses moral courage to face hardships involved in living up to the moral "ought," and does not wilt in the face of continued difficulty.

Humans have an obligation to develop their various sense faculties. They acquire knowledge through their senses. Since human beings are morally bound to acquire knowledge, they are bound to the means to attain that end. The necessary means to attain the end herein involved are adequate development of sense faculties, so that these senses may perform their proper function of serving as a medium for the acquisition of knowledge.

Humans also have duties to their physical natures. The distinction between ordinary and extraordinary means arises. This distinction goes back to Domenico Banez, a sixteenth century Spanish Dominican phikospher cum theologian. A well-ordered love of body demands that humans adopt all ordinary means to preserve their lives and health. Both affirmative and negative moral obligations are entailed. Affirmative duties impose obligations to use ordinary means of preserving life. Ordinary means are those means which offer a reasonable hope of benefit and can be done without excessive hardship. Such means would include food, shelter, and clothing. Negative or prohibitive duties impose moral obligations to omit acts, which, if performed, would ordinarily be injurious to health or life. Humans can not for example go on a hunger strike to the point that it would endanger their health. However, human beings are not obliged to adopt extraordinary means to preserve life or health. Extraordinary means are those which either can not be borne without excessive hardship or offer little or no hope of success. Extraordinary means are more than a well-ordered love of body demands. Whether or not a given means is ordinary or extraordinary will depend frequently on the specific person involved, as well as time and place. What was extraordinary fifty years ago may well be ordinary today. A means which would be ordinary for one person might well be extraordinary for another because of differing circumstances. A political leader, for example, may well have the duty to use extraordinary means to preserve his health during times of crisis.

Since most healthcare today takes place at the hands of medical professionals and within the setting of medical facilities, to avoid confusion extraordinary means are sometimes termed elective means, that is means which may or may not be chosen by the patient under advice. Correspondingly, ordinary means are sometimes called mandatory, that is those means which must be taken to preserve one's health. This change in terminology has come about because many procedures which are quite common medical procedures today would, at least in certain circumstances, be called extraordinary by the moralist. Cardio-pulmonary resuscitation in certain circumstances might well be an example. Such a procedure is part of usual healthcare procedure in a hospital, but may well be regarded by a moralist as extraordinary, according to circumstance, because it would produce no certain benefit for a patient..

Contemporary discussion of healthcare includes a debate on man's right to healthcare and the state's role in providing it. This debate has arisen in the past fifty years or so because of significant advances in medical science and adoption of certain forms of socialism. The term science when referring to medical science has a meaning far different from the usual meaning of science. Inductive reasoning does not lead to as much certitude in the practice of medicine as in other sciences. The practice of medicine is as much an art as a science. Humans have a right from natural law to ordinary means to protect their lives. As a result, human beings have a right to a reasonable degree of healthcare. What determines a reasonable degree of healthcare changes according to time and place. Certainly a reasonable degree of healthcare is different, let us say, in Ruanda than in Chicago. A reasonable degree of healthcare at the beginning of the twenty-first century differs from healthcare a hundred years ago. It is estimated that highest cost item in the family budget at the turn from the nineteenth to the twentieth century was food, in the turn from the twentieth to the twenty-first the highest cost item is healthcare. The right to a reasonable degree of healthcare stems from distributive justice. Nevertheless, concern about individual healthcare has no doubt become exaggerated in the United States at the present time. Likewise, political policy has tended to exaggerate the role of government in providing healthcare. The individual has a right to a reasonable degree of healthcare, but has no right to the "best possible healthcare."

Modern healthcare discusses the "right to die." Often healthcare and legal professionals are called upon to determine whether a person is dead. In the late 1960's, Harvard Medical School's *ad hoc* Committee to examine the Definition of Brain Death developed the following criteria: (1) total unawareness of externally applied stimuli; (2) no spontaneous muscular movement or spontaneous breathing; (3) no reflexes except those mediated by the spinal cord. A flat electro-encephalogram (EEG) for at least ten minutes should confirm the other three tests. The validity of the Harvard criteria is still discussed. Moralists can accept these criteria. The absence of consciousness and self-control are ordinary signs of death. In any event, the distinction between ordinary and extraordinary means stands moralists in good stead in determining the morality and necessity of healthcare measures to be taken for the dying. In terminal cases, there is no need to prolong life unnecessarily, especially when that life will have no human quality to it. Modern hospice care has eliminated much of the pain, psychological, spiritual, and physical, which can accompany some deaths. Death is seen as the last part of life. All things being equal, death should take place within the family. Care is given to all members of the family during and after the death. However no act which directly results in death may be morally performed.

In cases of terminal illness, at times legal and moral obligations may well diverge. For a moralist, no difference exists between not placing a patient on life sustaining equipment and taking him off. The moral point in each case is the same: the unnecessary use of extraordinary means. Legally however, the case may be somewhat different. The state must protect terminally ill individuals from being taken off life sustaining equipment by decisions of those whose interest clearly lies in the person dying. Therefore, prospective patients may be encouraged to make living wills. In such wills, an outline of what measures are to be taken, or are not to be taken, in cases of terminal illness, is stated. In general such wills have a legal status. In making such wills, designees should be made aware of a distinct possibility that their ideas might well change when directly faced with decisions at the time of serious illness.

MURDER

Murder is the unjust taking of an innocent person's life. It is not the mere taking of another's life. Several factors are involved. The death of the other must be directly intended. An innocent person is one who has not forfeited his right to life by commission of some act. Innocent is understood in an objective sense: a maniac who does not have control over his actions may perform acts by which he objectively forfeits his right to life, though he is not responsible for them. Murder is the taking of life without legitimate authority. The state has claimed the right to take person's life under the right of capital punishment or just war. The very existence of a right to capital punishment is under intense discussion as we write. A soldier killing in war does so under the authority of the state. Killing in self-defense is not murder since the other has given up his right by some act he is committing.

The argument against murder is theistic. Its immorality lies in the fact that human beings deliberately destroy what does not belong to them, namely life. Every being depends upon God. God alone has dominion over all other beings, and alone possesses absolute property rights over these beings. Human beings are simply guardians of their lives and health, obliged to take ordinary precautions to preserve them. Humans can only attain their final goal of happiness by acts which they knowingly and freely perform. When one human being takes the life of another, or indeed his own life, he decides for himself what is God's alone to decide: how many acts are sufficient for a human beings to achieve their ends? Murder is therefore a violation of God's supreme dominion over human life. It involves the assumption on the part of a human beings that right which belongs to God alone. Further, each person has a right of use ownership over his own life. Murder violates this use right. Finally, if capital punishment is moral, then murder may violate the right of the state in both the administration of justice and preservation of public order. For all these reasons, killing an innocent person except on divine authority is immoral.

An innocent man may never be directly killed, not even by public authority. But it is morally justifiable to kill someone indirectly or even to endanger one's own life for a proportionately grave reason. Thus, it is moral to jump from a burning building to escape a fire, even if one is morally certain of dying. For a just reason and in the exercise of virtue, it is moral to fight fires, to fast, or to perform other ascetic works for the sake of the kingdom of God, for a doctor to work among those with contagious diseases, or for workers to expose themselves to danger in construction.

One who voluntarily and unjustly kills another is bound to restitution. But one who kills in self-defense, justly in war or by chance under other conditions, is not held to restitution. Likewise restitution is obligatory in cases of mutilation or physical harm to another. The obligation of restitution passes to the heirs of the murderer. The heirs of the murdered person are due restitution unless they release the killer from the obligation. A judge's punishment does not take away an obligation to restitution. The person who was killed is able before his death to forgive any restitution due himself, but can not forgive restitution due his heirs or others. Persons to be considered as harmed by murder include the spouse, children, parents, relatives, friends, poor to whom he might have given money, and his creditors. Murderers are morally bound to repair all temporal damage arising to murdered persons before their deaths. They must restore any necessary expenses for care or expenses which arise from the fact that such persons could not work at the time of their infirmity. Murderers do not owe the amount of money which a person is earning at the time; but a precise quantity of money owed is difficult to determine. A murderer is not bound to pay for pain endured by the person he murdered since restitution can not be made in the same order. But a judge may render a decision concerning money in light of pain. A murderer must also restore to persons directly affected by the murder any damage which they incur by reason of the direct cause of death. Therefore, a murderer owes restitution to the spouse, children, and parents who depended upon the murdered person for sustenance. However, circumstances or the direct will of the family may well be such that no restitution is due. If widows and children receive state sustenance, little or no restitution may be due. The poor and more distant relatives are not subjects of restitution. Nor is a murderer held to pay debts of the murdered person which a murderer could in no way foresee or could foresee only confusedly. If a murderer directly intended to harm creditors, he is bound to restitution. But he who kills another in a duel is not bound to any restitution, since the other person in the duel is thought to condone the action.

SUICIDE

Suicide is direct taking of one's own life on one's own private authority, that is the "direct" killing of oneself. A human being may "indirectly" risk his life or health and is justified in doing so for a sufficiently grave reason. The justifying reason must be proportionate to the gravity of the risk. One may even put himself in circumstances from which death might result for a proportionate reason. But a human may never directly take his own life. The double effect principle is applied in both cases. In the case of direct death, the first principle of the double effect, that the act must be good in itself, is violated. In the case of risking one's life, the fourth principle of the double effect, proportion between good and evil, must be weighed.

The argument against suicide is essentially the same as the argument against murder. One does not have power over his own life. Only God does. Since the time of Plato, the philosophical argument against suicide has been theistic. Further arguments against suicide must be left to consideration of divine revelation.

SELF-DEFENSE

An unjust aggressor is anyone who, without sufficient and appropriate authority, encroaches upon human rights. The right to life can be violated by an aggressor, one who makes an unjust attack. The unjust attack must be understood in an objective sense. In such cases, the one whose right is violated has some right to self-defense. Otherwise, only the aggressor would have rights. The principles on self-defense are in essence taken from Thomas Aquinas' article on the subject in *Summa Theologiae* II-II, q. 64, art. 7. (1) The motive must be self-defense; (2) force may only be used at the time of the attack; (3) force must be used only as a last resort; (4) only so much force as necessary to repel the attack may be used. The principles concerning self-defense are closely associated with the principles of the double effect—in fact the double effect principles derive essentially from this article in the *Summa.* A question arises concerning principle one. Thomas Aquinas himself held that one could not intend the death of the attacker. Some later thinkers consider that an agent possesses a right to will means to an end. Therefore a killing may be directly willed. The above principles hold also against unintentional aggression, for example attacks by the insane. Under the principles of self-defense, goods as dear as life may also be defended. Otherwise life would be intolerable: the right to life extends to a certain quality of that life. Liberty, sanity, chastity, and functional bodily integrity are usually numbered among these goods. Material goods of great worth are also considered worth defending with one's life. If such defense were not morally allowable, a thief in an act of stealing would have all the rights, the defender none. The fourth principle of the double effect is also directly involved: one may not kill to defend small material goods nor to protect honor or reputation.

Coaction, that is the use of force, is a property of a right, that is, human beings are justified in using force to retain what is rightfully theirs. That the use of violence or force in protection of rights be morally justified, certain factual conditions must be verified. First, with regard to time the aggressor may only be opposed during an actual aggression, that is an anticipatory or pre-emptive strike against the aggressor is not justified. It is sometimes questionable precisely when aggression has begun. Further, violence must cease as soon as one has succeeded in repelling aggression, that is one may not continue the violence as a punishment after an attack has been halted. Secondly, with regard to manner, human beings are justified in using only as much force as is necessary, that is what will result in the least injury while still repelling the attack. For example, if flattery would curtail the unjust attack, a human is not allowed to injure an attacker physically. Killing an attacker is not morally justified if a lesser form of physical violence would succeed in curtailing the unjust aggression. But it is not immoral to defend one's life, or goods as dear as life, as much and as long as necessary when they have been threatened. An individual has not acted immorally if he fights an aggressor to the death when his life or very notable possessions have been endangered.

In unjust aggression, a collision of rights exists. The collision arises between an innocent person's right to life or property and the aggressor's right to life and physical integrity. In such instances, the right of an innocent person takes precedence over the right of an unjust aggressor. The former is innocent. The aggressor can retain his right to life and physical integrity by stopping aggression. When a person has a true right to something, he also has a right to preserve it.

According to the third principle of the double effect, the defender must never directly will to injure the aggressor or kill him. Man may only will to stop the aggression. The nature of the defensive act is to stop the unjust attack. The intention should be similar. Man may not directly will the death or injury of an opponent. If death follows, such an injury is indirectly voluntary, not directly intended.

Human beings may use force in the protection of goods of great importance to which they have a strict right. Such goods which may be thus protected include a woman's right to protect her virginity, liberty, for example incarceration, or notable material possessions. Just as human beings protect rights through recourse to force, so may they use force to help others protect their rights against unjust attack. It is immoral to kill for the sake of injured honor or reputation, or to impede an injury or to recuperate one's honor. Human beings may morally recuperate damages done to themselves if they are unable to recover them through the legal system, but they may not kill to do so. Human beings are bound in justice to help those who are under their care in some way. They are bound in charity to help friends, acquaintances, and neighbors.

According to the fourth principle of the double effect, recourse to violence is not justified if the resistance will probably result in a loss far greater than the good to be protected. For example, a man may not risk his life and the life of an unjust aggressor over a small amount of money. Such incidents occur and have occurred not infrequently. Human beings are certainly justified, however, in risking their lives over goods as dear as life.

MUTILATION

Mutilation is related to suicide. Mutilation is destruction of a healthy part of the human body. Except for proportionately grave reasons, mutilation is immoral. Immorality of mutilation is of the same species as suicide. The philosophical argument against mutilation is similar to the argument against suicide. Since the human right over one's own life is a right of stewardship, the human being is obliged to take ordinary means to preserve that life. The only difference from suicide lies in the fact that in mutilation a man takes it upon himself to destroy part of the body, not his entire being. Mutilation is a grave or slight moral offense according to the gravity of the destruction. If a vital organ is destroyed, or if mutilation noticeably injures bodily integrity, mutilation is grave, and a grave moral offense. If mutilation injures the body only slightly, the moral offense is slight.

Obviously surgery is a mutilation. For a proportionately grave reason, man may undergo surgery. In the state of modern medicine, some surgical procedures may be considered ordinary means under most circumstances. Pius XII declared that such mutilation is morally justifiable under the principle of totality, that is a part may be sacrificed for the good of a whole. This principle had existed among moralists for some time, but was first given papal approval by Pius XII. The principle of totality applies only to an individual, not society as a whole.

Directly related to the moral obligation to preserve health is the matter of dieting and fasting. Bulimia, eating and then vomiting, and anorexia, an unhealthy lack of nourishment usually for cosmetic reasons, are not uncommon contemporary diseases or conditions. According to the second principle of the double effect, a good effect can not come directly from a bad effect, that is the end does not justify the means. Human beings may not perform an immoral act for any motive or end whatsoever. They may not fast or diet to the point of injuring their health, no matter what the goal: knowingly to fast or diet to the point of injury is morally wrong. Virtue is characterized by moderation. Within moderation, fasting is helpful to human beings both spiritually and physically. Spiritually, fasting helps a human being to develop his will, to develop temperance, and to accustom his rational nature to control his lower animal tendencies. Unquestionably, many men and women in the western world eat too much and in the normal case curtailment is helpful to health. Obesity has become a major problem. But sacrifice must take place moderately. A human being can offend against the virtue of temperance by excess as well as defect, that is by eating too much or too little. If excessive dieting arises from mental or psychosomatic illness, an individual may have diminished moral responsibility.

Human experimentation concerns modern moralists much more than in previous centuries. On the one hand, scientists understandably want freedom of scientific inquiry. On the other, patients have the right of privacy and self-determination. When experimentation deals with an individual patient directly for his own benefit, as long as a patient is aware of dangers present in the experimentation, there is no ethical problem. Ordinarily, such experimental treatments are used only when no other useful treatment is readily available. Problems arise with experimentation on human subjects. Human beings are specifically different from irrational animals. Humans may use animals for experimentation to the advantage of the human race. In such cases the fourth principle of the double effect is usually verified. Animals, as God's creation, may not be abused, but may be used for experimentation, because of advantage to the human race. Human beings may not be so used, whatever advantage to the race as a whole may come about. A humam being may not give permission for use of his person in experimentation which has little or no value to the human race or is highly dangerous to the individual himself. Such experimentation is subject to the fourth principle of the double effect. When the fourth principle is verified, informed consent from a patient must be received. Guidelines for consent in human experimentation have been issued by the Department of Health and Human Services in the Unites States of America. Discussion of the precise nature of informed consent continues.

DUELING

A duel is combat between two or a few persons waged for a private cause by mutual agreement with deadly weapons. Dueling has the same essential immorality as suicide. In a duel, a mutual bestowal of rights over life exists on the part of the persons involved. But neither person possesses such a right. One accepts "rights to kill" another. One bestows on the other the right to kill. Neither has the right which he is apparently bestowing on the other person. Such rights belong to God alone. Above and beyond the immorality, dueling is obviously quite foolish. Winning a duel establishes nothing. Dueling rarely ends a quarrel. In fact, the quarrel is often carried on by the family. Honor is not restored. Insult still remains. One's good name is not restored.

It is important to distinguish dueling from war. Dueling is private, war is public. In former times dueling took place mostly in Europe. Dueling was not uncommon in France. Both Voltaire and Napoleon opposed it. In 1855, the Council of Florence prohibited it. The Council regarded persons killed as suicide victims and the person killing as a murderer. Pio IX condemned the practice in 1869, Leo XIII again in 1891. In Germany, especially in the universities, dueling often occurred. In 1890, duels were condemned by the papacy, even when there may have been agreement to stop the duel as soon as any blood was spilled or any wound incurred. Injuries stemming from dueling were viewed as mutilations. Those who participated in, challenged, or accepted a duel, those who fostered or were immediately present at a duel, or those who served as seconds were subject to civil and ecclesiastical penalty. Those who were inflicted with fatal wounds were denied Christian burial. In English civil law, all deliberate duels have been outlawed since 1614. From 1819, duels have been outlawed everywhere. According to current American and English civil law, dueling is murder and seconds are accessories. Dueling, however, is morally allowable on public authority when it takes the place of war

Today, dueling is infrequent. But the morality of prizefighting is similar to dueling. Distinction should be made between amateur boxing, which is a sport, and professional prizefighting. In the second case, the very purpose of the gladiators is to injure an opponent, at least temporarily. A prizefighter's hands are in fact lethal weapons and can inflict untold damage. As such, prizefighting is immoral. The one against whom the injury is done puts himself in a position that grave injury may be done to him. The other inflicts damage. There can be no justification for either act. Prizefighting is therefore immoral on the first principle of the double effect: the act is immoral in itself. The amount of money which one receives for this practice is irrelevant. The same can not however be said for amateur boxing. There, the purpose is not to maim or injure the other, merely to practice the manly art of self-defense. In fact, a knockdown counts no more than a well-defended punch. Amateur boxing can be defended on the grounds that it is a sport.

EUTHANASIA

Euthanasia, sometimes termed "mercy-killing," derives from two Greek words, *eu* and *thanatos,* meaning "good death." Euthanasia could be classified under suicide or murder, depending on circumstance. The practice is ancient, going back to Athens of the fourth century before Christ, to the time of Plato and Aristotle. In the twentieth century, euthanasia was more common in England and the Netherlands than in the United States, but euthanasia has become ever more popular in America, witness referenda in various states. In several places, passage of civil "right to die" legislation has been attempted. States have had various court cases over euthanasia. Ordinarily one distinguishes between active and passive euthanasia. Active euthanasia can be further divided into either affirmative or negative euthanasia. In active euthanasia, direct means are taken, by either performing or not performing an act, to take another's life. Passive euthanasia is the denial of extraordinary means to let a patient die in peace. Some moralists do not entertain this distinction since passive euthanasia is really not euthanasia in any normal understanding of the term. Such a distinction, so they believe, only creates confusion. On the other hand, several see no distinction whatever between active and passive euthanasia on the grounds that the effect is the same. It is best to preserve the distinction.

While we may have some sympathy with the ends of euthanasia, in the final analysis active euthanasia, whether positive or negative, is immoral in itself. Euthanasia offends against the first principle of the double effect. The act of killing is immoral in itself. Further, according to the second principle of the double effect, a good end never justifies an evil means. Passive euthanasia however is morally acceptable. One does not need to intervene medically where there is little or no hope of success. There is no moral necessity to use extraordinary means.

Founded in Great Britain but now spread over the Western world, the hospice movement has shown the distinct difference between active and passive euthanasia. With medical advances in pain control, in most cases little need exists for a dying patient to suffer physical pain. Especially in cancer cases, pain is rarely the problem it was fifty years ago. The purpose of the hospice movement has been to enable patients to die in peace without pain, at home or in a medical facility designed for the purpose.

ABORTION

Abortion is expulsion of a fetus from a mother's womb before viability, that is before a fetus is capable of living outside a mother's womb. After twenty-four weeks some fetuses are viable. After seven months or twenty-eight weeks, nearly all are viable. If in this period when a fetus is viable it is removed, the process is termed "premature delivery." Several kinds of abortion exist. Abortions may be spontaneous or induced. A miscarriage is often called "spontaneous abortion." Induced abortions are direct, if the intention is to expel the fetus either as an end in itself or a means to another end. Induced abortion is indirect, when a fetus is expelled, but the death of the fetus is not directly intended.

When spontaneous expulsion results from an accident or disease, there is nothing immoral about the action. Directly induced abortion however is always objectively immoral. It consists in any direct act or attempt to procure expulsion of a fetus which is not viable where the expulsion is desired as an end in itself or a means to another end. Such abortion is never morally allowable since it is never moral to kill an innocent person. Indirectly induced abortions in which an action is done to cure or remedy a medical condition and which accidentally results in expulsion of a fetus is moral. Likewise an operation which is designed to cure a disease, but which results in the death of a fetus, is moral. For example, a cancerous uterus may be excised even though a woman is pregnant. For a proportionately grave reason, a premature delivery may be induced. Likewise, a caesarian section is morally justifiable for sufficient reason.

Since abortion consists in killing a human person, it is vital to understand what a person is and when it exists. There are several philosophical opinions concerning the moment when a human being begins to exist in the mother's womb. Aristotle, himself a biologist, held that the human soul enters the body only after some weeks. Thomas Aquinas followed him in this opinion, but did not therefore approve abortion. Biologists are unanimous today that the fetus within the mother is human: the DNA is a human DNA. The life of the fetus is a life distinct from the mother's, though certainly not separable for some period of time. According to the theory of body and soul, philosophers will probably never be in full agreement as to the time when the soul enters the body. This does not however change the morality of abortion. Under moral principles concerning conscience, man is never allowed to act on a doubtful conscience.

The morality and legality of abortion have given rise to extensive debate in the United States and world-wide. Much of the discussion is at the very least not well informed. Well over a million abortions are performed each year in the United States. There is general agreement, among abortion foes and proponents alike, that this number is far too large and that means should be taken to decrease the number. Since 1973 and the Supreme Court decision of Roe versus Wade (in this case, there was deception on the part of the plaintiff who represented that she had been raped when in fact she had not been. She is now deceased, but died an abortion opponent), the constitution of the United States has been interpreted as protecting the supposed right of a mother to abortion. In a complex and at times contradictory decision, the Supreme Court of the United States interpreted the constitution of the land to mean that a right of privacy on which the right to an abortion has been based supercedes an unborn child's right to life. The right to abortion comes under the "penumbra" of the right to privacy. To consider abortion a private matter is on its face bizarre. What more social matter could there be than bringing a new member of society into the world? A father and other members of a family are involved. Obviously, there can be no such right to abortion on the basis of privacy. In fact, an unborn child's right to life is being transgressed. In directly induced abortions, the first, second, and most likely the third principles of the double effect are violated. Politicians who seek legislation to protect the right of abortion are objectively involved in cooperation in evil. Their acts violate the first and second principles of the double effect. Whether there should be a national law concerning abortion is of course another matter. However, the Supreme Court of United States has ruled that it is a constitutional matter and therefore subject to federal laws.

The discussion of the objective immorality of abortion should not obscure the fact that many proponents of abortion, even of abortion on demand, are sincere. For some reason, the morality of abortion appears obscure to contemporary human beings. All should hope for a rational discussion of the matter at hand. The partial purpose of the above has been to clarify points for discussion.

STERILIZATION

Sterilization renders a person sexually sterile in a physical sense. It is therefore mutilation. Direct sterilization renders a person impotent precisely for the reason of not procreating. This procedure is not a cure for any known disease. Contraceptive sterilization, either for purposes of avoiding pregnancy or overpopulation, is immoral. Such sterilization is permanent contraception. Eugenic sterilization attempts to breed humankind, somewhat like horses. Voluntary sterilization is a major mutilation and thus is immoral. That sterilization involves only a minor operation is beside the point. Futher the state has no right to impose involuntary sterilization, even for reasons of bettering the genetic situation of the human race. The state has a duty to protect its citizens, but has no right to take away an individual's natural right to procreate. Therefore, eugenic sterilization is obviously immoral. Indirect sterilization may be moral according to the principles of the double effect. The fourth principle of the double effect must be verified. But a man has no right to castrate himself or mutilate himself for money.

There are various types of sterilization. Voluntary sterilization is the medically accepted operation which removes the power of procreation. Voluntary sterilization may be therapeutic wherein diseased organs are rendered sterile. If there is medical ground for the surgery, sterilization is certainly moral. Sterilization may also merely result from an operation sought for other reasons. Sometimes, therapeutic sterilization is used as a permanent means of contraception, sometimes for the reason that child-bearing would be dangerous. The sterilization of a healthy organ is a serious mutilation and therefore morally evil.

Sterilization of mentally defective persons is immoral since the state has no authority directly over the bodies of its citizens. These people have committed no crime and therefore a state can not justly sterilize them. Punitive sterilization usually does not fulfill the purpose of punishment. Rather many of the criminals glory in their punishment.

ANIMAL RIGHTS

Irrational animals do not have intellect and will and therefore do not attain their ends by means of them. Duties and rights extend to human beings because of their constitution of intellect and will. Animals have no such constitution. Therefore, animals do not strictly speaking have rights. But that animals do not have rights in themselves does not imply that irrational animals may be treated without due regard by human beings, willy nilly. Since God is a person, God has rights. God has a right that his creation be treated with due regard. The right resides in God, not in animals. Since modern and post-modern intellectual society either does not believe in God or is agnostic about his existence, man has attempted to find another basis for treating animals humanely. Thus, the argument concerning animal rights. Though animals are lacking reason and free will, they experience pain. To torture animals is therefore immoral. Experimentation on animals for the good of mankind is morally allowable as long as there is utility for humankind and the experimentation is necessary or at least reasonable for attaining this end.

CHAPTER 4

Truthfulness

Veracity is a moral virtue by which humans are inclined to tell the truth, that is to bring conformity between what is in their minds and the signs by which they explain their respective minds to other people. The matter of this virtue is the signs by which humans proffer their minds. The essence of the virtue of veracity lies in the harmony between the human sign and the reality it signifies. Under the virtue of veracity, humans are bound to love and seek truth, especially when something must be affirmed or denied. Humans are morally bound to be careful lest what they say be not in conformity with their minds. Humans are bound to express their minds when the occasion demands it, though they are not bound at all times to say what is on their minds. Demanding such openness is more a contemporary phenomenon, owing little to the tradition of true speech.

Man should keep his promises. Veracity has much in common with fidelity. Fidelity is the moral virtue by which man is inclined to conform deed and word. One who promises something means to oblige himself to fulfill what he wills to do for another. But ordinarily such promises do not bind in justice. Therefore, the duty to fulfill one's promises is a lighter obligation than obligations imposed by commutative justice.

A lie is speech against the mind (*locutio contra mentem*), as Augustine of Hippo defined it some sixteen hundred years ago. Speech here means any external sign by which concepts are signified, such as words, motions, or even deeds. Four factors are involved in a lie. (1) speech not in conformity with the mind; (2) the will to speak falsely; (3) the will to deceive; (4) the actual deception of another person. A lie differs from an error: in an error there is no intent to deceive. A person who speaks the truth, thinking that it is false, formally lies. A person lies if he says a state of affairs exists which he knows does not, or if he says a state of affairs does not exist which he knows in fact does, if he says a state of affairs is doubtful when it is in fact certain, or a state of affairs is certain when it is in fact doubtful.

Various kinds of lies exist. A pernicious lie is one that injures another person. A profitable lie is one which is proffered for the speaker's own benefit. A jocose lie is one whose object is humor. Lying is directly opposed to the virtue of veracity. The immorality of a lie is intrinsic. The essence of a lie consists in opposition between outward expression and inward thought. Whether an outward expression harmonizes with an inward thought is sometimes difficult to determine. Words, phrases, and expressions are arbitrary signs which human beings use by common consent to convey their thoughts. At best, they approximate thought. The inadequacy of words to express thought has the subject of many a philosophical and theological exercise from Plato to Jacques Derrida. The ethical standard is that, if a given statement does not portray a person's thoughts, to a hearer who analyzes the expression with normal diligence, that expression is opposed to the internal thought and is therefore a lie. If the expression conveys the opposite of objective truth, it is a lie.

Discussion of the morality of lying goes back to the time of Plato. Plato, and the Stoics after him, believed that lying was moral to avert great evils or to achieve great goods. Ordinarily these goods were understood as social. In the Old Testament, objective lies were told. Jacob lied to Isaac to obtain the birth right of primogeniture due Esau. Abraham lied concerning the true identity of his wife. Thus many of the early church fathers, for example John Chrysostom and Origen, agreed with Plato and the Stoics, as did some early heterodox thinkers.

Augustine of Hippo was however the first Christian thinker to analyze lying in detail. He saw the intrinsic immorality of lying. Lying could not be practiced in defense of truth. So great was Augustine's influence that his opinion has endured until the present day. Some Protestant thinkers have distinguished between a lie which is morally evil and a false *eloquium* by which the speaker intends to deceive, but which is in fact moral.

The human obligation to tell the truth arises on several grounds. First of all, the purpose of the faculty of speech is to reflect ideas in a person's mind. The existence of the intellect in man is the reason that human beings men have speech, but animals do not. When human beings lie, they speak what they know in their minds not to be true. This is why Augustine of Hippo defines a lie as *locutio contra mentem,* speech against the mind. Secondly, society could not function if one human being could not trust another's word. Society is built on the foundation that human beings must tell the truth to each other. The proper ordering of society demands that human beings have faith in one another. The same is true of the court system. Without the integrity of attorneys, judges, and witnesses, the judicial system falls apart, as we are witnessing in our own day. Immanuel Kant suggests a third reason, that lying goes against his second principle of morality, that persons should not be used as means to one's own end. When a man lies, he uses the other person for his own ends. This third reason must be seen within the logic of Kantian philosophy to judge its validity.

Human beings should observe the virtue of veracity at all times, however difficult it may be. Nevertheless, situations continually arise in which to tell the truth would be improper. Indeed, in some cases speaking the truth will do more harm than good. In such cases discretion demands that man keep the truth to himself. Sometimes man is accosted by someone who literally demands an answer to his question and will not tolerate silence. Yet in such cases, according to the first and second principles of the double effect, man may not lie. Therefore, a predicament arises. He can not tell the truth, he can not keep silence but must speak, and he may not lie. In such a situation how may truth be preserved?

First of all, amphiboly may be used. Amphiboly is the use of words or expressions which of themselves are equivocal. For a sufficient reason, one may always use amphiboly. Secondly, mental reservation may be used. This method is more traditional. Broad mental reservations are distinguished from strict mental reservations. The former is the use of words which have a two-fold meaning, one more common and obvious, the other less obvious, but intended by the speaker. The more obvious meaning is not intended by the speaker, but he hopes the hearer will infer it. Broad mental reservation is not a lie since the outward expression is true and betrays the thought of the speaker. A cautious person analyzing the answer could detect the thought of the speaker from the speaker's actual words. The speaker does not deceive the hearer—rather, through hasty interpretation, the hearer deceives himself. The deception is not caused, but permitted, by the speaker. For a just reason, a person is allowed to use broad mental reservation. Indeed sometimes it must be used. For a sufficient reason, one may use broad mental reservation even in affirming an oath since no lie is involved. The use of broad mental reservation is necessary for the proper functioning of society. But the use of broad mental reservation is never morally permissible when the other has a right to the truth.

Since the social effects of broad mental reservation are in practice the same as a lie, it may be employed only for a good purpose. Broad mental reservation may not be used indiscriminately. The well-being of society demands that men have reasonable trust in one another's words. Two conditions must be verified if broad mental reservation is to be used. First, according to the fourth principle of the double effect, there must be a proportionate reason for using it, for allowing the other person to deceive himself. Secondly, the hearer must have no right to the information. For example, broad mental reservation may not be used by the ordinary citizen in a court of law. If a hearer has a right to a piece of information, a speaker has a duty to give it to him. What knowledge a person has a right to can be difficult to determine in an individual case. For example, a child answers the telephone and and tells the person on the other end of the line that his mother is not "at home." The expression "not at home" has two meanings. It may mean that person is not at home in a physical sense. But the expression has come to mean in ordinary parlance that "callers are not being received." The latter meaning is well established. The phrase is therefore a broad mental reservation. When the caller takes the obvious meaning, he is deceiving himself.

For professionals, the standard is different than for ordinary people. Many professionals find the use of broad mental reservation indispensable in their professional practices. Ministers and priests, physicians and nurses, attorneys and accountants must use broad mental reservation professionally. The seal of the confessional, for example, is inviolable. If a priest is asked, even in a court of law, about a matter of which he has only "confessional" knowledge, he must answer "I do not know." This statement has two meanings. The obvious meaning is "I really do not know." The other meaning is less obvious: "I do not know for publication; I am not free to say." From the fact that the witness is a priest, this second meaning would, or might easily, be inferred. The priest has used a broad mental reservation. There is good reason for the concealment. The intention of the agent is honest. Therefore, his use of mental reservation is morally justified.

Strict mental reservation is the use of words which have two meanings, but whose true meaning can not be perceived by the normal intelligent person. Strict mental reservation is in actuality a lie. The outward expression is not in agreement with the internal thought. The outward expression conveys an impression contrary to one's thought to a person exercising normal prudence and due caution. Strict mental reservation is never morally allowable.

A jocose lie is not immoral if the outward expression clearly bears no relation to objective fact, but is pure fiction. Words possess only that meaning which men agree to attach to them. Since in a joke everyone understands that the outward expression bears no relation to factual reality, no lie is told. A jocose lie might contain slight moral fault when the fictional character of the outward expression is such that it could not be discovered by the ordinary person and he would thus believe that the speaker was dealing with objective fact. A profitable lie bears only slight moral fault. However, many lies told for our own benefit also harm others. In such cases, the lie is not merely profitable one, but also pernicious. In itself, however, a purely profitable lie is only slightly unethical. An injurious lie is slightly unethical if the harm done or intended is slight. Injurious lies are gravely immoral if serious harm is intended or inflicted on another.

According to the Aristotelian theory of the golden mean, the virtue of veracity or truthfulness may be violated by excess or defect. Veracity is violated by excess when a person indiscriminately reveals true matter which may injure someone else, for example another's reputation. The virtue of veracity is violated by defect when a person fails to make known truths in their clarity and fulness which he is obliged to make known. The intellect seeks truth. No person may morally withhold truth from a neighbor who has a right to that knowledge. Further, a person may not deprive another of the good which the other has the duty to achieve. Lying is an offense against the virtue of veracity.

CALUMNY AND DETRACTION

The natural law forbids anyone to injure the reputation or honor of another. Reputation is the estimation held by many people concerning the spiritual or corporeal excellence of someone (his virtue, knowledge, health or strength). Honor is the external manifestation accorded a person because of his reputation. A person's reputation exists in the minds of his fellow men; the external tribute paid a person because of his reputation is called honor.

A person's reputation or honor may be injured in several ways. (1) Detraction is injury to the reputation of another person by publicizing hidden faults to those who have no right to know them. It is telling damaging, true facts. Detraction may be done directly with malice, or indirectly without malice for reasons of humor or conversation. Gossip is a common form of detraction. (2) Calumny is injury to the reputation of another by publicly attributing to him crimes or faults of which the other is not guilty, that is making false damaging accusations. Calumny may come about in several ways. (3) Contumely is injury to the honor of another by failing to pay him due respect or by actually insulting him. Contumely is opposed to honor, as detraction and calumny are opposed to reputation. All three involve external acts. Contumely is directed against one who is personally present. Calumny and detraction do not necessarily imply the presence of the subject of the denigration.

Both detraction and calumny are offenses against commutative justice. Persons have a strict right to their reputation. Theft is considered a grave moral evil; in history one's reputation in the community is thought to be a higher good than wealth. The seriousness of the offense is judged by the damage done to the reputation of the other, by the person who tells the stories (for example, a prudent man is more believable than a garrulous one), and the people to whom the damaging stories are told. It is more serious to detract a person of one profession, for example by saying a clergyman tells lies, than another, for example saying that a soldier is a heavy drinker.

When defects are already widely known or may be presumed from human inclination, for example greed, little if any personal damage is caused. To reveal faults to a prudent person for sufficient reason is not an offense against justice. Contumely is morally wrong because respect is owed to all men—because of the dignity of human nature itself. Contumely increases in moral guilt when done in the presence of others.

Reputation and honor are truly human goods. All human beings prize themselves highly, even above abundant material goods which they may possess. A decent, happy, peaceful life in society can not be led unless a person possesses these goods in some degree. Obviously then a strict right of another is violated by destruction of his reputation or honor. Such an act is far more unjust than depriving someone of material possessions—for it deprives him of something more valuable than material goods. Obviously, anyone who injures the reputation of another is obliged in strict justice to do everything possible to restore his good name. That a given person does not really deserve the good reputation which he possesses is not to the point. Indeed, to take the stand that such a person does not deserve his reputation is analogous to holding that money could be stolen from another person without moral fault on the grounds that he stole it form someone else. However, the good of society, in court cases for example, may at times demand a loss of reputation.

Honor is the good estimation concerning the qualities of another person. Honor is an external witness to the perfections of another. Qualities could be natural and internal such as wisdom or intelligence or external such as wealth, beauty, or natural legitimacy. Reputation is the common estimation of another by spoken word. It may be good or bad. Everyone has the right to the good estimation of others due to the human person itself or to merited honor due him. This good estimation can be either positive or negative, that is presence of virtues or absence of vice. Further, every person has the right to a good reputation, even when such an estimation is false. That a person has a right to his good name when true is obvious. This right may never be justly contravened. But the right to a false reputation is limited to the common good. Many evils would come about in society were the hidden defects of people to be made manifest continually and publicly. The peace and tranquility of society would be constantly tested and many people would be unable to perform their duties. Everyone ordinarily has the right to a good name. Man has a right to that reputation which arises from talents or from activities performed only if they are manifestly true. Indeed, even dead persons have the right to their good name, *de mortuis nil nisi bonum.* Dead persons still have rights. The right to a good reputation extends to moral persons such as cities or monasteries.

There are of course times when one may or even should reveal the defects of another. Hidden crimes are those which are not commonly known to the community as a whole. Some people may know them, but there is a well founded hope that they will not be spread to the rest of the community. A crime is public or notorious when it is known by many in the community. A crime may be public due to a judge's decision or merely when it is *de facto* widely known. A crime may be known in a closed community, such as a church, or in the wider public community, such as a city. Crimes or misdeeds of government or public officials are ordinarily thought to be public. For a sufficient reason, one may reveal the hidden crimes of another. Sufficient reason would include damage to the public good, to the good of a speaker, to those who hear it, or to some other third party. Precedence of public good over private right to one's reputation is apparent, One may reveal a child's misdeeds that they be corrected. Revealing injury to oneself in order to console a friend is morally justifiable. Two conditions should be fulfilled for the revelation of other's hidden misdeeds. Damage done to the reputation of a person should be in proportion to the good to be brought about. The rights of the innocent are thought to take precedence. Secondly, a revelation should take place with as little damage done as possible to a person's reputation. For example, a revelation should be made to as few people as is necessary to promote the common good. The person's name should not be disclosed if avoidable. A public crime already prosecuted by law may be manifested so long as it has not been forgotten or the individual has made amends. Such, however should not be done without public utility. A crime *de facto* already public may always be revealed without any cause in communities in which it is known, so long as the crime has not been forgotten and amendment made. One may not reveal crimes *de facto* known in one community to another community where they are not known. One who provokes another to detraction offends against justice. One who hears detraction and does nothing to impede it when it is possible without grave injury to himself offends against charity.

The obligations of journalists in revelation of misdeeds or crimes of others, especially government officials, has become most important in the last decades. A free press is of course essential to proper functioning of a democracy. An educated and informed community is the backbone of democratic rule. The media have great influence on political and social life. Therefore, journalists, be they in newspapers, magazines, or on radio or television, or on the internet, have professional obligations to the community, public officials, and private individuals. The media have an obligation to report all public crimes and misdeeds of public officials. They should not however divulge private crimes unless public good or grave harm to an innocent third party demands it. Journalists should bring some judgement to the public crimes of public officials. In political campaigns and elections, journalists should also divulge private crimes of candidates which bear on their office, not only since public good demands it, but also since a candidate is thought to yield his right to privacy in favor of the public good. Nevertheless, for a journalist to divulge private prurient misdeeds of public officials for sensationalistic reasons is morally reprehensible and brings grave harm to the state.

Historians have even greater latitude is probing misdeeds and crimes of historical figures. They may publish hidden crimes of historical figures and raise the issue of public crimes now forgotten. By doing so, academic historians diminish influence of bad rulers. Indeed, such is the general purpose of their professions, to research, teach, and judge truth. Historians must investigate causes and effects of human actions. In writing recent history, historians should be careful not to injure innocent relatives of recently deceased public officials.

Those who detract unjustly or calumniate another are bound to restitution. The detractor or calumniator is personally bound to repair the personal damage to the other's reputation as soon as possible and to repair any damage which he foresaw at least vaguely. The heirs are bound to repair any property damage arising from the detraction or calumny. If one foresaw spread of detraction or calumny to others, as least vaguely, one is also bound to restitution to those who heard the detraction. A calumniator is bound to restitution even at the cost of his own reputation since rights of the innocent take precedence over rights of the guilty. But, if damage that would come about to his own reputation would far exceed damage done, he is excused from restitution. A detractor can not strictly speaking retract what he said since he did not lie. However, he can say that he spoke unjustly or erred. He may also attempt to restore the reputation of the other by praising him in other ways. A detractor or calumniator at times is excused from restitution. If no real detriment has come about by statements, if damage is taken away by a judicial decision, if a person detracted expressly or tacitly condones the statements, if restitution is morally impossible, or if the one who is detracted or calumniated returns the offense in kind, one is not bound to restitution.

Akin to detraction and calumny is rash judgement. Rash judgement is a firm assent of the mind concerning evil actions or motives of another without sufficient reason. It is more than opinion, doubt, or suspicion. Assent of the mind with sufficient reason is not morally reprehensible, even if erroneous, Rash judgement is a judgement of the mind whereby evil is judged of another on light and insufficient grounds. This is an internal act, but chances are that it will be externalized in the form of detraction, calumny, or contumely. It differs from rash opinion in which no actual judgement is made. Rash judgement is an offense against commutative justice. In order to be an offense against justice, the judgement must be firm, with due deliberation, rash, that is without sufficient reason, and over grave matter. It is not morally reprehensible to act as if some one might do evil. To lock one's precious possessions when guest arrive, for example, is not a rash judgement.

Insulting behavior is also against justice. Insult consists in an external action which indicates contempt because of some actual or presumed vice. Insult differs from detraction in that insult offends against the honor of the other person, not his reputation. Also, an insult takes place either in the presence of the other or in such a situation that the other will soon know of the insult. This condition is not true of detraction. Honor is a greater good than either reputation or wealth. Insult can be either positive by word or external action or negative, by omission, for example the omission of a salute or greeting. When insult occurs, restitution is due. The one who insults must restore the reputation of the other insofar as he can. The one who suffers an insult ought to bear it with equanimity. In some serious cases, however, he may demand restitution.

SECRETS

Secrecy is a moral obligation of not manifesting something hidden concerning another person. The matter of a secret is something known only by one or a few persons. The person who knows the secret may be a physical or moral person. For example, a medical staff or a corporation may possess a secret. Thus hidden knowledge may be known by many individual persons and yet still be a secret.

Three general types of secrets exists. A natural secret involves matter which is by its very nature secret. Such a secret can not be revealed without harming another person. The injury may be to a natural right, such as the right to reputation, honor, or property. By natural law man is bound not to reveal such secrets. A promised secret is one in which a promise is made not to reveal the matter of the secret after the matter has been divulged. The matter is not naturally secret, that is if the secret were revealed, no harm would follow to anyone. A man freely binds himself in the case of a promised secret. No obligation exists from the nature of the matter. A promised secret is not based on the virtue of justice, but rather on the virtue of fidelity, that is fidelity to our promises. An entrusted or committed secret is based upon agreement or contract. Before a person obtains the information, he agrees that the matter will remain secret. The information is given only upon condition of the agreement and would not otherwise be given. The agreement may be either explicit or implicit. A professional secret is a type of implicit entrusted secret. Lawyers, physicians, accountants, nurses, and ministers are among professions that are involved with implicit entrusted secrets. Both parties understand that one party is giving information which the other is bound in justice to preserve in secrecy. The reason for professional secrecy is that the ability of such professionals to practice their profession would be severely compromised if secrecy were not involved. No one would use an accountant who betrayed one's financial condition to the newspaper the next morning. The profession itself would be compromised.

Everyone has a right to his secrets. Were this not to be true, life would be intolerable. Everyone's life would become an "open book." Thus, one who has a secret is bound not to explore it, not to reveal it, and not to use the knowledge. A scientific secret may be explored by further research or other just means since the owner of the secret should not be unwilling that such research take place. The secret however may not be explored by unjust means. Ordinarily a secret may not be manifest. Knowledge from a secret or from secret knowledge unjustly obtained may not morally be used to one's own advantage. If the secret knowledge has been justly acquired, one may use it. Keeping a natural secret obliges from commutative justice and from charity. But one need not keep a natural secret when it is unable to be kept without grave hardship to oneself. Promised secrets normally oblige only in fidelity. As such, they may be revealed if it entails grave hardship to keep them or if the matter should be manifest without the promise.

When a natural secret is violated, one's fellow man is injured. The moral fault is great when serious injury against natural rights arises. Otherwise, only slight moral fault is involved. Violation of a promised secret is also only a slight moral fault. Fidelity to one's word has been violated, but no harm has been done. The essence of a promised secret is that its revelation will cause no harm to our neighbor. Hence, the only ethical problem involved is breaking one's word which is a slight moral fault. Violation of an explicit entrusted or committed secret is always at least a slight moral fault. Such a violation involves failure to live up to one's word. When revelation does grave harm to the person, a second ground of moral fault exists. When revelation of an entrusted secret involves grave harm to or for another, serious moral fault is attached to violation of secrecy.

Any violation of professional secrecy very probably involves grave moral fault. Even though revelation might bring only slight harm to a patient, client, or parishioner, social harm is grave. Estimation of the profession suffers seriously in the eyes of the community. Through its lack of confidence, the community tends to deprive itself of necessary services of a particular profession. Society at large suffers grave losses in addition to that suffered by an individual about whom something has been revealed.

Normally one may not inquire into others' secrets. The matter of a secret is personal and private. A parallel exists between secrecy and property rights. Secrets are more personal than property. One's property rights may not be violated; nor may one's secrets. Before one can morally investigate another's secrets, two conditions must be verified: the investigator must have a right to the knowledge and he may use only morally good means to discover the secret. The investigator may not lie or blackmail the other person.

The morality of reading another's mail falls under the category of secrecy. In itself, opening another's mail or reading secrets in his letters is an offense against justice. If what is contained in the letter is personal, one is not justified in reading or revealing it. Nevertheless there are cases when it is morally acceptable to open others' letters. If the very nature of a written message is obviously not intended to be private or if permission of a sender or a person to whom a letter is sent can be presumed, a moral obligation not to read a letter does not exist, for example postcards. Letters that are received and left in some public place may be read. To read letters that have been torn up and thrown away is probably not a grave offense against justice, but if it contains something hidden, it should not in charity be revealed. In cases of national emergency, a state may censor mail in so far as it is necessary for preservation of the state. A private person may open and read letters of another when he reasonably judges that they may contain something which does him severe damage. Finally, a person may give formal or implicit consent to have his mail read.

Secrets may at times be revealed. If from the beginning no obligation to keep a secret existed, one may reveal a promised secret. For example, if a promised secret was based on the use of force, the secret may be revealed. If an obligation to keep the secret has ceased because the matter has become publicly known, no obligation to keep a secret exists any longer. If a person has promised to keep a secret for a specified time and the time has elapsed, no obligation any longer exists to keep the secret. If an owner of a secret desires to make it know, once again an obligation to keep the secret no longer obtains. Man is not bound to preserve others' secrets when grave danger will come about to the one keeping it. If an owner of a secret has failed to keep faith with a holder of a secret, if he has failed to live up to his part of the agreement in some way, entrusted secrets may be revealed.

Cases exist where a secret must be revealed. When grave harm would come to society by retention of a secret, it must be revealed. For example, if a physician knows of a contagious disease, he has an obligation to report this information to proper authorities. If retention of a secret would result in grave harm to an owner of a secret, a secret must be revealed. For example, if a patient were to confide to a nurse that he was about to commit suicide, the nurse would be obliged to give that information to those who could prevent it. If retention of a secret would result in grave harm to an innocent third party, a secret must be revealed. For example, if one knew that a person was about to murder an innocent man, a keeper of a secret would have a moral obligation to take steps to safeguard the life of an innocent party. Finally, if one can not keep the secret without grave hardship to himself, he is not morally bound to keep the secret. An owner of a secret is not thought to want to bind a holder of a secret in such cases, unless there was an explicit promise to do so.

CHAPTER 5

The Right of Private Property

A person's right to possess and use his property, unless otherwise legitimately prohibited, is his dominion over it. Dominion signifies that a thing belongs to someone. A person who has perfect dominion over a thing has a right to possess it, use it, sell it, change it, give it, or destroy it. Dominion gives a right to an owner to do with a thing as he pleases. A thing could be either material or immaterial. The owner possesses a thing as his own, and is not merely a curator of it. Dominion is perfect when an individual retains a right to possession and use of the object. For example, a man who both owns and lives in his own house has perfect dominion over it. Imperfect direct dominion occurs when a person owns an object, but does not have a right of use. For example, a man who owns a house but rents it to another has imperfect direct dominion. Imperfect indirect dominion occurs when a person has a right of use, but does not own the property. For example, a tenant of a rented house has imperfect indirect dominion.

The right to private ownership is an exclusive right to possession, use, and distribution of thing at will. Property is any external good capable of distribution among human beings to serve their utility. These goods are usually, but not exclusively, material or bodily goods. Property is a tangible and external object morally joined to a person that he may rightfully call his own.

Ownership deals with the substance, use, and fruits of a thing. Private ownership is perfect or full ownership when the owner has power over all three. It is limited when the owner has a right over one or two but not all three. Limited direct ownership occurs when a person owns the substance of a thing, for example a house, but not the use of it. The renter has limited indirect ownership. A limited indirect owner can also have a right to fruits of a thing, for example a farmer who rents property. There are various kinds of indirect limited ownership which need not concern us here. Ownership is private when vested in a physical person. Ownership is corporate when vested in a corporate person, that is some group of human beings united together for some purpose. Ownership is public when vested in a community, that is a state. In public ownership, a state has a basic right to use the property of private citizens even without their consent, when public necessity or great utility requires such use. This right of the state to do this is the "right of supereminent domain." Ordinarily, a state is required to indemnify a private citizen for property which it takes over from him. A person who owns a thing possesses a right of ownership. Any living physical person, even if not yet born, can possess a right to ownership.

That which a person owns is usually called goods. Such goods may be internal such as his life and members, mixed, such as reputation or honor, and external, such as material things which a person possesses. Over internal goods which are not distinct from the human being himself, such as his life, a human being does not possess direct dominion. He has only use of them. Over internal goods distinct from his person, such as whatever acts he may commit, a human being has direct dominion. Over mixed goods such as honor and reputation, man has complete dominion, since they follow from his own work. Thus, restitution is due if such goods are taken from him.

From natural law, certain principles apply to ownership of exterenal goods. (1) A thing cries out for its owner (*Res clamat ad dominum*). When a thing is not in the possession of its owner, it is not in a natural state. A thing should be returned to its owner. (2) A thing fructifies for its owner (*Res fructificat domino*). This principle follows from the first. The increase of a thing belongs to the owner. (3) A thing perishes for its owner (*Res perit domino*). This principle can be more accurately stated. A thing which perishes by chance perishes for its owner; a thing which perishes by fault perishes for him who committed the fault. This principle also follows from the nature of dominion. Since the owner has dominion over a thing, what occurs to the thing affects him. Restitution also comes from this principle. (4) It is not moral to increase one's wealth from the property of another (*Ex re aliena non licet ditescere*). This principle follows from principle number two. In application of this principle, it must be determined if another's property is a cause or merely a condition of another's increase in wealth

TYPES OF PROPERTY

Property can be either movable or immovable depending upon whether an object may be moved about or not. An automobile is movable, a hundred acre farm is immovable. Property can be either consumptive or non-consumptive depending on whether it is consumed through use or not. Food is consumptive. Some consumptive things are consumed through first use, such as bread; other consumptive things are consumed only through repeated use, such as clothing. Property is productive when it produces further goods, for example a machine. The right of ownership belongs to a person, be it a physical or moral person.

Ownership entails possession of something. Possession is retention of something not prohibited by law with an intention of keeping it as one's own. Possession begins with actual apprehension of an object, These good can be either corporeal or incorporeal. The actual possession of an object is not sufficient; one must intend to take at as his own. The law must not prohibit possession. One may be either in legitimate or illegitimate possession of a thing. A legitimate possessor has a right to a thing. An illegitimate possessor is either in good faith, if he possesses something belonging to someone else, but does not know it, in bad faith if he possesses something of another which he knows belongs to another, or doubtful faith, if at the beginning he thinks it to be his own, but later comes to doubt his title to possession. In cases of doubt, the condition of a possessor is to be preferred. A possessor in good faith is subject to prescription.

Intellectual property presents special problems, especially in the global market place and with the rise of technology. With the common use of computers in the western world, problems with intellectual property have become even more complex. Civil law is attempting to deal with these problems, but there is some cultural lag. Under the name of author is generally taken those who write books, who compose music or paint, or discover scientific theories. An author has a natural perfect ownership of what he writes, paints, or discovers. Therefore he has a right to the thing itself, its use, and its fruits. Further, an author has a right of divulging the thing to others. All however have the right to use a work once divulged. At times, a price must be paid by those who use a divulged work, since an author has a right to the fruits of his work. Copying a work for private use only is not immoral. Civil law speaks of a lapse of time after which works become part of the common treasure of mankind. A period of time must elapse after the death of an author before the work of an author is part of the public domain. Many particularities of authors' rights are determined by civil law

Whether private ownership is a natural right or a right arising from the *ius gentium* has been a matter of historical dispute. In the first place, every philosopher of whatever stamp claims that a human being has a right to clothing, shelter, and nourishment. These things are necessary to sustain life. A human being must take these things to himself if he is to avail himself of them. The question over private property disputes whether, in the ownership of other property, private ownership is natural to man.

A human being has a natural right to perfect his entire physical, mental, and spiritual person. To achieve these objectives, human being must possess things as his own. Human beings have a natural need for private ownership. Private ownership is an incentive or inspiration to work, study, and develop various talents. Without private ownership, an individual's dignity can be lessened. He could become a vassal of a state, completely dependent on a state for his well-being. A human being has a natural right to the fruits of his labor. He perfects objects with his mental and bodily powers. In perfecting these objects, a human being projects his own personality, something of himself. These arguments are strong and probative. The question remains: of what are they probative? Philosophers such as John Locke and Thomas Jefferson claim these arguments prove the natural right of private ownership. On the other hand, Thomas Aquinas thinks these arguments prove only that private property is a moral system; it need not be the only such system.

Capitalism is an economic system, but not the only one, which holds to a natural right to private property. Capitalism holds that an individual and private corporations are the source of creation of wealth. The role of government should be to let individuals create wealth. *Laissez faire*—"let them do as they will"—has been its clarion call. Adam Smith is credited with founding capitalism in its modern form, but elements of capitalism go back as far as early communal monasticism. *Laborare est orare.* In the last century, various abuses in capitalism arose such as exploitation of workers and consumers alike. The rise of labor unions, writings on social responsibility, and governmental interventions to restrain abuses have largely eliminated at least the more extreme abuses of *laissez faire* capitalism in the western world. Capitalism in its purest form probably does not exist anywhere in the western world today. General recognition of social aspects of property has taken place. But the principles on which such recognition is based have existed since the Middle Ages. Capitalism is only one form of private property and should not be confused with the concept of private property itself

Marxism or communism is opposed to private ownership. Karl Marx's thought evolved over many decades, but from the beginning he held that private ownership of the means of production created problems. The means of production should not be in private hands, but in the hands of a state. Marx over-emphasized the importance of economics in human life. He was a materialist who thought that the driving force in individual man, in society, and in history was the satisfaction of material needs. As a theory, Marxism has never been put into practice in its pure form anywhere. Probably, it can not be. It may remain a purely theoretical system, more at home in an academic milieu than the workaday world. Insofar as it has been put into practice, communism has failed miserably. It has remained in existence only by denying in practice its theory of prohibition of private property. Communism gave, and still does give, its members innumerable possessions to use as their own. The rulers remain in power only by an iron hand of fear and violence. In practice, a human tendency toward ownership works strongly against communism.

Various kinds of socialism exist. State socialism holds that the means of production should not lie in private hands, but should belong to a state. In practice state socialism has also had an unproductive history. Utilitarianism is a kind of socialism. It holds that the purpose of government is to produce the greatest good for the greatest number. Utilitarians understand good in terms of pleasure. A community is understood merely as a group of individuals. Shortcomings of utilitarianism in all its various forms have been examined earlier.

TITLES TO PROPERTY

A title to property is a means by which persons come into lawful possession of property. It is the cause of conferring ownership. Property which a human being can own is either vacant, abandoned, or lost. Ordinarily titles to property are listed as seven:

(1) Occupancy: the taking of a thing that belongs to no one with a manifest intention of holding it as one's own. Requirements for occupancy are normally three: The thing must not actually be owned by anyone, that is the object is vacant or abandoned. The object must be actually possessed with an intent to own it. Such an intention must be made known by a suitable sign. Obviously, occupancy is the original way that all property has been gained. A right to possess animals by occupation arises. Domestic animals, such as dogs and cats, belong to their owner. Animals are free by nature, but can be tamed, such as birds, bees, and fish in a tank. They are the property of their owner as long as they remain in his custody. But once freed, they are subject to occupancy. Wild animals enjoy natural freedom and therefore belong to the one who first catches them regardless of place. However, an owner of land has a right to prohibit hunting or fishing on his property. Laws concerning hunting and fishing are probably penal laws.

Finding or discovery is a kind of occupation. Treasure, vacant properties, and abandoned or lost things are subject to finding or discovery. Treasure by its nature belongs to the one who finds it. If he finds it on another's property, civil law determines what part belongs to each. Vacant lands belong to the one who occupies them, subject to civil law. Likewise, abandoned property belongs to the one who occupies it unless civil law determines otherwise. One who finds an article has no obligation in justice to take it, though perhaps there is some obligation in charity. Once he takes it, a finder is bound in justice to seek the owner, but not at his own expense, He is morally bound to take reasonable care of the object. Once the owner is found, he must return the object. The finder has a strict right to restitution for expenses involved in finding the owner and the reward, if one has been offered. If a finder can not discover an owner, after a lapse of time determined by civil law, the thing becomes his.

(2) Labor: the human industry which is suitable to producing goods. Labor may be physical or mental. By physical labor man transforms raw materials into useful goods. New value is thus created. A person has a natural title to the fruits of his labor. If he works for another, he has a right to payment, though the fruits of that labor may belong to another. Therefore, work is a legitimate means of acquiring property. Karl Marx, and many modern socialists, maintain that labor is the only true title to property. They also believe that human beings can not sell their work and thus become alienated, but must directly receive part of the fruits of this labor

(3) Gift: the gratuitous transfer of ownership to another. Gift is a unilateral contract. The natural law basis for a gift is that an owner may dispose of his property at will. Thus, a person must own the property in order to give it. If the one to whom a gift is given realizes that the gift is not the property of the one giving it, he is bound to restitution. Gift is more than a promise since ownership is actually transferred. For a title to be transferred, a gift must be offered and accepted by some exterior sign. Acceptance is necessary since otherwise one could be given all sorts of unwanted things. A gift is sealed by acceptance of the gift. Acceptance is irrevocable. Before acceptance, an offer can be revoked. One to whom a gift is given ordinarily owes a giver a debt of gratitude. If a receiver shows enormous ingratitude to a giver, if a child is born to a giver, or if legitimate heirs are deprived of their rightful inheritance, a gift may be revoked.

(4) Trade: a form of exchange. Barter, purchase, and commerce are all means of exchange. Trade is in actuality a mutual gift. Since trade always involves a contract of some sort, this form of title to property will be considered in detail under contract.

(5) Inheritance: property of an owner upon his death passes to designated persons. Inheritance is the sum total of goods of a dead person. An heir is the one who receives a dead person's goods. Heirs are either necessary, if they have some natural right to the inheritance, or arbitrary, if an inheritance depends upon the will of the dead person. Inheritance is usually made by written testament, but can be done orally. If there is no will at all, property passes to natural heirs, usually husband, wife, or children. The natural law basis for inheritance is existence of family. Property is for conservation and support of a family. Without inheritance, a family would not be preserved at all or would not be preserved so well. Particularities of inheritance are determined by civil law. As with a gift, inheritance is sealed by acceptance. An heir may repudiate his inheritance. Ordinarily, heirs are bound to pay debts incurred by a dead person, but are not obliged to use their own wealth to do so. Many personal debts are extinguished by death. There is no natural duty in justice to make a will, but to avoid various inconveniences after death there may be some obligation in charity. A maker of a will is bound by natural law to give to his children an inheritance which is due their state of life. Not to do so is an offense against justice. A testator is bound to give to his wife, brothers and sisters enough to alleviate grave indigence. To remote relatives, he may have some slight obligation. The rest he may do with as he will.

(6) Accession: ownership of the increment of one's property. Fructification, birth, and new soil are examples of natural accession. In general these natural additions belong to an owner of a property. Accession by another's work, such as building a house on another's property, follows the maxim that the increase belongs to the principle owner. The title to ownership by accession other than natural accession is generally settled by agreement or civil law.

(7) Prescription: extinction of a previous owner's title and its transferal to another by lapse of time. Several types of prescription exist. Easements or mining rights, for example, are included under this title. Prescription may at first seem a strange title to property, but prescription is a legitimate title to property. If prescription were not moral, many evils would come about in society. Ownership would become uncertain. Legal processes concerning ownership of property would not be easily terminated. Many true owners would possess things in doubtful conscience or would fear losing their property. Many people would fear the payment of debts long overdue and uncollected. Lack of adherence to principles of prescription has led to contemporary wars, and many invalid claims to restitution.

For prescription to take place under natural law, several conditions must be present. The property must have an owner, unknown to the new possessor. The property must be suitable for prescription, that is it must not be protected against prescription. Public properties, for example, may be protected against prescription. In general, stolen goods may not prescribed. For various reasons, civil law may impede prescription. A possessor must intend ownership and be in good faith, that is over a period of time he must be morally certain that the thing belongs to him. Good faith of a previous possessor generally extends to the one who obtains the goods from the first possessor. A possessor must think that he has a legitimate title to the property. A person must be in continuous possession of the thing. Finally, a time determined by civil law must have elapsed.

INJURY

Injury is violation of the strict right of another, either by action or omission of an action which is owed strictly speaking to another. One may be injured in three ways, by theft, by detraction, or by murder. Injury differs from injustice in that injustice is a vice opposed to justice while injury has to do with an actual act. One might offend against legal justice, against distributive justice, or against commutative justice. Offences against commutative justice are our concern here. One may damage another's rights by offending against justice or charity. We are concerned here with offenses against justice. A positive injury is done by performance of an action, a negative injury by omission of an action. A personal injury injures another person; a real injury brings about harm to external goods. Injuries are in themselves serious matters, though they may become light if the matter with which they are concerned is light. The seriousness of an offense against justice arises from damage done to one's neighbor and to the community. In regard to property, rights may be injured either by theft or by damage done to property. No injury comes about if the person knowingly and willingly yields his right. In order that this state of affairs come about, the right must be able to be ceded, for example one may not yield his right to life, and the person must wish to yield it. If an action does harm to another, but does not strictly speaking offend against a right, no injury in a moral sense occurs. There can be no injury where there is no right. But an act indifferent in itself can become unjust by an agent's intention.

THEFT

A thing can be stolen in two ways, by theft or by robbery. Theft takes place in a hidden manner, robbery openly by force.

Theft is the occult taking of something which belongs to another, with an intention of keeping it as one's own, at least for a time, against an owner's reasonable will. Stealing is taking a thing to retain it as one's own in order to sell it. An owner may be unwilling not only as to the substance of an article taken, but also as to the manner in which it was taken. An owner must be reasonably unwilling. Whoever takes something out of extreme necessity does not steal because the owner is not thought to be reasonably unwilling. Nevertheless, for example, someone who takes pleasure in a pornographic magazine is thought to be reasonably unwilling that the magazine be taken.

The gravity of a particular theft depends upon the gravity of the loss. The gravity of theft may be judged on either a relative or absolute standard. An absolutely grave standard is that which is judged by the value of thing itself without consideration of the person from whom the matter is stolen. The absolute standard is used with regard to moral persons, that is corporations, institutions, the state, and the very wealthy. Absolutely grave matter is that matter the loss of which inflicts a grave loss to society, but does not necessarily inflict a grave loss on a particular person. Some maximum amount of money must exist which by its very nature should be regarded as grave regardless from whom the money is stolen. There must be a maximum amount beyond which to steal would result in destruction of the social order. Human beings need an orderly society. If thefts above a certain amount were to be universally regarded as only slight, hummn beings would act accordingly and the order of society would be destroyed. To set a precise figure as a standard is difficult. The value of money differs in various places and at various times. In the United States in the year 2018 this standard may lie between two hundred and fifty and three hundred dollars. When money was scarce, for example in the Great Depression, the standard may have been five dollars. During the boom before the Great Depression, the absolute standard had been placed at twenty dollars. Inflation over the course of the past hundred years must be considered in reckoning this figure.

A relative standard is determined by the loss inflicted upon a particular victim. The relative standard is that amount of money which inflicts great damage upon the person injured. A grave loss is usually considered the loss of a day's wages or the amount of money it takes to support an ordinary family for one day. But if a theft inflicts a grave loss upon a poor person, it is for that reason in and of itself a grave evil. To steal a hundred dollars from one person might be a grave evil. But to steal ten dollars from another might also be a grave evil. The relative standard is certainly to be used in judging the gravity of thefts against persons of average means and should be applied in most thefts against individuals. The relative standard obviously can not be valid in the case of great losses.

Certain circumstances can reduce moral gravity of theft, When children steal from their parents, ordinarily moralists reckon that they must steal twice as much as the relative standard to reach grave matter. Wives or husbands are to be judged even more liberally, especially if they use the money for the family. Often parents in a family are not concerned so much with what was stolen, but only that a child stole something. With regard to people working within a family, if they steal precious gems or the like, an absolute standard is to be used. If they steal things to eat or drink, especially if they consume these things and do not sell them, the matter is not thought to be grave since a head of a household is not thought to be unwilling. With regard to stealing fruits and wood, ordinarily there is no grave fault. Human beings may ordinarily pick grapes or apples from a tree owned by someone to stave off hunger. If an owner does not specifically prohibit it, taking strawberries, raspberries, and the like does not constitute a theft. Laws prohibiting such fruit-picking should be thought penal and not binding in conscience. Likewise, laws against gathering small amounts of wood from a public place are penal.

Ordinarily, small thefts do not coalesce into one grave theft. A number of small thefts usually remains a number of slight moral offenses. However, small thefts coalesce into a grave moral offense when they are morally united. Small thefts may morally unite in various ways. Small thefts coalesce when they are a product of an original intention made at the outset, an intention in which a person decides to commit a number of small thefts which he knows will total a grave amount. Small thefts are morally united when they are intentionally committed at short or longer intervals against the same or different persons or institutions. For this kind of theft to be grave, a greater quantity is not required than if the object were taken at one time, if it is taken from one owner. But if it is taken from several owners, the absolute standard must be used. A butcher who takes away a small portion of meat from each customer or a wine merchant who places a small amount of water in each bottle begins to commit a grave evil at the point when an absolute standard is reached. Small thefts can coalesce when committed by a number of persons acting jointly. Each takes only a small amount, but the total amount taken is grave. A relative standard is used against one owner, but an absolute standard against many owners. Small thefts may coalesce into a grave offense by mere multiplication, if the object is retained by the thief and a great interval does not take place between each theft. A relative quantity is required if the material is taken from one owner. If taken from several, an absolute standard is to be used. For example, a tailor who is in the habit of taking some extra material from every customer commits a grave injustice when an absolute standard is reached. If one steals property which belongs to many people, he offends gravely against justice when an absolute standard is reached.

Two types of cases exist when taking something in the possession of another is not theft. A human in extreme necessity or quasi-necessity, that is facing starvation for himself or his family or some other matter threatening death, may take enough from one who himself is not in the same state to preserve his life without committing theft. If there is a socially sanctioned method for procuring the aid and the person has time and opportunity to avail himself of that channel, the person does not have moral recourse to outright appropriation. If he has time and opportunity, a person in need must ask for the needed object. When the period of necessity ends, if the thing still exists, a person is bound to restitution. If the thing does not exist any more, but the poor man is able to give back its equivalent, he is also bound to restitution. Civil law also recognizes that such an act is not theft. Civil law imposes upon a person an obligation of showing that he was actually in such dire and immediate need. During cases of extreme necessity all goods become common. Each one has the right to preserve his own life. The cause of extreme necessity may arise from nature or human malice. If the danger is a common one, an individual does not retain this right. The wealthy have an obligation in charity to help the poor and not impede the poor from gaining things by occupation.

Occult compensation is an act by which someone secretly takes something from another which the other person owes him. Occult compensation is morally just when five conditions are verified. Public and private order demands that, when the proper conditions are present, a person can recover his possessions. First, the thing must be owed in strict justice, not merely in charity. One may not use occult compensation for gifts that are not given, or promised for inheritance, but not given. Secondly, the thing must be certainly, not probably, owed. The condition of a possessor is to be preferred. Everyone has a right to possessions until proved that they are not his. Thirdly, circumstances must be such that no legal means exist of getting back what is owed. There must be no other way to gain possession of a thing than by secretly taking what is owed. Occult compensation must be a last resort. This condition implies that a person can not prove by legal process that the object which he is taking back actually belongs to him. Such impossibility is a moral impossibility. If a fight or enmity would occur, this condition is verified. If this condition is violated, there is no violation of justice and thus no necessity of restitution. Fourthly, the thing which a person recovers must be of the same nature as the thing owed to him. For example, a person may not take money in lieu of the thing itself. Finally, by the act of occult compensation one must take from the debtor only what is owed. The compensator may not inflict further loss on the other. Domestic help may avail themselves of occult compensation. Domestic help can recover justly due salary. An employer owes nothing beyond a contract, even if a contract is for some reason below a lowest just salary. If a salary is the lowest just one, occult compensation can not be used. If domestic help were compelled by fear or force into contract or if they are unjustly burdened with more work, not in the contract and which he is unwilling to do, occult compensation may be used. Likewise merchants are not morally justified in diminishing goods sold for an agreed upon price which they later consider to be too low.

UNJUST DAMAGE

Property rights may also be injured by unjust damage. Unjust damage is an action by which someone brings harm to the goods of another with an owner receiving no compensation in return. Unjust damage also occurs when one person impedes another from obtaining a good which is due him. In order that a person be obliged to make restitution for unjust damage, three conditions must be present. First, damage must have actually ensued. Secondly, an individual's act must have been a real physical cause of damage. Thirdly, damage must have been knowingly and willingly inflicted, deliberately and consciously done. Obligation of restitution can only arise from a human act, one done with knowledge, voluntariness, and freedom. No moral obligation to make restitution arises from pure accidents. However, damage which arises from a careless habit demands restitution. When someone has a habit, knowledge, voluntariness, and freedom are present, at least indirectly. In cases of pure accidents, persons may forfeit their right not to make restitution. For example, many types of workers and students agree at the outset of their employment or course of study to pay for accidental breakage, whether or not deliberately inflicted. A moral obligation exists to live up to a contract such as this.

One who impedes another from obtaining something to which he has a strict right offends against justice and is bound to restitution. It makes no difference whether a person has used just or unjust means to impede attainment of the good. For example, if a person impedes a son from gaining his due inheritance by entreaty to the father, he does unjust damage and is bound to restitution. If one impedes another from obtaining a good to which he has no strict right, but uses unjust means, he is also held to restitution. If he uses just means, no moral fault arises. For example, one may by entreaty persuade someone to leave another out of a will. If one impedes another from obtaining a good of which he is unworthy, no fault against justice by reason of unjust damage is committed, even if he uses unjust means. Calumny and detraction are of course offenses against justice for other reasons. Likewise, if a person impedes another by helping a third party avoid payment of unjust damage, he offends against justice and is bound to restitution.

RESTITUTION

Restitution is restoration to another of what is unjustly taken from him. When no injury occurs, there is no obligation to restitution. The obligation of restitution arises from natural law, in commutative justice. From charity, the golden rule demands restitution. One should have an intention of restoring the goods. One who can not restore goods of the same order is not held to restore goods of a different order. For example, one is not morally bound to give money to someone whose reputation he has injured. Commutative justice demands that equity be restored. Restoration of equity can not occur when goods are of a different order. One's reputation is not restored by money. However, a judge may order a punishment from goods of another order, for example that money be given for an injury. A moral obligation to restitution is serious, but of course may admit of light matter. A moral obligation to restitution can be lessened in several ways. The moral basis for restitution lies in the unjust possession of another's property, unjust damage to another's property, or unjust participation in either.

Ordinarily offenses against distributive justice do not bind to restitution. It is too difficult to find both the offender and the injured and to determine the amount of the injury incurred. Rather the wrong must be remedied as soon as possible for the future.

Man may possess goods in one of three ways: a possessor in good faith objectively possesses another's goods, but does not know that these goods belong to someone else; a possessor in bad faith knows at the outset that goods which he possesses belong to someone else; a possessor in doubtful faith does not know if an object in his possession belongs to him or not, or does not know to whom the goods belong. When articles are found, ordinarily one does not know who the owner is.

A possessor in good faith is invincibly ignorant concerning the ownership of an object. He has a moral obligation simply to restore goods to their rightful owner as soon as he learns that these goods belong to that person, unless the object has become his by prescription. If their value has been lessened, no matter the cause, he is morally bound to restore them only in their present condition. If only part of a thing exists, he must return the part that still exists. He has no obligation in justice to restore any damage done while he possessed the object. In charity, but not in justice, he may make good any depreciation the goods may have suffered while in his possession. If their value has significantly increased due to the labor which the possessor in good faith has expended upon them, he has a moral right to the wealth, but he must return the object. He can keep the wealth. If however the object naturally fructifies, he is held to compensate the owner. If there is no hope of finding the owner, the person becomes owner of the object by prescription. If he has bought the object, he must return it to the owner and try to get his money back from the person to whom he paid the price. If he can not get his money back, he must bear the loss. If he does not know the owner, he can give it back to the person from whom he bought it and get his money back. But he must bear the loss if he can not get his money back. If the goods have been lost, stolen, or destroyed, no obligation in justice exists to the owner. If the goods have been improved, the possessor is able to deduct all necessary expenses. If the thing has been only accidently improved, no expenses may be sought.

A possessor in bad faith is a person who unjustly retains possession of a thing which he knows to belong to someone else. In general, a possessor in bad faith has the moral obligation to restore the goods in question or their equivalent in money and make good any damage done to an article and any depreciation that occurred because the article was stolen. He should return the thing itself, if possible, not another in its place. He should return it in the same condition in which he first found it. If he does not possess the thing, he must return the equivalent in money. If the thing has perished through an internal failure or through an incident where it would also have perished for its owner, the thief is not bound to restitution. But if the thing would not have perished had it been in the possession of the owner, he is morally bound to restitution. If the thing has increased in value, he must return the thing as it now exists, but may deduct the price of his industry and labor involved in the increase. If the thing has decreased in value because of his own fault, he must make up the difference. But if it would have suffered decrease in any event, he is only bound to restore the object. If at the time of the theft, the thing could have been sold for a greater price than now, the thief is bound to restore the difference in price. If the object has less value now and the thief does not possess the thing, it is sufficient to restore the present value. He must give back any fruits which naturally or civilly were produced by the object, but is not bound to restore the fruits of his own industry. He is morally bound to repair any damage to the article. The possessor in bad faith is allowed to deduct any expenses that he incurred which an owner would also have incurred.

A possessor in doubtful faith is one who for serious and probable reasons doubts whether an object which he possesses belongs to him. This doubt can arise at the beginning or during the course of the possession. If his doubt arises during the course of his possession, he must make an effort to find the true owner, an effort in proportion to the value of the articles involved. If he makes a good faith effort and can not find the true owner, he becomes possessor in good faith and acquires the right to dispose of the article as he pleases. If the possessor in doubtful faith fails to make this effort and thus fails to find the owner, he becomes a possessor in bad faith with all the obligations attached. If he finds the owner, he must restore the article, If the doubt remains, he may keep the article in question. If he in all good faith does not make an effort, he must restore the article and any increase in value if the owner is found. In the case of doubt from the very beginning of possession, he is morally bound to return the thing to a possessor in good faith. He may have recourse to a judge. If he knowingly receives an article in doubtful faith, he must restore it to the probable owner, or give the object or its equivalent to the poor or a pious cause. If he buys such an article and is not able to make any diligent inquiry, he may keep the article.

One must make restitution for any unjust damage that one does. Unjust damage is understood as damage to the goods of one's neighbor unjustly done without the owner receiving recompense. Such damage can be both positive or negative according as something is done or omitted which brings damage to one's neighbor. That one have an obligation to restitution for unjust damage, three conditions are necessary. (1) The act must be unjust and deprive the other of something to which he has a strict right. If commutative justice is not injured, one has no strict duty to restitution. If one causes damage unintentionally, he is still bound to restitution. One is bound to restitution, even if he knows that the owner may abuse the object. If giving the object back will result in a grave evil, one is not bound to restitution. (2) The person must be the cause of the damage. Only the person who causes the damage is bound to restitution. If a person is only the occasion or an essential condition for the damage, he is not bound to restitution. If the damage is only vaguely foreseeable, a person is not bound to restitution. For example, if one is thought to commit a crime for which another is truly guilty, only the judge, not the criminal, is bound to restitution since the guilty person is only the occasion of the injustice. If one returns a gun to another who uses it to murder someone, the giver of the gun is a condition but not a cause of the murder. However, if the giver of the gun knows that the person will commit murder, he is bound not return it. If one lights a match to cook a meal in a picnic place and this light causes a fire of great damage, the person is not morally bound to restitution. However, if one foresees the damage and intends it, he is morally bound to restitution. (3) One must be responsible for the damage in conscience, that is he must have intended the damage. Juridical fault is merely penal. Before a juridical decision, one is not bound to restitution. But after a juridical decision, one is bound to restitution, if the judge so decides. If one doubts after due diligent investigation that he is the cause of unjust damage, he is not bound to restitution. If one is intentionally part of a group which does unjust damage, a person is bound to restitution. But if the group does unintentional damage, no one is bound to restitution. One who doubts whether he has paid a bill and has no positive reason to think the bill has been paid is bound to restitution. A creditor may seek a judicial decision, but the debtor has the same rights as the creditor. A debtor is not morally bound to a judge's decision. If one brings about damage out of invincible ignorance, he is bound to restitution insofar as the damage comes about voluntarily, but no more. The question concerning whether one is bound to restoration to someone whose property is damaged, although brought about by invincible ignorance, is disputed. In practice, one is not bound, though arguments in favor of restitution are strong.

In spiritual goods, such as knowledge, the arts, the use of reason, or free will, one who impedes another by unjust means is bound to restoration, if reparation in goods of the same order can be made. For example, if one damages another's reputation, he is bound to restitution. However, if one damages another's use of reason or memory or free will, he severely offends against justice, but is not bound to restitution since he can not restore in goods of the same order. However, he is bound to repair any temporal damage that he who has lost his reason or memory may have incurred. The same would true for one who deprives another of pursuit of education by force, fear, or fraud. If one offends against spiritual goods by just means, he is not bound in justice to restitution, but is bound in charity if he is able.

One who cooperates in bringing about unjust damage to a third party may also be bound to restitution. Cooperation can arise from either the commission or omission of an act. Unjust cooperation in evil demands restitution, since a cooperator is a partial cause of the unjust damage. Such restitution must be made in cases when the damage done is unjust, the person is the cause of the damage, and the unjust damage is directly intended. One who commands unjust damage be done in his name is the principal cause of damage and therefore owes restitution insofar as he influences the will of him who carries out the actual act. Further, he is bound to restore those things which he who carries out the mission is unable to avoid. If one commanding damage revokes his order and informs the one who is to perform the act, the one commanding is no longer bound to restitution. But if the revocation does not reach the one who is commanded, the one commanding is still bound to restitution. The one commanding is bound to restore all goods, even to the one he commands, and repair damage of which he is the cause, that is which he could in some way foresee. If he who is commanded freely and willingly takes up the act, he is owed no restitution by the one who ordered. He who encourages or gives advice by word or deed to another to perform unjust damage is bound to retract his evil counsel. He is also bound to tell the one who is about to be damaged. He is bound to restoration for that damage which came about from his advice. He is not generally held to restore anything to the perpetrator of the damage, unless the advisor or counselor acted by deceit. One who is morally bound to give good, not bad advice, for example a lawyer, a doctor, or a psychologist is bound to restitution, whether he gives bad advice intentionally or through vincible ignorance. One who approves by external acts, such as voting or giving one's opinion, also consents to unjust damage. One who consents is bound to restitution insofar as he efficaciously influences the act. If one withdraws his consent, whether in good faith or in bad, he is held to nothing. He who errs in good faith is held to revoke his consent, But if he is unable to do so, he is also held to nothing. Politicians whose votes are necessary for an unjust law are bound to restitution. But if the numbers are already there for passage, the particular representative is bound to nothing, Indeed, one who votes for an unjust law to avoid a more unjust law does a morally good act, providing the act for which he is voting is not immoral in itself and it is known that he is voting in this manner only to avoid a greater evil. One who encourages an evil act is bound to restitution if his encouragement is an efficacious cause of damage done. Those who help someone after unjust damage is already done are held to restitution if they cause damage to be brought about or something stolen to be retained. One who approves unjust damage after it is done is not bound to restitution. One who approves unjust damage before it is done in his favor and fails to stop it owes restitution.

Negative cooperation in evil occurs when one does not impede damage to a neighbor to which he is held from justice to impede. This situation may come about by either keeping silent before an action is done, not standing in the way when it is being done, or not revealing damage after it has been done. One is morally bound by commutative justice to impede damage occurring to his neighbor. Examples of such would be those damages arising from explicit contract or from office. If he does not impede damage, he is bound to restitution. One is not so bound if restitution involves grave hardship. In all other cases he is also not bound to restitution.

When one is part of a group which cooperates in evil, the question of restitution of each member arises. In general, those who act together as the principal cause of the damage are bound together to restitution. If the principal cause pays the entire damages, others are then not morally bound. If the principal cause refuses to make restitution, then the others are still bound to restitution of the entire damage. If there were several principal causes, for example in a conspiracy, if one pays, the others are not bound to pay, but the one who paid may seek money from the others. If many together are partial causes of damage separately, they are each morally bound to pay part of the damage in proportion to the degree they have participated in the damage. If all have equally participated in bringing about damage, one is as bound to restitution as the other. If all have not participated equally, the following order is recommended: (1) the possessor of the thing; (2) the one who commanded the operation; (3) the executor of the plan; (4) the positive cooperators; (5) the negative cooperators. If the principal cause pays restitution, the others are not bound. If one of the secondary cause pays restitution, the principal cause must pay him. If the principal cause is many people and one pays, the others owe him money. If the owner forgives the debt to the principal cause, all are freed from the obligation of restitution. However, if the debt is forgiven to equal or secondary causes, it is not to be presumed that the principal cause owes no restitution.

Ordinarily, when an owner is certain and known, restitution must be made to him, as long as restitution is able to be made without serious hardship. Restitution to the poor ordinarily does not supply. Restitution is not due organizations with an evil purpose. Restitution must be made directly to the owner, not his creditors. If an owner has died, restitution should be made to his heirs. If an owner is unknown or for some reason can not receive restitution, a possessor in good faith owes nothing. A possessor in bad faith must give to the poor. Likewise, one who does unjust damage to an unknown person must make restitution to the poor. If the owner is uncertain, an effort must be made to find the owner to whom restitution is due. Once investigation is made, restitution should be made to the probable owner. Otherwise, one may make restitution to the poor. Positive civil law ordinarily determines the order in which restitution is to be made. According to natural law, an owner takes precedence over creditors.

For restitution to be valid, the justice violated, and only the justice violated, must be restored, if it is able to be done without serious injury to the debtor. The act of restitution need not be a human act; it is sufficient that *de facto* justice be restored. One is even able to simulate a gift. A possessor in good faith is not bound to expenses of restitution—the owner is bound to them. However a thief is bound to incur expenses of returning property. If a thing perishes, a possessor in good faith is bound to nothing: a thing perishes for its owner. A thief is held to nothing if a thing perishes through a third party of mutual agreement sent to restore the thing stolen. If an owner or creditor did not agree to the third party, the thief is still morally bound.

Restitution must be made *in toto* as soon as possible. The retention of another's property is a continuation of damage done. It is immoral to delay restitution or give back only in part with the intention of making restitution to heirs. But if restitution can not be made in whole, it must be made in part. If restitution can not be made immediately, it must be made as soon as possible. He who intends to make restitution, but can not do so at the present time, commits no immoral act.

Various reasons excuse from restitution. Forgiveness by the damaged person, impossibility of the debtor paying the debt, or giving over goods on the part of the debtor to the owner excuse from the obligation of restitution. Forgiveness excuses from restitution absolutely; impossibility or giving goods in lieu of restitution only suspends the obligation as long as the inability remains. In the latter two cases, an owner of property is not able to be reasonably unwilling that he not receive his property at the present time. Forgiveness of a debt obviously removes any obligation of restitution immediately, since a person who owns something can do with his property as he pleases. Forgiveness of a debt may be done either expressly or tacitly and at times may even be presumed. That forgiveness excuse from restitution, the one who forgives the debt must own the object and must freely forgive the debt. He is making a gift and a gift to be a gift must be freely given. Forgiveness of a debt may ordinarily be presumed within a family. Likewise, in the case of a number of small thefts by a poor person against several owners, forgiveness of restitution may be presumed. When a person does not have the article or the money to make restitution or can not make restitution without grave hardship to himself or his family, he is excused from restitution. Likewise, giving goods instead of the article itself or money equal to the value of the article or the damage done can be considered restitution. Giving goods can be done either voluntarily or by judicial decision. Such a judicial decision binds in conscience, The creditor becomes owner of the goods. A debtor can morally retain part of the goods if he needs them in grave necessity. Ceding goods does not excuse from an obligation of restitution when one is later able to restore the goods, unless the debtor so decides.

CHAPTER 6

Scandal

Every person has a strict right in justice not to be led into moral evil by deeds, words, or omissions of others. Scandal is any word, deed, or omission which by its very nature presents an occasion of spiritual harm to another. Indirect scandal is any word, deed, or omission which by its very nature is morally good or indifferent, but which, due to certain circumstances, may be a source of spiritual harm to one or more persons. Direct scandal is any word, deed, or omission which by its very nature or by the intention of the agent leads another into evil,

In indirect scandal, the principles of the double effect are applied. The first three principles are verified. The fourth principle, that a due proportion exist between the good and the evil, will often be difficult to verify. In direct scandal, every person has a strict right in justice not to be hindered in pursuit of his final end. Rights and duties are correlative. Therefore, other people have a duty not to interfere or hinder another in the attainment of his final end. Moral evil, of which scandal is an example, hinders man in the attainment of his final end. Therefore, every man has a strict right not to be led into moral evil by the words, deeds, or omissions of others.

Scandal of the weak is not scandal. Scandal of the weak takes place through acts which of themselves should not scandalize, but do so because of ignorance or frailty in the person who is scandalized. The act, by its very nature, should not cause scandal. Furthermore, the intention is not to cause scandal nor does the person foresee that scandal will be taken.

Direct scandal contains a two-fold evil: on the one hand, the act is itself immoral; on the other, there is spiritual harm which the moral agent foresees will come to a second party. These facts create four-fold possibility: (1) if the act done is a slight moral offense and a slight harm to the second party is foreseen, two slight evils are committed; (2) if the act done is a grave moral offense, but only a slight harm to another is foreseen, two evils arise: a grave evil of the type of the act committed and the lesser evil of scandal; (3) if the act done is a slight moral evil, but a grave harm of scandal is foreseen to another, two evils arise: the first is a slight evil of the type committed, the second a grave evil of scandal; (4) if the first act is a grave evil of one species and grave harm to another is foreseen, two grave evils arise: one form the act itself and the other of scandal.

In indirect scandal, the act itself is morally good or indifferent. In such cases, the fourth principle of the double effect comes into play. Applied successfully, no moral guilt exists. However, if the proportion is questionable, moral guilt is measured by the degree of harm (slight or grave) which the moral agent foresees will come about to the other person.

II

B. SOCIAL ETHICS

In individual ethics, rights and obligations belonging to individual persons have been considered. In social ethics rights and obligation proper to human beings as members of society are considered. Individual rights are often matters of commutative justice. Social ethics often concerns distributive justice.

CHAPTER 1

The Nature of Society

Society is a stable, moral union of a number of persons using common means, under a common authority, to attain common objectives. A society is a stable union—permanency is characteristic of societies. A society is a moral union of persons since intelligence and free will are the basis of societies. Human societies are in direct contrast to the union of animals evidenced in herds and flocks. The latter union, though in some sense analagous to human society is the result of a gregarious instinct in animals. On the other hand, human beings unite into societies because they know that their common use of certain means, under a unified authority, will enable them to attain a desired objective. Human beings freely will to enter such a union.

According to mainstream western tradition, man is social by nature. Various proofs for this position have been proposed. Plato argued that we need one another's talents, that one man alone can not care for himself. Aristotle thought that man's faculty of speech argues for his social nature. Human beings communicate ideas only to other humans. Augustine held that humans are social by nature. "Nothing is so social by nature and so anti-social in its perversion as the human race." Thomas Aquinas also held to the social nature of man. Man is born into a society; domestic society is responsible for his rearing and education.

During the Enlightenment, establishment and protection of individual human rights became the great project and man's social nature was called into question. Thomas Hobbes especially held that human beings were anti-social by nature, not by perversion. Hobbes thought that man was satisfaction-seeking animal. He thought that humans entered into society by social contract to prevent chaos, a complete breakdown of human relations. Other such as John Locke and Jean-Jacques Rousseau thought that man was not anti-social by nature. But they too thought that man entered society and produced government by contract. Such theories have been called human atomism. The governments of the United States and the European parliamentary democracies, among others, were founded on social and governmental contract theory. The state is not natural, but a human convention for his own protection and well-being. In our own day, when even the natural basis of the family has been called into question, if the state were not natural to man, there would be no natural societies. All societies would be conventional.

In every society, a common objective is sought by all members of the given society. In fact, the nature of a society is determined by the nature of its objectives, by its final causes. All members have an obligation to strive for the end or objective of the society. There are many societies to which humans need not belong. However, if one becomes a member of a given society, he lives up to his obligations only in so far as he strives to accomplish the purpose of the society. Human beings belong to certain societies by nature. In such cases, a human being violates an obligation imposed by natural law when he does not strive for the goals of such societies.

All Catholic philosophers hold that man is social by nature. Whether or not man would have needed an authority had he not sinned is a matter of some debate. Augustine of Hippo for example held that any subjection of man to man, especially in its more coercive aspects, resulted from sin. Thus, political authority stemmed from sin. Thomas Aquinas held that, even in his pristine state, human society would have needed an authority.

But in the state of man as he presently exists, the mere fact that the members of all societies have an obligation to strive for the objective of each society implies that there is one principle in the society which constantly and effectively directs them towards the objective. This principle is an authority. Authority is defined as the right possessed by someone to oblige members of a society to act in such a way that the common objective of the group will thereby be attained. This authority must be one, that is unified in some manner. Such unity may be found in varying degrees in various persons, but ultimately it belongs in the highest way to one physical or moral person, for example a king, a president, a parliament, and so forth. Authority is the proximate, active cause of the unity of a society and therefore no society in the present state of human nature can exist without one.

Societies are natural or artificial. A natural society is based on, and necessitated by, the very nature of the human being. Only two such societies exist: (1) domestic society (the family) and (2) civil society (the state). In a certain sense, the church is a "natural" society since it is necessitated by man's spiritual nature. However, the church is a supernatural society in so many respects that it does not directly concern a student of ethics. An artificial society is one which is not necessitated by human nature, for example a drama society.

Societies are perfect or imperfect. A perfect society is supreme in its own sphere and contains within itself all necessary means to attain its objectives. Only the state and the church are perfect societies; the former is supreme in the material sphere, the later in the spiritual sphere. These two societies arise out of man's two-fold nature, the material (physical) and the spiritual. Corresponding to his material nature is material welfare (the object of the state); corresponding to his spiritual nature is spiritual welfare (the object of the church). All other societies are imperfect. They seek some phase of man's material or spiritual welfare. Accordingly, men are dependent on the state or the church for aid in achieving their objectives.

Given man's social nature, two natural societies exist: the state and the family. Although maintaining that man is social by nature, Augustine held that the state, especially in its coercive aspects, is the result of sin. Nevertheless he held that in his present state man must live in a state. The state can take several forms. Plato lists five in descending order of merit: aristocracy (the rule of the best, the wise man); timocracy (the rule of honor or the military); oligarchy (the real of the wealthy few); democracy (the rule of the mob who prize freedom); tyranny (the rule of the dictator who enslaves the entire population). Aristotle thought that three good forms and three bad forms of government exist: The good forms are monarchy, aristocracy, and constitutional government. The three bad forms are tyranny, oligarchy, and democracy. Augustine of Hippo spent no time on the various forms of government in this world. His main philosophical and theological aim was to bring about peace which could only come ultimately as a gift from God. Thomas Aquinas held the benign monarch to be the best form of government. Today, many hold that democracy is the best form of government. Such an evaluation must be approached critically and await the judgement of history. So many forms of government can exist that it is difficult, if not impossible, to list them all. Various authors have used the terms by which they describe various forms of government differently. Perhaps all governments are variations on either monarchy, aristocracy, or democracy or some combination of all three.

Given the existence of the state, how does political authority come to legitimate power? This question has largely arisen during the Christian dispensation. In the Gospel of St. John, Christ says to Pilate: "You would have no power over me except from him who sent me (Jn 19:11)." Augustine of Hippo himself held that political power comes to the rulers from God, but he did not expend much effort on how this power was mediated. Giles of Rome, a student of Thomas Aquinas, held in *De ecclesiastica potestate* that there were two swords (cf. Lk 22:38), the source of authority on earth. The pope held them both. The king ruled only through the power given him by the pope. Boniface VIII gave this theory papal approbation in the Bull *Unam sanctam* (1308). Needless to say, secular powers reacted to this theory. Kings maintained that they also held power directly from God. There were indeed two swords, the religious and the secular. The pope held the former, the secular ruler held the latter, both directly from God. The theory of the "divine right of kings" reached its high point in the writings of Sir Robert Filmer. In his *Second Treatise on Civil Government,* Filmer was John Locke's principal adversary. Rejecting the divine right of kings, Locke held that power comes to the ruler by the consent of the governed. Both society and government come from contract. The people may withdraw consent from one ruler and give it to another. Locke's theory was the philosophical foundation for the "Glorious Revolution" (1688) in England and indirectly for the American revolution and the consequent constitution. Today, most Christian theorists maintain that political power comes to the ruler from God, but is mediated through the people. Such a theory may well have its roots in late scholasticism.

Rulers and representatives have obligations toward their subjects. They must strive to promote the common good. Rulers must maintain the freedom of the individuals in their states in so far as possible and avert both internal and external temporal evils from the state. Rulers are bound to remove disruptive individuals for the common good and are held to administer justice without reference to persons. They are further held to maintain religious freedom of individuals in their state. Rulers are held to have sufficient knowledge to perform their duties especially for repelling outside danger to the republic. They are duty bound to avoid unjust laws. If unjust laws are proposed, representatives are bound to vote against them, since they are the efficient cause of law. Citizens have the obligation of honoring their rulers and of obeying the just preceptive laws of the state, Patriotism, that is fidelity toward the state, is a virtue and only extreme causes justify rebellion.

Since a government has the right to just means to attain its ends, rulers have the right to levy taxes. Such taxes are both direct and indirect. Direct taxes are those directly levied upon the population, such as income taxes. Indirect taxes are those which are imposed upon the occasion of business or inheritance, for example sales tax and tariffs. That taxation be just, there must be a just cause, taxation should not be excessive, and taxes should be proportioned according to the subjects' ability to pay. All moralists maintain that indirect taxes are penal laws. That sanctions are attached to them is sufficient that they be obeyed. With regard to direct taxes such as income tax, two opinions prevail. Because of the right of the government to levy taxes, some moralists hold that payment of income tax is a duty in legal justice, and thus a taxpayer would be morally held to pay taxes. Others maintain that there is a general obligation in legal justice to pay some income tax, but that individual laws may be regarded as penal laws. The second opinion is solidly probable and may be followed. One who collects taxes owed in legal justice is morally bound to collect them. Generosity to the poor is to be recommended.

There is no moral obligation for restitution if one does not pay indirect taxes such as sales taxes, prior to a judge's decision, since these laws are universally regarded as penal laws. Concerning income tax, the situation is more complex. Those who hold that there is a moral obligation in legal justice to pay income tax hold that there is a moral obligation to restitution if one does not pay his taxes. Others would hold that one is morally bound to restitution only after a judge's decision, at least with regard to partial income tax payments. Tax collectors have the moral obligation to restitution if they culpably neglect collecting taxes. In all these cases, restitution need not be made to the government, but can be morally satisfied by giving money to the poor or charitable causes.

In general, voting is a privilege, not an obligation. However, an individual has an obligation to vote when use of the privilege promotes the common good or impedes the election of bad rulers or representatives. Excessive hardship excuses from this obligation. A citizen has the duty to inform himself concerning issues and candidates. One is morally bound to elect good candidates, but there is no obligation to elect the best. Avoidance of a grave evil, avoidance of an even graver evil, or promotion of public utility may render it licit to vote for an inept candidate, according to the fourth principle of the double effect.

Military service is also a matter of moral obligation certainly on the part of the state and at least in certain cases on the part of the individual. The state has the obligation to conserve the state and to protect and defend its citizens from internal and external threats. One means to this objective is the maintenance of a military and legislating military laws. Methods of providing a stable military are either voluntary entry or conscription. Conscription is either universal (if it extends to all eligible for the draft) or particular (if it is done by lottery). With regard to universal conscription, the state has a right and indeed at times a duty to exempt some from service, for example clerical students. Military laws should be just so that only as large an army is maintained as necessary for the security of the state. The citizens should not be taxed beyond reason for the support of an army. Nor should soldiers be forced to live in generally unsuitable conditions. Conscription should be legislated only when voluntary service does not provide the necessary soldiers. Citizens have a general obligation to support a just state. However, particular laws concerning military service are probably penal laws; they do not ordinarily bind in commutative or legal justice since sanctions attached to them are sufficient that the laws be observed. In certain circumstance, conscriptions may bind in legal justice. Voluntary soldiers have an obligation in commutative justice to serve according to the conditions of the contract. The state is obliged to pay them a just wage. When bound by legal justice, in particular conscription, conscripts are obliged to honor the draft lottery. If drafted, they are bound in legal justice, but not in commutative justice, to serve. When universal conscription binds, it does so in legal, but not in commutative justice. Those who feign health reasons in order not to serve do not offend against justice, since one is not bound to place himself in grave danger. For a proportionally grave reason, one can desert the military. However, for no proportionally grave reason, if the conscription binds in legal justice, deserters offend seriously against the virtue of justice.

Those avoiding military service are generally not bound to restitution. One who attempts to avoid military service by unjust acts is not bound to restitution since he injures no one's rights. Nor is one bound to restitution if he avoids military service either before or after another since no one's rights are damaged. However, they who corrupt physicians by bribery offend against commutative justice. Physicians are held to restitution toward those who are called to military service since others have a right of demanding that these officials perform their functions honestly. However, these physicians do not owe restitution to the state.

CHAPTER 2

Domestic Society: The Family

Marriage is defined as the union of one man to one woman for the purpose of procreating and educating children and of mutually helping one another. This definition of marriage first occurs in Augustine's *De bono coniugali* (400 a.d.), *On the good of marriage.* Augustine considered Christian marriage primarily and finds three goods in marriage: procreation and education of children (*bonum prolis*), the mutual love and support of the participants (*bonum fidei*), and the permanency or indissolubility of the union (*bonum sacramenti*). Permanency is an attribute of Christian marriage as the sign of the union between Christ and his church.

The use of matrimony consists in performance of the conjugal act, carnal copulation. It is sometimes called the marriage debt (cf. 1 Cor 7:3). On the part of the man, carnal copulation consists in the penetration of the vagina with the penis and implanting his seed. On the part of the woman, the act consists in the reception of the male seed and the effusion of vaginal fluid. Venereal pleasure occurs in each partner. The purposes of the conjugal act are the procreation of children, symbolizing marital love, and allaying concupiscence. The conjugal act is obviously good in itself, when used for the proper ends. This is true both when the act in a natural manner is open to procreation and when it is not. The proper ends of the marriage act are the procreation of children, the conservation and cherishing of marital love, the satisfaction of the obligation of the marital contract, or the avoidance of incontinence, and the satisfaction of sexual desire. Engaging in intercourse for any of these reasons is licit so long as generation of children is not excluded. The sexual act should be performed in places suitable for the act. It may be performed at all times not threatening the health of one of the partners. Danger of spreading contagious diseases is a valid reason for not performing the marital act.

Natural law lays down monogamy as the only moral form of marriage. Unity is therefore an attribute or property of marriage. Opposed to the unity of marriage is polygamy, marriage of one mate to two or more members of the opposite sex. Two types of polygamy exist. Polygyny is the union of one man to two or more women. Polyandry is the union of one woman to two or more men.

Polyandry is contrary to the purpose of marriage and is therefore always opposed to the natural law. Polyandry is never permissible under any circumstance. Under polyandry, neither purpose of marriage is achieved. Polyandry does not help to increase the race to any greater extent than does monogamy. The child does not know its father, nor the father the son. Thus the right of the child to know its father is violated and the obligation of the father to educate and love his child is violated. Polyandry also destroys the mutual help and love of the partners in marriage. It destroys the possibility of mutual love between spouses. The home could well be characterized by competition between spouses of the same sex; jealousy and strife might well be rampant. Several persons would be head of the family. Nothing good can be said for polyandry since the objectives of marriage can not be attained.

Polygyny is not opposed to the procreation and education of children. Since both the father and mother are known, children can be born, the children know their parents and the parents know the children for whom they are responsible to rear properly. But polygyny is evidently opposed to the mutual help and love of one spouse for another. Domestic peace and happiness would likely be impossible. There can be no complete and mutual love for one another. Jealousy and strife might well characterize such a marriage. Thus, polygyny is also opposed to the natural law regarding marriage.

In certain periods of Jewish history, God revealed the temporary permissibility of polygyny. The reason behind this dispensation lay in the danger of the dissolution of the human race. Marriage is instituted for the preservation of the human race. The "natural" form of marriage is the form by which the objectives of marriage would be best achieved. Due to the scarcity of men, polygyny best served to propagate the race. If polygyny had not been allowed, the institution of marriage would not have served its purpose of preserving the human race. Temporarily, the secondary goods that usually flow from marriage had to be risked or even forfeited, in the interest of achieving the basic and more important objective of preserving the human race. As soon as the emergency ceased, the "natural" form of marriage was reinstituted that best achieves the end of marriage, that is monogamy. At the beginning of the human race, God emphasized monogamy as the natural form of marriage: "they shall be two in one flesh (Gen. 2:24)." Upon his coming, Christ emphasized that the divine dispensation for polygyny had long since ceased (Mtt 19:5; 1 Co 7:4).

Domestic society or the family is a stable moral union of persons of the opposite sex, made under contract, for the procreation and education of children, and for the mutual support of the participants. The physical basis of marriage is the bodily adaptation and attraction of each sex to union with the other. The moral basis of marriage is the ethical principle, admitted by even the most primitive peoples, that a man and a woman may not legitimately enjoy sexual union unless they are pledged to each other by some formal agreement making them husband and wife. The spiritual basis of marriage is the love of the partners for the character, ideals, interests, and aspirations of each other. The first philosopher to speak of love as a part of marriage was Augustine of Hippo.

One of the greatest sources of evils prevalent in society today is the failure on the part of many adults, even Judaeo-Christians, to appreciate the purposes of marriage. Many tend to think of marriage as purely personal, individual, and physical. They lack an appreciation of its moral, and particularly, its spiritual basis. When humzn beings regard marriage as physical for their own interests rather than for the social objective intended by the creator, that is the propagation of the human race, it is not at all surprising to find selfishness and sensuality becoming alarmingly prevalent. This is not to deny that love for one another should be an essential element of marriage.

Marriage is a contract—Christians believe it to be a particular kind of contract, namely a covenant. As a contract based in the natural law, marriage is a pact of mutual agreement whereby a man and woman give each other the right to sexual relations and to other normal features of conjugal life, such as cohabitation and collaboration in mutual needs and interests. Every contract presupposes that the parties enter the agreement knowingly and freely. If either knowledge or freedom is entirely absent, even if the parties actually go through the rites of marriage, there would be no marriage. For example, a young and innocent girl might go through the form of marriage without knowing its nature. The mentally defective may be so devoid of knowledge that they are incapable of making this contract. A girl might be subjected to the influence of great fears, threats against her life, and so forth, to the point that her freedom would be essentially impaired.

One who is permanently deprived of the physical power of sexual intercourse prior to marriage is barred by the natural law from marriage. The inability must be permanent and antecedent. The essence of marriage involves a bestowal of the right to sexual intercourse. One can not give another right to something which is physically impossible *Nemo dat quod non habet.* The impossibility of intercourse refers to an inability to perform the sexual act, not to an inability to have offspring.

The fear necessary to render a marriage invalid need not be so great as to destroy freedom totally. Of course, grave emotional fear invalidates marriage since there is no human act. But both state and church have the power and the right to place conditions on the validity and legality of contracts. Both place fear as invalidating marriage. As is the case with other contracts between human beings, the marriage contract must be externally expressed. Normally such expression is given by spoken word, but could also be done by sign or writing.

So far as the natural law is concerned, the parties may marry without having met one another. A couple could marry by proxy, that is through representatives who go through the marriage ceremony in their name. At the moment that the representatives complete the ceremony, the two persons would be husband and wife. Conditions laid down by the church for such a marriage are the following: (1) a sufficient reason for marriage by proxy must exist; (2) the one who appoints another as a proxy must sign a document to that effect; (3) an authorized priest and at least two witnesses must also sign the document If the principal revokes the commission or becomes insane before the ceremony takes place, there is no marriage.

Indissolubility of the marriage means that a marriage bond is intended to last until the death of either husband or wife. Thus, divorce with a right to remarry is prohibited. The true nature of marriage as an institution involves the procreation and education of children. Whatever is indispensable to attaining this purpose must be a property of marriage. The birth and proper education of children certainly necessitates a degree of permanence to the union of husband and wife. In lower nature, animal nature rather quickly reaches maturity and full development. There is no prolonged dependence on "parents." Even the animal "parents" remain together until their young are no longer dependent on them. In decided contrast, the human child has a complex nature, both spiritual and physical. The development of this nature needs years of careful management on the part of the parents. A moderate estimate is that a child depends upon its parents until it reaches the age of twenty. Nature obviously places the obligation of permanent union on husband and wife until at least twenty years after the wife is capable of child-bearing. Practically speaking then, the intention of nature is that marriage is a union until the death of the parties. Nature does not merely make a child physically dependent on its parents, but also instills affection in the heart of the child for its parents and in the hearts of parents for the child. Evidently nature intends husband and wife to remain together until at least the age of seventy, that is twenty to twenty-five years after the wife can bear children. To a reasonable person, this should be evidence in abundance that nature intends the union of marriage to be permanent.

The above argument would hold also in the case of a childless marriage. The nature of marriage is not dependent upon individuals for its nature and properties. Rather the nature of the institution must be regarded. The nature of marriage is as unchangeable as human nature is unchangeable. Even though a given couple may not have children, they have entered an institution which is necessarily, according to the natural law, an indissoluble and permanent union. Reflection on the other ends of marriage, the dependence of one on the other, the mutual help and support of one for the other and so forth, indicates that nature intends that marriage be a permanent union even into the most extreme age, even unto death. There would hardly be a marriage if an enduring commitment of one to the other did not exist.

The emphasis on the indissolubility of marriage in the New Testament is evident. "Whosoever shall put away his wife and marry another, commits adultery against her. And if the wife shall put away her husband and be married to another, she commits adultery (Mt 10:11-12)." Of course, separation is justified under extreme circumstances. For example, Christ mentions a justification in the event that one party commits adultery: *"Whosoever shall put away his wife, except it be for fornication, and shall marry another, commits adultery* (Mt 19:9). Those Christians who desire a pretext for divorce pervert the evident meaning of that passage. The above offense is not a justification of divorce with the right to remarry. The italicized phrase is clearly presented by Christ as a justification for separation.

The marital debt may be sought by either partner, either explicitly or implicitly. At times even an interpretive intention suffices. No obligation exists to seek the marriage debt. From charity one may be bound to seek the debt if it is necessary to preserve love or to preserve one's partner from incontinence. But a grave obligation exists to render the debt as many times as it is seriously demanded, whether expressly or tacitly. To render the debt is a matter of commutative justice. One of the partners should not render himself impotent voluntarily on a continuing basis, for example through excessive work. Absence for protracted periods can have the same effect.

By commission of adultery or incest, a spouse loses the right to demand the marriage debt. The right is lost only when the adultery is known. Faith is not due to one breaking the contract. But the right to request is not lost, merely the right to demand. That the right be lost, the adultery must be certain, not committed by both, and neither explicitly nor implicitly condoned. If the innocent party seeks the debt, he is thought to have implicitly condoned the adultery. The right to demand the debt therefore has been restored. Within marriage all actions which lead to successful completion of the marriage act are morally good. Such preparatory actions are also morally good even when the partners do not want to or for some reason can not have intercourse at the time. Such acts promote the other ends of marriage, for example a mutual love for one another. Incest which does not arise from force or fear annuls the demand of the marriage debt. However, the one who committed incest is bound to render the debt if requested. If the one seeking the debt is drunk or has otherwise lost the use of reason, the other is not bound to render the debt, since there is no human act present.

The obligation to render the marriage debt ceases under certain circumstances. Immoderate demand or grave danger to health excuses from rendering the debt. Ordinary foreseen inconveniences do not excuse. But some obligation not to be burdensome to the other in requesting the marriage debt remains. What is too often may differ from to place and person to persons—in present day America three or four times per week appears to be normal. The spouse who does not fulfill the obligation to care for the family loses the right to the marriage debt. The existence of many children in a large family excuses from rendering the debt. But proximate possibility of damage to children to be born does not excuse from rendering the debt since existence is better than non-existence. If intercourse would harm a fetus in the womb, spouses should not engage in it. Various forms of artificial insemination have come to the fore in recent years. Artificial insemination is placing the male seed within the woman by means other than copulation. Scientific help for married couples to conceive is in general to be encouraged. Some forms of help to inseminate the woman are moral and at times to be encouraged. But the immorality of many forms of artificial insemination lies in the means by which the male seed is obtained. The ordinary means are various types of masturbation. As such, they are to be avoided. The objection against many forms of artificial insemination is that it renders a human act mechanical.

HUMAN SEXUALITY

The most controversial part of contemporary ethics involves human sexuality. Human sexuality involves biological, social, and personal levels. Since the work of Sigmund Freud the role of human sexuality in the development of the human person has been grossly over-emphasized. So strong has the influence of Freud been in the last century that contemporary society is almost certainly not in a good position to judge the importance of sexuality in human life. From ancient Greco-Roman times mankind has known the importance of human sexuality. The role of sexuality in human life is more important than was judged to be the case in Victorian times. Freud aside, the most influential factor in sexual practice in the last half of the twentieth century has been the discovery and ready availability of contraceptive measures. In the western world, sexuality has been torn from begetting and rearing children. We need only look at the population of large American cities and the composition of the American family to observe the influence of this separation. Further, contraceptive practices have influenced the entire western world in such a way that few western countries are replacing their populations by reproductive means. Combined with excessive individualism, a result no doubt of a certain lack of protection of individual rights in previous centuries, such contraceptive practices have led to the demise of the family in many quarters.

Chastity is the moral virtue by which humans control their sexual lives. By it they moderate or at times exclude venereal pleasure. It is an aspect of the cardinal virtue of temperance. The practice of chastity varies according to states of life: celibate or married. Modesty is the aspect of the virtue of chastity by which man abstains from acts which ordinarily lead to intercourse. A natural human disposition toward modesty is not virtue, but can be nurtured to inculcate and preserve the virtue. Purity is the aspect of the virtue of chastity by which one proposes to abstain from voluntary pollution.

Virginity is a firm proposal of the will by someone who has never had intercourse to abstain from all venereal pleasure, licit or illicit. It can be a virtue or a vow. Virginity can be lost through any grave offense against the virtue of chastity or through the proposal to marry. Virginity is irreparably lost through any voluntary sexual violation of the body. The proposal to marry offends against virginity, but does not irreparably take it away if the marriage is not consummated. St. Augustine particularly praised the practice of celibacy and virginity.

Humans have the propensity to preserve their own livee and the lives of the human race. By nutrition humans preserve themselves, by intercourse humans preserve the human race. Just as pleasure accompanies nutrition, pleasure accompanies intercourse. Man offends against the virtue of chastity by excessive appetite for or use of venereal pleasure. Venereal pleasure arises from movement of the reproductive organs which could include the flow of fluids which serve to aid generation. As such, it is a sense pleasure. Licentiousness is the disordered appetite or use of venereal pleasure. Such disorder can take place inside or outside of marriage.

Immodesty consists of voluntary occupation with matters which lead to venereal pleasure. Impurity consists of the effusion of seed within or outside of copulation.

Understanding of chastity as a virtue developed mostly in Christian times. Augustine's view of sexual life evolved to the position that, in the original state of man, sexuality was under the control of reason. Man would have procreated physically, not spiritually (whatever that might have meant), with concomitant pleasure. But the procreative act would have been under the control of reason. Among the results of sin is that human sexual life went beyind reason's control. A glance around contemporary society, not to mention Augustine's times, confirms this view. A comparison with human nutrition is instructive. Before sin humans would have nourished themelves with the concomitant pleasure attached. Such nutrition would have been under the control of reason. After sin, the taking of nourishment went out of reason's control. The same holds for human sexual pleasure.

During the second half of the twentieth century and into the twenty-first, artificial birth control has become a central topic in western society. Artificial means of birth control have been in existence since the ancient world. But former methods to interfere with procreation were primitive and unreliable. Since the growth in biological understanding of procreation, more effective means of avoiding conception have been produced. Extensive use of these means has led to the severing of the performance of the sexual act from reproduction. The Christian philosophical understanding of the sex act has taken its teleology, that is it natural purpose, into account. A rudimentary analysis of the biological process of reproduction indicates that the purpose of human intercourse is the procreation of human offspring. To interfere with this process and to block the process from attaining its natural conclusion is therefore immoral. In actuality, artificial birth control can be considered a kind of masturbation.

Since the progress in contraceptive means, objections to this view have come from all sides.

(1) Many have spoken of a unitive function of the sexual act. It is a means of expressing the close unity that a married couple has. The mutual help, support, and love of one for the other reaches its symbolic expression in the act of intercourse. A couple should be able to engage in sexual intercourse for this purpose without attempting to have children. This argument has much merit. For some time, the unitive function of the sexual act has been recognized by Christian philosophers. Nevertheless, a problem arises: if the purpose of the sexual act is purely symbolic, expressive of love, why should this symbolism be limited to married people or even to people of the opposite sex? Indeed, such use of the sexual act beyond the union of man and a woman has become more popular, and, at least on a philosophical level, has been justified on the same grounds. Clearly, the biological purpose of intercourse is procreation of children. Sexual intercourse makes sense as an expression of love only within marriage together with the procreation of children.

(2) A second objection to the teleological view is that human beings often interfere with the processes of nature, indeed to human advantage. For example, human beings cut their fingernails and do not let them grow unattended. Man shaves and cuts his hair. Some medicines are taken or medical practices undergone so that natural functions do not, at least for a period, take place. This argument also has some merit. Nevertheless, the sexual act is central to marriage. It is the matter of the contract. Certainly intercourse is more essential, vital, and central to marriage than is hair to the human being.

(3) The essential question is whether each and every instance of sexual intercourse must be open to the procreative end. What is certainly immoral and unethical is the entering of marriage without an explicit or implicit intention of having children, when such is possible. The very purpose of marriage is to bear and rear children. Two men or two women can be good friends, but they can not marry simply because they can not produce children. The contraceptive mentality, widespread in the western world in the beginning of the twenty-first century, is certainly immoral. The traditional literature of marriage, at least in the most outstanding authors, may certainly be read in this manner. To enter marriage and exclude the possibility of bearing and rearing children in a positive manner is to invalidate marriage. Following natural rhythms in sexual matters in marriage is of course in order. Responsible parenthood should be encouraged. Urban life of the twenty-first century is considerably different from rural life of the nineteenth century. On the farm a large family was advantageous; in the city a large family is sometimes a liability. What constitutes responsible parenthood will differ according to time and place. There is no moral obligation to have as many children as possible, but there is a moral obligation to have children in marriage when possible.

Understanding human genetic composition progresses almost daily. One can not pick up a newspaper without reading about genetic discoveries. Such genetic understanding has influenced contemporary sexual life. Prediction of hereditary disease or serious physical or mental defect has become usual. Genetic modification of a fetus is on the horizon. Such advances in medical science are to be encouraged. Nevertheless ethical considerations must remain paramount. Abortion of a fetus because of knowledge gained through new methods is to be avoided. A fortiori, abortion because of gender considerations is unethical. Artificial insemination outside of marriage is immoral. Within marriage, help to couples to conceive is a good to be sought. The manner by which a man's sperm is to be obtained should be moral, that is masturbation is to be avoided.

Surrogate parenthood has become a not uncommon phenomenon in the twenty-first century. By means of uniting a sperm with an ovum and implanting the fertilized egg in a woman's womb, some couples who can not conceive or maintain a fetus can have a family. The practice is open to abuse. A fertilized ovum can be placed in the womb of a woman who is not the natural mother. At times, a fee is charged. While at times one can sympathize with the couple who wants to conceive but can not, the practice of surrogate motherhood is immoral. The process of conception is cheapened and may degenerate into a business. Women are many times treated as chattel. The same is true of the fertilized ovum. A human process becomes a scientific event. Science should help the natural process of conception, but not replace it. Human beings are not merely mechanisms.

Sexual relations between unmarried heterosexuals is more common today than in previous times. The availability of artificial contraceptive means has promoted such relations. A couple may engage in sexual activity without concerning themselves with reproduction. The unitive symbolic function of the sexual act can remain with unmarried couples. But marriage is a public as well as a private matter. Both the state and the church have the right and the duty to control social and public matters dealing with marriage. Prior to the Council of Trent, much social confusion reigned over marriage. There were few public records. Church law changed this situation. The state has followed. Nevertheless, many couples have made commitments to one another without official documents. In many cases both church and state, for example in remote areas where no church or state representative exists, recognize such unions as marriages. Some argue that the same is true for the so-called single couples. However, the social and public nature of the effects of marriage demand public record. Thus the ordinary situation should be marriage as it is commonly understood.

Restitution by reason of rape or fornication is a difficult and complicated problem. If a man and woman mutually consent, there is no obligation to restitution on either part either toward the woman or toward the parents. The couple maintain obligations toward the child. With regard to rape, if the man did not promise marriage to a virgin, he is bound to restitution for all the damage of which he is the cause. He may do this by marriage, but the woman is not bound to accept. If he offers her money and she refuses, wanting to marry, the man is not bound to marry. He may offer her some amount of money or otherwise take care that she can marry as well as she would have if she had not been violated. If he can not marry her, he must provide for her as he can. If he promised marriage, the man is bound to the promise, unless there is a great disparity in class, the virgin knew that the promise was frivolous, or the parents reasonably do not consent. Since the man can not restore virginity, he is bound only to keep the matter private so that the woman suffers no further damage. Toward a child arising from the act, a rapist is held in justice to pay the expenses of birth and to provide for the child. In charity he is bound to recognize the child as legitimate if there is a subsequent marriage. In the case of fornication, the man is not held to expenses of birth because there was mutual consent. But the onus of raising the child falls upon both parties. If the woman has had relations with more than one man, if the father can not be determined, none of the men is bound to care for the child.

In the case of adultery, if no child arises, there is no obligation to restitution. However, if the adultery becomes known to the husband or wife, there is moral obligation to restitution. If a child arises and the woman's consent was forced, the man is bound to restitution. If the woman consented, both are bound to restitution. If the husband consented to the adultery, there is no obligation to restitution. Ascertaining parentage is easier today because of examination of DNA. Nevertheless, if the woman is unsure if her husband or lover is the father of the child, and the true biological father of the child can not be ascertained, no restitution is necessary and the child is believed to be legitimate. If the child is certainly illegitimate, but the true father is doubtful, there is no moral obligation to restitution on the part of the lovers, except in the case of conspiracy among the men. If a child arising from adultery is separated from the family, such as being placed in an orphanage, no further restitution is demanded. Otherwise, the adulterer is bound to the expenses of birth and rearing the child. Restitution is also due the other children if they lose part of their inheritance. The woman is not bound to reveal the illegitimacy to the child. But the mother is bound to repair any damage done to the legitimate children because of the existence of an illegitimate child in the family. If the man can not make restitution without grave inconvenience to his own family, he is not bound to restitution.

Piety is the moral virtue by which honor is due parents and country. Natural reason indicates that the special relationship between parents and children is the basis for this virtue. This virtue includes special acts by which children honor their parents. It also includes obedience children owe them. In marriage, spouses incur special obligations toward one another. They are held to mutual love and mutual help one for the other. They are held to render the conjugal debt and to cohabitation. Ordinarily husband and wife are bound to care for the physical and spiritual well being of each other.

Over the past century, women's emancipation has come to the fore. Originally confined to the political sphere, today the women's movement includes domestic, economic, and social goals. Certainly abuses against women have existed in the past. Both men and women possess the same human nature. They both have the same destiny. They therefore should have equal rights. Nevertheless, certain differences of men and women exist in the concrete, both of body and soul. Thus equality does not demand uniformity. Political, social, and economic goals of emancipation are to be encouraged. Equal opportunity of education should be an aspiration. But the women's movement unfortunately has become involved in abortion on demand. The so-called right to abortion was not espoused by most of the early proponents of women's emancipation. Such groups are morally bound to proper means to attain their ends.

Both parents and children have obligations toward one another. Children should respect, love, and obey their parents. Children should respect and love their parents both internally and externally. A child is held to pay the debts of his father from any money left to him, but is not held to pay the father's debts from his own personal wealth. Minor children have the duty to obey their parents in all serious matters which are not immoral. Minor children should obey their parents in morals and those matters necessary for the maintenance of order in the family. In choosing a way of life or a person to marry, however, children are free, though out of respect they should consult their parents. Parents do not have the same power over illegitimate children as they do over legitimate ones. Further, illegitimate children do not enjoy the same rights nor do they have the same duties as legitimate children unless and until they become legitimate. Nevertheless, parents are obliged to feed, clothe, and shelter their illegitimate children and to educate them according to their own economic conditions. Parents are held to love and educate their natural children. As a matter of duty, parents must feed, clothe, and shelter their children. They should offer a moral example to their children, correct them, and be vigilant in moral matters. Parents have a further obligation to see that the schools which their children attend foster morality.

Families and members of the family own property. Today the situation is much different than in former times. Neverthcless, ownership of the family property is ordinarily still determined by civil law. In general a child owns what he has earned from his own labor, but he owes something to the family for his food, clothing, and shelter, if the parents so desire. That which he has earned not from his own industry, but as part of the family belongs to the family. In former times, husband and wife jointly owned the family's common goods, but the husband and father was administrator of the family property. In strict justice he owed the family proper administration of these goods. Ordinarily he ceded some of his power in running the household to his wife. A dowry belonged to the husband, but what the wife inherited was given to her personally. What she earned by own industry outside the home belonged to her. Today husband and wife are generally regarded as having joint ownership and administration of the family's goods. A wife certainly has ownership and administration of what she has earned by her own private industry. Both husband and working wife have a moral obligation to contribute to the family and to administer the household jointly. Some families still follow the traditional model

In earlier times, servants were a part of the larger family. Today, at least in the western world, servants are not ordinarily part of the family. Domestic workers are more common. Heads of the family and domestic workers have mutual obligations. A domestic worker must promote domestic welfare, do work assigned in a reasonable fashion, and observe conditions of his contract. Heads of a family must pay a just wage which should include some provision for retirement. They must take care that working conditions do not promote bad health.

OFFENSES AGAINST CHASTITY

Inordinate desire for and pursuit of venereal pleasure outside of marriage is a grave evil. Venereal pleasure is ordered toward procreation. Such procreation should take place only within marriage. Protection of marriage is a great good for the human race, the endangering of marriage a great evil. All directly willed offenses against this good of marriage, that is directly willed pursuit of venereal pleasure outside of marriage, are grave evils; slight evils do not exist. Indirectly willed offenses against marriage may be grave or slight evils, according as these actions proximately or remotely give rise to the possibility of exciting human desire. Human libido may be either strong or light. Obviously some difference in individuals exists. Among young men and women, invincible ignorance may excuse from responsibility; vincible ignorance lessens responsibility.

Offenses against chastity may be divided into those according to nature and those against nature. Offenses according to nature include fornication, adultery, incest, and rape. These offenses differ among themselves only by reason of circumstances. Offenses against nature include masturbation, sodomy, and bestiality.

Carnal movements in the sexual organs of both men and women arise either voluntarily or involuntarily. They are necessary for the act of intercourse. When they arise voluntarily outside of this purpose, they offend against the virtue of chastity, when involuntarily they do not; when voluntary in cause, a proportionate reason is necessary. Resistance to involuntary movements or movements voluntary in cause is necessary only when consent to them is likely.

FORNICATION

Simple fornication is copulation by a single man and a single woman with mutual consent. A single person is one who is bound by no other law than natural law to observe the virtue of chastity, that is bound by neither marriage nor religious vow. Concubinage is frequent copulation between two single people of the opposite sex with each other. It differs from simple fornication in that copulation occurs with the same person. These two people may or may not live with one another. The particular evil of concubinage lies in the intention to persevere in the offense. A prostitute is a human being who gives him or herself sexually to many others for money. A whore is someone who does the same merely for satisfying sexual desire. All the above are kinds of fornication.

Whatever the variety, fornication is a serious offense against chastity. It offends against the natural law because fornicators seek venereal pleasure without attendant obligations of bearing and raising offspring. Fornication seriously endangers society which is fundamentally based on procreation and proper education of children.

Prostitution can be public or private. Sometimes prostitution is tolerated by state law in larger cities to avoid greater evils. Both St. Augustine and St. Thomas thought that greater civil evils could possibly be avoided by legalizing prostitution. In contemporary society public prostitution is an evil; it does not achieve its proposed purpose of public health and in fact many times spreads disease.

ADULTERY

Adultery is copulation with the spouse of another. One or both partners can be married. Adultery may, but does not necessarily, include intercourse. Adultery is committed even if the other spouse consents. It is an offense against commutative justice since the right of the marriage contract is violated, and against chastity.

INCEST

Incest is copulation with family members or close relatives with whom marriage is prohibited. Normally marriage is prohibited through third cousins. Incest can also be committed with legal relatives, that is relatives through legal process such as adoption, or with spiritual relatives, for example godchildren. Incest is an offense against chastity and piety, that is reverence due to parents and relatives. Much more scientific knowledge: concerning genes has served to demonstrate what was known intuitively for centuries

RAPE

Rape is the violent abduction of any person for the purpose of satisfying sexual desire. Rape is essentially violence. It is an offense against chastity since it involves illicit sexual pleasure, and against justice since violence is involved. If the person involved is a virgin, rape is particularly odious. It deprives the other person, normally a woman, of what is hers by right, namely her virginity.

MASTURBATION

Masturbation is a voluntary experience of complete venereal pleasure without engaging in intercourse. Male masturbation consists in the flowing of seed without the possibility of its achieving its purpose, thus against nature. Female masturbation consists in causing the flow of vaginal fluid. The precise evil consists in the use of sexual pleasure not for its destined end. At times the flow of fluid is involuntary; in this no offense is involved. Many contemporary physicians recommend masturbation for health reasons. Such grounds are medically questionable and objectively morally objectionable. When sexual pleasure is only voluntary in cause, sufficient reason allows it.

Masturbation within marriage is copulation in such a way that generation can not take place. Withdrawal before the flowing of the seed or impeding the seed from reaching the woman by instrumental means are both forms of masturbation within marriage. Insofar as artificial birth control is a kind of masturbation, it has been treated above. To discontinue intercourse before the flowing of the seed by mutual consent is not immoral. But formal cooperation in such practices for the purposes of birth control is immoral. Material cooperation in withdrawal is possibly moral. Masturbation in marriage, when it takes place by oneself, is particularly evil since it impedes the successful completion of the marriage act.

SODOMY

Sodomy is intercourse with persons of the same or opposite sex in a place of the body not naturally destined for performance of the act, It can take place between persons of the same or opposite sex. Sodomy is against the natural purpose of intercourse and conjugal faith which demands that spouses use each others' bodies in the manner suitable for generation. The act may or may not be consummated. The participants can he active or passive. Homosexual acts are a type of sodomy. Such acts are unnatural since the purpose of intercourse can not be achieved.

BESTIALITY

Bestiality is sexual intercourse of a human being with an animal. It can be with any animal of either sex for whatever purpose. Such a practice is against natural law. As such, it is a serious evil. The offense against nature consists in frustration of a natural end of human sexual intercourse, the continuation and preservation of the human species. Therefore bestiality is especially repugnant to human nature. Recently, some philosophers have consider the traditional moral judgement on bestiality as a type of "speciesism," that is an arrogant regard for human beings as superior to other types of animals. The foundation of ethics is precisely that human beings, because of his intellect and will, differ from other species.

SEXUAL PERVERSION

Sadism, masochism, and fetishism are types of sexual perversity. Little is known about the causes of these phenomena, but may be presumed to be a combination of nature and nurture. Sadism is the taking of venereal pleasure from performing actions of cruelty and violence: strangulation, flagellation, and so forth. These actions are not performed to induce intercourse, but to excite lust. Masochism is the taking of venereal pleasure from suffering acts of violence or cruelty. Fetishism occurs when lust arises from dreams or actions which ordinarily do not pertain to sexual activity. Examples include finding hands or feet objects of sexual attraction.

HOMOSEXUALITY

Homosexuality consists in sexual attraction for persons of the same sex. If the attraction is for young boys, it is called pederasty or pedophilia, if to youths ephebephilia. Homosexuality has existed in western society at least since ancient Greece. However, there is much contemporary misunderstanding concerning its role at that time. Education began with the military class. Schools as we know them did not exist—Plato's Academy and Aristotle's Lyceum are exceptions. Such education took place between a younger man and his mentor. The purpose of education was essentially moral. The relationship was to inspire virtuous noble deeds. Part of this relationship was at times sexual; but sexual relations were not the fundamental purpose of the relationship. For this reason, there was understanding and tolerance of homosexuality in Greece and Rome.

More is known today of the causes of homosexuality, but much still remains to be learned. Evidently heterosexual and homosexual tendencies exist within all men and women. In approximately five per cent of the population, homosexual tendencies predominate. The causes of this predominance are not well known. Some speculate concerning a genetic cause; others speak of the childhood relationship with one's parents; some have even speculated about life in the womb as a cause. The probability is that nature and nurture both play a role. Homosexuality is not necessarily a sign of mental sickness. Sexual attractions of this type can ordinarily be repressed just as sexual attraction to the opposite sex.

The problem arises with sexual relations within a homosexual relationship. Obviously the reproductive purpose of the sexual act can not be realized between two members of the same sex. Thus a marriage can not exist between them. But the unitive function of the act can be maintained. Since the finality of the act is procreative, this symbolism should take place within marriage. The act of intercourse is not symbolic of any loving relationship, for example between brother and sister, but only of the marital relationship. Two men or two women can be good friends, but they can not be married to one another. There is some similarity with the inability to marry one's brother or sister, though they may of course be good friends. One cause of the discussion about marriage between members of the same sex is that various social benefits are accorded married couples not accorded to single people. In the United States, healthcare benefits are an example. But solution of healthcare insurance is not a reason to recognize homosexual relationships as marriages. In fact, it may be a reason to rethink the manner in which healthcare benefits are given. Obviously there are untenable social repercussions in representing homosexual union as a social ideal on the same level as marriage. With such a policy, society ultimately could die.

CHAPTER 3

Contracts

Contracts have both moral and legal status; at times the legality and morality overlap. Morally contracts arise out of the virtue of justice, specifically commutative justice. A contract is a mutual agreement between two or more people concerning the transfer of a right. The immediate effect of a contract is the transfer of a right. A contract differs from a promise in that a right is actually transferred. Certain notes belong to the essence of a contract; others accrue to contracts by reason of custom; still others are accidental and do not belong to the essence of the contract.

Several types of contracts exist. Contracts can be unilateral or bilateral according as one or more of the contractors are morally bound. Somer contracts bind only morally, others bind both morally and legally. Contracts may be gratuitous or onerous depending upon whether one or more take on an obligation. To be binding morally a contract must be both valid and licit. A valid contract is one which is a real contract. A licit contract is one which both parties are legally and morally allowed to make. An invalid contract may look like a contract, but in fact is not. Several types of contracts exist, but there is no need to enter into all of them here.

Four conditions are required for a valid contract: (1) suitable matter; (2) capable persons; (3) mutual consent; (4) agreement on cause. Any object of ownership can be the matter of a contract.

(1) The matter of a contract must be possible. No one can oblige himself to what is impossible. A human being may of course oblige himself to something difficult. If part of the object becomes impossible, the contractor is held only to the part which is possible. The object of the contract must exist either in fact or in prospect. The object must belong to one of the parties. No one can give what he does not possess. The object of the contract must be morally permissible. Otherwise, there would be an obligation to do and not do the same thing at th same time and in the same respect. Therefore, a contract to do evil is immoral. Morally speaking, a contract need not contain a consideration or transfer of money. If a contract does contain a consideration, the object must be estimable by price. One who has received money to perform an evil act is morally bound not to perform the act, but in practice is not morally bound to return the money. There is an ongoing dispute among moralists concerning this latter matter.

(2) The parties to a contract must be capable of making that contract, that is they must be capable of performing a human act. The contractors must be capable of consenting. Infants, the insane, drunks, or those lacking the use of reason from some other cause are incapable of making a contract. The civil law may determine who is capable or incapable. Ordinarily, contracts made by minors are voidable in civil law.

(3) Mutual consent is necessary for a valid contract. The consent must be true and not feigned. One who feigns consent voids a contract but is held to any unjust damage arising from this false consent. In the external forum, feigned consent may not be presumed; it must be proved. The consent must be free and deliberate, that is from a perfectly voluntary act. Thus those who are semi-drunk or half-asleep can not enter into a valid contract. The consent must be mutual, that is, both parties must agree to the same thing. Without voluntary agreement there is no contract. All must agree to the same thing. But mutual agreement is not sufficient. The two parties must make the agreement relative to one another. Consent need not take place at the same time, but one must not have revoked his consent when the other consents. The consent must ordinarily be manifest by some

external sign. The sign may be written, oral, or by some other means. External consent seals the contract offered by another. If the contract is favorable, silence is presumed to mean consent. If the contract is onerous, and one is easily able to signify lack of consent, silence is also considered to be consent. *Qui tacit consentit in favorabilibus.*

Error, deception, or violence may void a contract or at least render it voidable. An error may be one's own or another's. An error is substantial if it concerns the substance of the thing, for example, a dead horse instead of a live one. An error is accidental if it does not pertain to the substance of the thing, for example the color an object. Deception is prior error on the part of one contractor. Absolute violence voids a contract under the principles on violence. Substantial error voids a contract. The contracting parties must agree on the matter of the contract. Substantial error means that there is not agreement as to the matter. The same is true concerning accidental error if the quality of the object was the reason or a necessary condition in the contract. Usually, the parties do not have to agree on the worth of the matter. Accidental error of itself never voids a contract. Accidental error on the part of one of the contracting parties brought about by deception before the contract renders a contract voidable at the discretion of the one who was deceived. But an accidental error accompanying the contract does not render it voidable, if the person would have contracted if the error were known. If a horse is dead or dies soon after the purchase because of a pre-existing condition, the contract is void. If a mistake is made over the color of the horse, the contract is not invalidated unless the color was stipulated as the reason for the contract.

A contract arises from fear when fear gives rise to the contract in such a way that one would not have contracted without fear. Ordinarily contracts arising from fear are valid unless fear takes away the use of reason. Fear leaves a human act intact. Grave fear does not render a contract invalid. Fear, unjustly brought about, however may render a contract voidable at the discretion of the one who suffered it. Fear brought about by a third person without the consent of the contracting parties does not render a contract invalid. Ordinarily, the state or the church makes regulations voiding contracts made under duress or intimidation. For example, marriage or religious profession brought about by fear is voided by positive civil or church law.

(4) Consent seals a contract. Therefore the cause of the consent must be the same. The motive behind a contract may be principal or primary, if it is the main or only reason for the contract, otherwise it is secondary or impulsive. If the primary cause is not present to both, the contract is invalid. The lack of the secondary motive in one of the parties does not render the contract invalid.

Certain obligations arise to the contracting parties. Some obligations arise from natural law, others from civil law, still others from both. Obligations arising from natural law oblige in conscience, civil obligations do not. Every valid contract imposes a moral obligation in conscience by reasons of commutative justice. Such obligations have to do not only with codicils in the contract, but to conditions which are implicit in the contract either by natural law, by positive law, or by custom of the area. Such an obligation is grave or light according to the matter, A voidable contract obliges until or unless the one who is able to void it does so.

Contracts may be made specifying certain conditions. Past or present conditions constitute valid contracts if the conditions exist. A future condition which is possible does not impede a contract, but if it is or becomes impossible, the contract becomes void. A contract for a prescribed objective is valid. The contract is immediately valid. One party accepts the onus of fulfilling the purpose. For example, a person gives money to a charitable organization for a particular purpose. A contract with a particular motive is valid if the cause actually exists, and is the primary motive of the contract. For example, a person gives a gift to his cousin precisely because he is a cousin. If the motive does not exist, the contract is void unless the motive is only secondary. Contracts to begin on a certain date are also valid. If the day is now certain, the contract becomes immediately valid, though the execution takes place on the day designated. A person may for example give a person a gift taking place when the giver dies. If the event is uncertain, the contract is valid only when the condition is present. For example, a person agrees to give a gift to a school if his son finishes his degree.

PROMISES

A promise is a contract by which one obliges himself gratuitously to do or omit something. A promise differs from a proposal because in a proposal one does not intend to take on an obligation. Promises are valid under the following conditions: (1) one must have the will to bind himself, even if he does not advert to the obligation;

(2) the promise must be manifested by an exterior sign and be accepted. Promises can oblige in fidelity or in justice. Ordinarily, promises oblige only under the virtue of fidelity. There is no transferal of right. Promises binding under the virtue of justice transfer a right. Promises obliging under justice cease if a notable condition comes about which would have impeded the contract had the condition been known. Every promise has the tacit assumption that a person binds himself only without grave hardship. If before the promised action the motive for the promise ceases, the obligation of the promise ceases. If the promise becomes impossible to fulfil due to no fault on the part of the one promising, the obligation to fulfil the promise ceases. If the person to whom the promise was made dies, the obligation ceases if it was a personal promise. Otherwise the obligation does not cease and it should be done or omitted to the heirs. If the one promising dies, a personal promise dies with him. Otherwise, the obligation is inherited by the heirs.

BILATERAL CONTRACTS

A deposit is a contract by which someone is given something to take care of it and to restore it in its present form to the one who gave it. A deposit can be gratuitous or onerous depending upon whether the deposit is done for money or not. Tacit consent is sufficient for the deposit. Companies who carry freight have a contract of deposit. The one who accepts the responsibility of a deposit agrees to guard the thing with the same diligence which he is accustomed to guarding his own possessions of equal value. He is not obliged to guard the deposit at grave peril to his own life. The one with whom the goods are deposited may not use the article unless with the express or tacit consent of the depositor. The consent of the depositor may be presumed if no danger of damage to the article is present. When the article is consumed through use, for example money, the depositee may use the article if there is likelihood that he can replace it. He is able to keep the increase as the fruit of his labor. The one who has the article is bound to return it when asked by the depositor, whether the time has been determined or not. He can not return it before the time determined, He should not return the goods if he knows that the thing has been stolen, if he knows the depositor will abuse the thing, or if the depositor refuses to pay the fee agreed upon. If the depositee does not return the goods, he is bound to restitution. The depositor is a morally bound to pay expenses incurred by the depositee in taking care of his goods. The depositor should also repair damages which the depositee incurred in the course of taking care of the object. Sequestration, by which some controverted thing is deposited with a third party until ownership is decided by litigation, is a type of deposit and generally is to be judged morally the same.

One may agree to carry out business in the name of another. This power can be gratuitous or onerous depending on the existence of payment. Examples include the power of attorney, the work of stock brokers, and sometimes the work of banks. Such persons must carry out the business with the same diligence that they use in carrying out their own business. One who receives money should use greater care than one who performs such duties gratis. The person must observe the limits of his mandate and should use all legitimate means to carry out the business. If he exceeds the mandate, he is bound to restitution. All profit belongs to the person he represents. What he acquires by extraordinary industry or by special agreement he may keep. He is bound to restitution for damages for which he is culpably negligent. The one for whom the business is carried out must fulfil his obligations toward the one who carries out the business and also observe the limits of the mandate. The former must pay the necessary expenses of the latter which he incurs, even if the business does not turn out as the former had anticipated. He is bound to pay the damages which the person with the power suffers without any fault of his own, but is not bound to pay damages which happen by chance.

Lending or borrowing is a contract by which a thing is given to someone for use for a period of time with the obligation of returning it to the lender after its use. Lending is always gratuitous. Lending differs from a lease in that a lease usually contains a provision to repeat the loan. The one who borrows a thing should not use the borrowed article for any other use than the designated purpose of the thing. If he does so, he is bound to reparation. The borrower is bound to the ordinary expenses incurred in keeping the thing, but not to extraordinary expenses. For example, he should feed a horse, but he is not bound to pay for a veterinarian operation. The borrower is bound to take better care of a thing than a depositee since the contract redounds to his benefit. He must pay for damages incurred for which he is responsible, but not for damages incurred by ordinary use of the object. He must return the thing at the time determined explicitly or implicitly, even if not demanded by he lender. He should not restore it before such time if the lender is unwilling. If he keeps the article beyond the time, he is responsible for all damages. The lender is morally responsible for all damages which happened by chance. The lender should tell the borrower about defects in the goods. He is morally bound to pay for all expenses incurred by the borrower for preserving the thing which come about without fault of the borrower. He is not bound to repeat the loan. If the thing perishes, it perishes for the owner.

One may also lend something consumable. One agrees to lend and the other agrees to use the thing and repay with a thing of the same kind in due time. Food and drink are examples of things subject to this kind of contract. For a time, the borrower becomes owner of the thing. The very nature of the thing borrowed is that it is consumable—it has no other use. Therefore, by its very nature, this kind of contract is gratuitous. If it were not, one would be demanding the return of the thing plus a price for its use. But the nature of the object is that it has no other value than its use or consumption. Since the borrower becomes the owner of the object for time, one asking a price for its use would be asking a price for something not his. One may not sell both a steak and it use. Nevertheless, there are times when the lender may ask a price from the borrower of a consumable item. If he loses money or suffers damage by not having the object for a time or if the person does not replace the thing in due time, the lender may ask a price.

USURY

A particular question arises concerning the lending of money. Is money a consumable? The origins of money go back many centuries. In ancient cultures, money had only representative value. It was sterile, that is it did not of itself increase. Money was a consumable. For example, if a person's salary was three bushels of wheat, rather than receiving the wheat itself at the end of the day, an employee might receive a coin for each bushel that he had earned. At some time, the worker could redeem these coins. However the value of the coins did not in themselves increase or decrease. With the rise of mercantilism and capitalism, the nature of money changed. In the mercantile system of the late Middle Ages and in capitalism in its industrial form, money began to have a value in itself. People pooled their resources to bring about production of goods and creation of wealth which was not available to isolated individuals. As companies grew, the value of one's money would increase. Later, inflation came about and one's money could also decrease in value. Thus money no longer had only a representative value. Money could increase and decrease in value and thus had a value in itself. Money could always have had this function, but in fact money took on this function only gradually due to historical circumstances.

May one take interest for lending money? In former times, the taking of interest on money lent was viewed as immoral. Since money was a consumable, taking interest on lending it would be like lending a bottle of wine and asking something for its use. The Latin term for such a practice was *usurus* from which the contemporary term usury comes. But today, usury is not the taking of any interest but the taking of excessive interest in lending money. A person should be allowed to take some interest in lending someone money. Not to be able to do so would entail man losing money by lending it. How much this interest should be depends upon circumstance of time, place, and individual. Interest rates may be set by the state, by common estimation, or by agreement between two people. Obviously a range can be established.

Taking excessive interest is immoral and is termed usury. Usury is against the natural law and offends against commutative justice. Credit cards which can entail interest of seventeen percent and more are obviously a modern example of usury. Credit cards with lower rates are moral. Circumstances may exist when one ought in charity to lend a poor person money without interest. The change in the morality of taking interest for lending money came not from an error about the nature of money, nor from the changes in civil law, but from change in the function of money in society.

BUYING AND SELLING

Buying and selling is a contract between two parties who agree to exchange a commodity for a price. Barter is still a usual form of exchange in many parts of the world and differs from buying and selling only in that money does not change hands. Products necessary for life such as food and shelter may be bought and sold. Products may also be sold merely for the motive of profit. This form of buying and selling is called business. The seller may merely sell the product without changing it in any way, or may through his own industry change it. For a true purchase, the buyer and seller must agree on the object, there must be an actual object in fact or in prospect, and money must change hands.

The seller has several obligations. The object to be sold must really exist and buyer and seller must agree on its substantial nature. A seller may substitute one thing for another if the purpose of the product is identical. Thus a pharmacist may sell a generic brand instead of the name brand if the purpose of the medication is the same. A seller may not however substitute an artificial product for a natural one. Secondly, the seller must own the object. If the seller does not own the object, the contract is invalid and the buyer does not become owner of the article. The object must be pure, not mixed. For example, watered down wine may not be sold as wine. The seller must manifest the substantial hidden defects of the object even if not asked. Consent seals the contract. Both parties must consent to the same thing. If the seller does not consent, the contract is invalid. The seller must reveal the accidental defects, whether manifest or hidden, upon request. If he does not do so, the contract is voidable. The seller is under no obligation to reveal the accidental hidden defects if not asked. But if the buyer is not well informed so that he does not know the accidental defects, he should be told. The seller must deliver the product as it was at the time of purchase. Otherwise, the buyer has the right to void the purchase. If the object suffers damage, the seller is morally obliged to repair it, even before a judicial decision. If the article is damaged by chance, both the buyer and the seller lose part of it.

The buyer also has certain obligations. If the seller is unaware of the value of the object, the buyer must advise him or offer him at least the lowest just price. Likewise, if the buyer is unaware of the value of the object and offers more than the highest just price, the seller must advise him of this state of affairs. Otherwise, the contract is unjust. The buyer must pay for the object at the time and place agreed upon; if no time and place was agreed upon, then at the time when the merchandise is delivered. If he does not pay, the seller need not hand over the merchandise. Custom or contract may determine what will happen if payment is delayed. The buyer must accept the object upon delivery. At that time, the seller has the right to demand the payment.

The determination of a just price is a matter of some dispute. Economists argue for a price dictated by whatever a particular market will bear. Businessmen speak of a fair profit for the seller after considering his own expenses. But the moralist speaks of a just price. The price of a thing is its value in terms of money. Value is the common judgement concerning a thing in a given region, which judgement depends upon it usefulness to man. A just price therefore is the true money value of a given product.

There are three kinds of just price: A legal just price, a common or natural just price, and a conventional just price. A legal just price is determined by public authority. A legal price is thought to be just until otherwise proved. It binds in commutative justice.

The natural just price is the price determined by the common estimation of men which they will pay for a given product at this time in this place. It is not mathematically determined but has a certain elasticity. Two extremes are to be avoided in determination of a just price. On the one hand, every commodity does not have an exact price. On the other hand, a commodity is not worth whatever a buyer would pay in a given circumstance. Situations vary according to time, place, and individual taste and desire. One might be willing to pay a king's ransom for a gallon of gasoline or a pint of water in the middle of the desert. The worth of one's money would be inversely proportional to one's need: the greater one's need, the less one's money would be worth. A just price therefore must be the price a commodity is worth to society in general. This price is determined on the free and open market. Obviously, the free market does not determine an exact price, but a range. Thus, there is a highest just price, above which a buyer is exploited, and a lowest just price below which a seller's need to sell would be exploited. When a legal just price does not exist, it is moral to buy and sell within this range. It is moral for a buyer to accept a price lower than the lowest just price, if a seller so offers. Whether it is moral for a seller depends upon his motive. Sales as business practices are of course moral. At times an object has special worth to a particular individual. If the article is of great sentimental value to the owner, he may sell over the highest just price because this sentimental value is worth something. Likewise, if the article has great sentimental value to the buyer, the seller is allowed to sell below the lowest just price as a favor to the buyer. Further, a price may be adjusted above the highest just price if payment is deferred, or lowered below the lowest just price because of immediate cash payment.

The conventional price is one determined by agreement of seller and buyer. The price of some articles is difficult, if not impossible to estimate. Articles such as rare paintings, manuscripts, rare gems, or antiques can hardly have a natural or legal price. It is moral to sell or buy for a conventional price, so long as the price is not beyond a reasonable sum. One might question the morality of the price received for various art works today on these grounds. One is of course allowed to make a profit because of his own insight into the worth of something. But it is immoral to buy something at a very low price because the seller is ignorant of the object's worth.

An auction is offering for sale an article to several concurrent bidders so that a greater price is gained by the seller. Prospective buyers bid on the object or even on a job. Sometimes private auction houses run the auction; at other times the state. Morally a seller has a moral obligation to sell the object to the highest bidder, even if the price is below the lowest just price, unless there was prior agreement to withdraw the object if a certain price was not met. The practice of sending bidders into an auction who have no desire to buy the object merely to drive up the price is unjust to a buyer. It is immoral for a seller to give a buyer an object of less worth. A buyer may not impede others by force or fraud from bidding so that the price becomes higher. However, the prospective buyers are allowed to ask or advise others not to bid so that the price remains lower.

MONOPOLY

Monopoly is exclusive control over a market. Monopoly is public when it is practiced by or controlled by a state. It is private when done by private corporations or even an individual. Monopoly is just when it is in the public welfare. In the United States, government monopolies have existed in energy ownership and distribution. At the present time, the situation is changing. In various countries or states, telephone, television, tobacco, and alcohol, to mention but a few, have often been under monopolistic control of a state. A monopoly is unjust when it is not in the common interest. What promotes the common welfare can differ according to time and place. Private monopolies are not of themselves immoral. However, they can sometimes establish an untenably low price to drive out competition, and then, after driving out all competition, demand an untenably high price for the same goods. Such practices are obviously immoral. In the United States, a judicial bias against monopolies unquestionably exists. Monopolies are not in themselves unjust, but must be judged in light of the public according to their results.

GAMBLING

Gambling or betting concerns some future event whose outcome is objectively uncertain and whose result comes from luck or skill or a combination of both. Betting is often referred to as a contract of chance. In general, gambling is not immoral since a person may dispose of his property as he wills. As a contract, betting must conform to certain standards. (1) One may bet only his own money. This may be obvious, but the father of a family, for example, may not bet the family's means of supporting itself for the necessities of life. Creditors must be paid before money is bet. (2) The matter of the bet must be understood in the same way by all and must be something morally allowable. (3) The outcome of the future event must be objectively uncertain. Subjectively, both parties may be certain. (4) Objective uncertainty must not be contravened. Cheating voids a contract of chance. Such things as point-shaving and doping of animals render gambling immoral. (5) The loser must pay. Where gambling is outlawed, it is probably a penal law and therefore does not bind in conscience. One may bet, but must put up with the legal consequences. Ordinarily such laws are framed so that it is illegal to take a bet, but not to place one. Examination of the wisdom of outlawing gambling is best left to social sciences. A person may also bet on a past event with a third party as the adjudicator, for example an encyclopedia. One who is certain must say so, but thereafter one may accept the money of another on the grounds that there is nothing wrong with receiving a gift.

LOTTERY

A lottery is a game of chance in which for a certain price one buys the right of winning a certain prize if the lot falls on him. Lotteries may be public or private. Today, the practice of government lottery occurs not infrequently. A lottery is per se moral. To be moral, the price of the chances must be proportional to the prizes offered and the chance of winning. The greater the prize, the greater the price for the chance may be. The greater the number of people participating, the price should be lessened. The money given out must not be equal to the money taken in. Often some object to lotteries on the grounds that money is taken from those who can least afford it. However, the money is often very little and the chance to win gives great enjoyment to those who participate.

PARTNERSHIPS

A partnership is a contract between two or more people who oblige themselves to work together and share any money received. Ordinarily partnerships must be affirmed by positive law to be valid. For a partnership to be moral, the purpose of the partnership must be moral. A contract over an immoral matter is always invalid. Even if a contract is signed, the persons are not held to perform an immoral matter of a contract, though they must pay those who have been legally and morally employed. Ordinarily, equality among members concerning money gained and damages is to be observed unless some peculiar circumstances dictate otherwise.

EXCHANGE

Exchange is the practice of changing money for money. The money exchanged must be of the same value. The money demanded for the service must be equal to the service provided. To ask an enormous price for the change of money is immoral.

STOCK MARKET SPECULATION

The stock market is a place, constituted by public authority, where certain business is transacted and certain contracts agreed upon. Besides stocks, stock options or options on commodities, such as farm products, are also traded. An option is an agreement to buy or sell a product at an agreed upon price at an agreed upon future time. Speculation in the stock market is itself a valid contract and a moral practice, Of its nature, speculation in the stock market is a contract of chance. As such, it is subject to the moral principles concerning contracts of chance. Speculation in the stock market is open to fraud and abuse. For example, the outcome of one's investment should be objectively uncertain. Investing from "inside information," that is from knowledge not available to the general public, is unjust. Spreading false rumors concerning a state, government, or private company in order to affect the stock is immoral. Manipulating stock prices even by just means is immoral if it affects the poor. It is against charity to seek to become rich over the demise of another. The common welfare demands that civil positive law protect a stock market and the individual investor against such immoral practices. The stock market can only work when the public at large has confidence in the project. Special insight into the worth of a stock from one's own intuitions is of course in order and speculating in the stock market on such insight is not immoral. Finally, on a personal level it is immoral for the head of a household to speculate the family treasure in the stock market.

INSURANCE

Insurance is a contract by which one party for a certain price obliges himself to compensate another for damages agreed upon, which the other party suffers by chance. Thus, insurance is in a certain sense a contract of chance. It differs from other contracts of chance in that the future event is some danger. Insurance has something in common with buying and selling In order to be moral, the price of insurance must be proportional to the danger against which one is insured. One might question the morality of certain automobile insurance policies on these ground. The danger against which one is insured must be clearly known. If one withholds certain significant information prior to the contract, the contract is invalid, since the matter of the contract is not substantially agreed. If the danger changes significantly during the course of the contract, the contract may be voidable. Often codicils of insurance policies are so esoteric that ordinary persons do not understand them. Automotive and property insurance of various kinds can be good examples of policies where, at least at times, the codicils are not well known or are not interpreted in the same sense by both buyer and seller. Since both parties must understand the matter of a contract, such policies are morally questionable. The one who insures must possess money enough to insure potential damages. The insurer is not bound to pay for damages arising from grave culpability on the part of the insured. The insurer is bound to pay for damages incurred by the insured according to the value of the thing at the time it perishes, unless other provisions have been made. For example, an insured person may demand more than the actual price at the time of the thing perishing if that agreement was part of the original contract. Insurance at its worst plays on the insecurities of human beings and, while stock brokers often sell greed, insurance companies many times sell fear. Therefore, selling unnecessary insurance is an immoral practice.

Life insurance presents special ethical problems. Several types of life insurance exist. One is simple life insurance in which upon the person's death money is paid to heirs or certain designated third parties. Term life insurance offers this service only over a certain period of time. Other life insurance becomes due at a certain age, for example sixty-five or upon retirement. Since life insurance is a contract, buyer and seller must agree on the matter of the contract. To be moral, the money to be paid by the insuree or the price for the policy must be equal to the danger undertaken by the insurer. Life insurance is immoral and the contract invalid when the insuree withholds certain necessary and serious information which he possesses from the insurer, for example the existence of cancer. But if this information is not available at the time of the contract, there is no moral fault. Withholding slight information does not affect validity of the contract, but payment may be reduced at the time due.

Automobile insurance is the subject of great controversy. Automobile insurance is a contract whereby the insurer agrees to pay, sometimes less a certain amount of money, for damages to a car or persons in an automobile accident or when the automobile is stolen. The insurer may also agree to pay damages arising from injury to persons in an accident for which the insuree is responsible. Since automobile insurance is a contract, both buyer and seller must agree on the substantial matter of the contract for the contract to be valid. The amount that a person pays for automobile insurance must be equal to the danger that an insurer assumes. Today, this principle is in some places honored more in the breach than in the observance. Also collusion between the auto repair shop and the insurer to the detriment of the owner is immoral. The practice of not offering automobile insurance necessary by law to some people for reasons having nothing to do with their ability to pay is immoral. Automobile insurance is subject to civil positive law.

CHAPTER 4

Work

The usual means of supporting oneself and one's family is work. Work is a contract by which one offers his labor to provide certain services to another for compensation and the other obliges himself to pay a wage for the agreed upon service. Work is based upon a contract between an employer and an employee. The object of the contract is the person's labor, that is human actions which produce a product. The object of the contract is neither the product produced nor the price of the object produced. Though socialists and communists deny the validity of such a contract, a contract to work is moral and necessary. Such a contract is moral since man has full ownership of his own acts and can dispose of them as he will. Work is necessary since it is ordinarily the sole means by which someone can sustain himself and his family. The natural end of work is the conservation of one's own life and the fulfilling of one's obligation to sustain one's family. Thus work is moral and necessary for human life.

Both employer and employee have obligations toward each other in commutative justice. The employee owes the employer a reasonable day's work as defined by what the job is. The employee does not owe the best possible job. Such would be impossible on a continuing basis.

The employer owes the employee wage. Wages are of various types. An individual wage is that which is sufficient to provide food, clothes, and sustenance for an individual for one day. A family wage is that which is sufficient to provide the same for a family in a given region. The family wage is absolute when it is sufficient to sustain a family of ordinary size in ordinary circumstances. A family wage is relative when one considers the number of persons in a particular family, and the various circumstances within any given family. When moralists discuss a just family wage, an absolute wage is what they have in mind.

In commutative justice, an employer owes an employee at the very least a just individual wage. Usually, a person supports himself by means of a job. He trades his work for money. The money earned from work is a wage (salary). This money is an extension of himself, since it represents his work. A just wage can not be elastic. If such were the case, a just wage would be almost impossible to determine in individual cases and would in any event produce almost an impossible task of bookkeeping for an employer. A just individual wage is one that allows a person to support himself in a given society. The human being has certain basic needs for clothing, shelter, and food. Above that, a certain number of luxuries, those things which are not absolutely necessary, should be part of human life. Thus a just wage is that amount of money which is necessary in a given society to perform these functions. This money is due both to those who have a family and those who, for whatever reason, do not. Otherwise hiring practices would be heavily weighted in favor of those with no children.

In commutative justice, an employer must pay an adult of sound mind and body a family wage for his work. Every man has a natural right to marry and rear a family. Without a family wage, he could not do so. If a man had no other means to support a family other than his work, he would have to remain celibate if he did not receive a family wage. By its very nature, work has a social value. Therefore he has a natural right to a family wage. This obligation of paying a family wage falls primarily on the major employer or the head of the firm. In commutative justice, the owner of the business is not obliged to share his profits with the workers. Though communists and some socialists deny it, a contract for work is a valid contract in commutative justice on the part of both the employer and the employee. The relationship of employer to employee is not a partnership. Nor is the relationship of a tenant farmer who has rented the property so that he might farm it and have its use and fruits to the owner a partnership. An employer has borne the risk of the endeavor. However, the employer and the employee can enter into a partnership if they so wish. Such a partnership is of greater danger to the employee since he can ill afford losses to his income. Equity, or at least charity, apparently demands that an employer share a part of his profits with an employee in the form of rewards or bonuses, especially if profits received from a business at a given time are quite high.

Ethical problems have arisen during the last century with the rise of women in the workplace. Among these problems is the question of wages. Should men and women be paid equal wages for equal work? On the supposition that the work is the same and the laboring conditions like, an employer is morally obliged to pay men and women the same wages for equal work. A lower wage may not be paid a woman on the grounds that she is a woman. If such were the case, grave evils would arise in the workplace and society; men and women would not be on equal footing in obtaining work. A man might have to accept a lesser salary or might not even be able to obtain work at all to support a family. Women are more suited to some jobs and men to others. A wage may be adjusted and agreed upon which takes these factors into consideration. A serious mistake is made in assuming that equality necessarily means uniformity.

A word should be said about contractors. A work is whatever has been taken up to be completed, such as a house or clothing. A contractor is the one who takes up the work. A contractor violates commutative justice if he does not pay a just wage. He is also obliged in commutative justice to honor terms of a contract, especially with regard to materials used. He must pay restitution if he does not do so. A contractor is obliged to finish work during the prescribed time at the prescribed price. He is not allowed to increase the price. He however can buy materials at the best possible price, even if he had not originally foreseen such a price. A person for whom work is done is not morally allowed to lower the price. The contractor can morally raise the price if he has suffered grave unforeseen and unforeseeable damage. He is responsible for ordinary, but not extraordinary danger. He may also raise the price if he has computed the price erroneously.

The contemporary world of corporations and labor unions has brought about several problems of ethical importance. Discriminatory practices in hiring are part of contemporary ethical discussion. To refuse to hire because of color, race, religion, or sexual practices is illegal in the United States. Affirmative action has become a favored practice in some areas. When affirmative action means equality of opportunity for education and employment, the practice is ethical and to be encouraged. When affirmative action means equality in outcome, the practice can lead to offenses against justice. In theory, offenses against distributive justice do not bind to restitution. The reason is that it is too difficult to determine who is responsible and who has been injured. When both are known, then restitution is in order. A judge who has erred in his judgement is duty bound to correct it and restore the moral order by some kind of restitution. But a son is not responsible for restitution for discriminatory practices which may have existed in his father's law practice. A government holds itself responsible to eliminate discriminatory tax practices; for example, a government does not pay restitution to those who have lost money. Rather, the government rectifies the practice at present. As a society, men are duty-bound to treat people with justice at the present time. However, men are not in general duty bound to restitution for offenses against distributive justice because it is too difficult to determine who has practiced discrimination and precisely who has been hurt. This principle applies to affirmative action.

Labor unions have become commonplace in the western world. We await their coming in the developing world. Labor unions have been effective in correcting abuses in work practices, working conditions, and wage inequities among other things. That workers have a right to unionize is today taken as easily proved. The gathering of workers into groups is the primary means that workers have to better their conditions. Such a practice helps to even the playing field against corporate powers. Questions arise concerning the means that labor unions may ethically use. In general, when greed operates on the part of either management or labor, the negotiating process becomes difficult and can easily break down. A closed or union shop whereby a worker must be a member of the union to work can be morally justified, but is open to grave abuse. Workers should not be forced to join a union. Sometimes local conditions dictate that as the only means to curb abuses. The human being has a right to work, but no one has a right to this particular job. Likewise right to work laws can be justified, but are open to abuse as a means of "union breaking."

Strikes can be justified according to the principles of the double effect. The direct strike is cessation of work in order to facilitate correction of abuses. Grave evils can be foreseen from a strike: loss of profits, loss of wages, lack of goods and services, and public economic discontent. A cessation of work is not in itself immoral. For a concerted cessation of work, there must a justifying cause. A strike must be properly authorized and must be a last resort. Only justifiable means may be used. However, if these conditions are met, there is nothing wrong with a cessation of work. The good effect of solving abuses does not come directly from the bad effects of loss of profits, lack of goods and services, and public discontent. The bad effects should not be intended. Problems can arise with the fourth principle of the double effect. There must be a proportion between the evils that are sure to arise and the good that will come about. A sympathy strike, wherein other unions join in a strike against the same employer, is legitimized according to the principles of the double effect. A sympathy strike against other innocent employers can not be so justified since the first principle of the double effect is not verified.

On the part of employers, a lockout, whereby an employer shuts down his plant rather than suffer injustice, can also be justified according to the principles of the double effect. According to the fourth principle, there must be a proportionate reason for a lockout. A sympathetic lockout is probably not so justified because of the disproportionate evil visited upon innocent people.

A boycott is a concerted effort not to patronize certain employers. A boycott can be justified on the principles of the double effect. A secondary boycott against those employers who do business with the intended employer can also be justified under the double effect. However, a sufficiently graver reason is necessary. When a boycott is perpetrated against a nation, it is called an embargo. An embargo against military weapons can be justified by the principles of the double effect. However, an absolute embargo, whereby no trade of any sort is allowed, is unjustified when the population, and not only the government, is injured. Such an embargo violates the first principle of the double effect. Innocent people are directly affected. Whether invasion or encouragement of revolution in such cases can be justified would be decided on the fourth principle of the double effect and especially on the likelihood of success.

CHAPTER 5

War

War is defined as open hostility with weapons of one nation to force its will upon another nation. Peace is the desired condition for individual persons and nations. Peace is the tranquility of order brought about by a right ordering of parts. In the individual, the body should be subject to reason and reason to truth (God). International peace should be a goal of world order. Nevertheless, mankind's history is a story of war. Three positions on the morality of war can be readily identified. On the one hand is militarism. This theory maintains that man is fundamentally war-like and anti-social. The English philosopher Thomas Hobbes (1588–1679) held this position. Only creation of a state by mankind keeps man from warring one against another. Nineteenth-century German philosophy in a certain sense idealized war. Like he did with all other matters, Hegel subsumed war into his dialectic. War was neither moral nor immoral, but a stage in the advancement of the Spirit. Karl Marx, or at least some of his followers, followed this notion, but placed the dialectic in the material world. Fichte, Hegel's contemporary, identified morality with struggle. Friedrich Nietzsche's *Übermensch* exemplified the will to power (*Wille zur Macht*) which often included war-like characteristics. Undoubtedly these German philosophies led directly or indirectly to Hitler's Germany. For militarists, war is neither moral nor immoral, but mankind's natural state.

Absolute pacifism is the direct opposite of militarism. Pacificism maintains that all war for whatever purpose, defensive or offensive, is immoral. Ordinarily such pacifism is based on religious grounds. The early church contained several pacifist groups. In our own century, Mohandis Ghandi in India was the great representative of pacifism. He maintained that through passivity against violent aggression the non-violent will ultimately achieve victory. His theory led to Indian national independence. His theory of non-violent resistance influenced several movements in the western world including the civil rights movement in the United States and the anti-war movements in the western world. Among religious groups Quakers are perhaps the leading pacifists. Obviously, a person may refuse to defend himself. A nation may also so refuse. But is it a moral imperative to do so?

A third group, standing in the middle between militarism and pacifism, maintains that war is undesirable, but some times unavoidable and in these cases moral if carried out in a correct manner. This position has been the mainstream position in western philosophy. In his ideal republic, Plato had a soldier class. Plato thought that even offensive wars were justified on the grounds that a state needed luxuries as well as necessities. Nevertheless, such was not the ideal. Plato did not want "a feverish state." Cicero maintained the justice of some Roman wars. In the Christian dispensation, Augustine of Hippo maintained that both offensive and defensive wars could be justified. Indeed, all traditional authors have thought that defensive wars against aggression were obviously moral. According to Augustine, the ideal state for man is peace. Man strives after peace. Peace is the ultimate goal of war. The definition of peace as the tranquility of order, mentioned above, is an Augustinian expansion of a Ciceronian idea. Often Augustine is thought to be the originator of the just war theory. In fact, several principles of what would later be developed into a just war theory are found scattered throughout Augustine's writings, especially *Contra Faustum* and *De ciuitate dei*. Augustine thought that some wars were just and consistent with the gospel of Christ. But he did not formalize the theory. Thomas Aquinas continued this tradition and based himself firmly on the authority of Augustine. Later thinkers such as Vittorio, Suarez, and Robert Bellarmine refined the just war theory into what we have today. The just war theory has many contemporary defenders and is generally thought to be the only means of intellectually grappling with the complexities of war.

JUST WAR

Wars are of two kinds. An offensive war is one taken up to punish injury or to recover a nation's possessions or territory. A defensive war is one taken up to repel an unjust attack against the state. Almost all moralists have agreed that a defensive war is moral. The philosophical basis is war's analogy to unjust aggression. Just as a man is morally allowed to defend himself, so is a nation morally allowed to defend itself against unjust attack. The question arises concerning an offensive war. Among nations, there is no higher power except God. Therefore, a nation through its leaders has the right to recover property and punish offenders. A nation is morally allowed all means necessary or useful which are not excluded either by natural law or *ius gentium.* Therefore, a nation is justified in using stratagems, tactics, and deceptions in prosecution of war. It is further moral to deprive cities of water, to explode bombs, and even to destroy monasteries if enemies are using any of these to defend themselves. Such matters are covered by the *ius gentium* and international law. It is not licit to poison a water supply directly. It is moral to kill soldiers, but it is not moral to kill innocent civilians. After recovery of territory and just punishment, a victor is held to make a just peace and the vanquished are held to accept a peace lest a nation be exposed to more harm.

The just war theory maintains that, for a war to be justified, several conditions must be fulfilled. First, there must be *ius ad bellum,* that is a *casus belli.* The offending against the rights of a nation constitutes such a cause. In a recent document from the John Paul II, genocide within a country constitutes such an occasion. Defense of the human right to life takes precedence over sovereignty of a nation. The statement was the first such statement by a moral authority in the history of mankind. Retribution against a nation has also been viewed as a justification for war, on the grounds that there must be some restoration of the moral order when one nation transgresses the rights of others. Only a nation or group of nations could obtain such a restoration. Personal glory or national aggrandizement do not constitute a *casus belli.* In an offensive war, the cause must be morally certain, in a defensive war at least probable.

According to the fourth principle of the double effect, there must be a sufficient proportion between the evil done and the good to be gained. Small evils are not grounds for war. However, a group of small infractions can coalesce into a major infraction of a nation's rights. A nation need not wait until aggression is actual. But a nation can act when it is morally certain concerning the intent of the other nation.

War must be a last resort. All other measures must be tried before a nation resorts to war. This principle is also an application of the fourth principle of the double effect. Besides negotiation and diplomatic measures, economic sanctions have become a common means to bring unjust attacks to an end. Though economic sanctions are an approved method, a nation must be careful lest the citizens of the offending country who are many times innocent bystanders be the prime victims of the economic sanctions.

For a war to be moral, there must also be hope of success. Moral certainty is not needed. But a ruler can not morally lead his people and armies into almost sure defeat. Small nations may resist larger ones, but leading soldiers to the slaughter is certainly immoral.

A war can only be morally prosecuted by a proper authority. Who the lawful authority is represents a legitimate question today. A legitimate authority is one who *de iure* has care of the community and *de facto* power to use it. In former times, the principle of legitimate authority constrained feudal lords from illegitimate wars. Some contemporary commentators hold that the United Nations is the only legitimate authority to authorize war today. This opinion is subject to question. It preempts the sovereignty of individual nations. Some modern military actions seem morally justifiable although the United Nations has not officially approved. Likewise, there is a role for international courts. But moral authorization and legal authorization are different matters. Guerilla actions should be able to be stopped within an individual country even if some international authority does not yet approve.

Those who prosecute wars must have a right intention. The right intention must be to repel or punish an unjust attack. By its very nature, right intention is subjective. A wrong intention can make an otherwise moral war unjust for a particular person or groups of persons. Ordinarily, citizens of a country and its soldiers can presume a right intention of their rulers until proved otherwise by facts. But a citizen is bound in conscience not to participate in a certainly unjust war.

Conscientious objection presents a problem in this area. One has an obligation to inform one's conscience. Once so informed, a person is morally bound to follow a certain conscience and suffer the consequences for it. Certainly a citizen or soldier can have objections to a particular war. But some wars can be just. It is difficult for a government to countenance objections to particular wars, but provision should be made for them, if possible. In a war of doubtful justice, soldiers subject to authority are bound to serve, but not those which are not so subject.

So much for *ius ad bellum. Ius in bellum* must also be investigated. Not only must there be a just cause for war, a war must also be prosecuted by moral means. In general, a nation is allowed to prosecute a war against the military machine of other nations, but not against the population. Combatants are those who are actively engaged in the prosecution of war, such as soldiers. Non-combatants are those not actively engaged in the war effort, such as the ordinary citizens of a country. In former times, this distinction was much easier to apply than now. A soldier was a combatant; but women, children, farmers, senior citizens, and merchants were not. Introduction of sophisticated weaponery has complicated the matter. Workers in a munitions plant should be considered combatants. Is a nation justified in attacking a transportation and communication network of an enemy? Its energy and power stations? These matters are certainly questionable. In judging morality of a military action, connection of installations to the war effort must be considered before they are destroyed. The amount of collateral damage must be weighed against necessity of bombing these areas. Such places as military airfields and naval shipyards are legitimate targets. If a ruler places civilians purposely in the way of military operations, he is morally at fault. Guerilla warfare becomes suspect on the same principle. Further, carpet bombing of a city is immoral since the direct killing of civilians is immoral. Direct bombing of a city is also immoral on the first principle of the double effect. Likewise, direct terrorist attacks on civilian populations are immoral. Soldiers are not morally allowed to plunder an enemy on their own authority. Prisoners of war may not be killed. The exact conventions of war at any given time are a matter for positive law, the *ius gentium,* or positive law such as the Geneva conventions.

The invention of nuclear weapons has brought an added dimension to war. Some weapons of mass destruction are largely indiscriminate in those whom they kill. Indirect long term effects of nuclear bombs, such as radiation, are not completely studied. However, devastating long term effects are becoming increasingly evident. Complete destruction of cities or parts of cities is certainly immoral. Is the notion of a winner and loser in a war outmoded since mutually assured destruction only produces losers? What possible cause could there be for such destruction? The fourth principle of the double effect could never be verified. Recent diplomatic efforts to base an international peace on some other foundation than mutually assured destruction are laudable. In the twenty-first century, local wars are more likely. Small nations may well have nuclear weapons. Nuclear bombs are actually merely larger guns and their use is guided by the principles of the double effect. Nuclear weapons have called offensive punitive wars into question. How can such destruction be justified by reference to restoring the moral order? In a defensive war, the use of nuclear weapons is justified if the principles of the just war and the double effect are verified. Total nuclear war whereby either the entire world or the greater part of it would be completely destroyed could never be justified because of the fourth, and perhaps the first, principles of the double effect.

In the present atmosphere of weapons development, great destruction, perhaps even destruction of the entire world, could arise. The moral imperative of reaching a world where such weapons will not be used is evident. Whether this effort would include mutual disarmament or some other means is a matter for diplomats and politicians. Systems of protection against nuclear weapons for nations and perhaps the entire world should not be ruled out of the question. The scientific and technical possibility of such systems is not a moral question.

REBELLION AND REVOLUTION

Revolution is open, organized, and armed resistance against a duly constituted authority. A civil authority has the right to put down revolutions. But revolutions against tyrannical powers can be justified. *Occide tyranum* writes St. Thomas. According to Augustine, followed by Thomas Aquinas, unjust laws are no laws at all. Both passive and active resistance to immoral authority are morally allowable. Passive resistance is required when citizens are ordered to commit immoral acts. One may suffer immoral laws, but may also passively resist them. Active resistance to unjust laws is morally allowable. According to the principles on self-defense, active resistance to personal injury from a tyrant is morally allowable. True revolution is allowable under the following conditions. The government has become habitually tyrannical. All other means have been exhausted. There is reasonable hope for success. The judgement concerning tyranny is objectively judged correctly. The harm to the public good must not be greater than the injustice which causes the rebellion. Civil protest is a minor form of rebellion. In general, the principles on protest should follow the principles of the double effect. Proportionally graver reasons must exist to disrupt the peace and harmony of society.

CHAPTER

6

Crime and Punishment

Sanctions are attached to laws to enforce them. Therefore, a state has a right to punish. Punishment is that harm inflicted upon one who has violated the law. There are three powers within the state: executive, legislative, and judiciary. Whether these three distinct roles should be represented by three separate branches of government is a problem which modern democratic theorists still discuss. The legislative enacts laws, the executive carries them out, and the judiciary decides whether the laws are justified or have been violated.

Traditionally, three purposes for punishment have been envisioned: correction, deterrence, and retribution. Correction strives to educate and rehabilitate an offender. Deterrence strive to prevent the same types of act from being performed by others. Retribution restores the moral order and envisions some proportion between offense and punishment. Without retribution, small offenses could be punished by great penalties since both correction and deterrence would be present when harsh punishments are meted out for small crimes. Punishment may not be inflicted unless an offense has been committed and may be mitigated for sufficient reason. Only one of the purposes need be present in order to punish. These three purposes are also involved in parental punishment of children although such punishment is only analogous to that of the state.

Much contemporary discussion has focused on the use of capital punishment for grave crimes. The state certainly has the right to punish. The state exists to maintain justice and it does this by punishing crime. The natural law allows retribution for serious offenses against individuals. Some crimes are so heinous that only death would be the proper retribution. One might think of the crimes of Mao, Stalin, and Hitler in this regard. The state must justify its use of capital punishment in particular circumstances. For capital punishment to be moral, a grave crime must have been committed, the commission of the crime must be certain, and the punishment must take place under juridical order.

Earlier attempts to argue against the use of capital punishment focused on a lack of deterrence of crime. Some sociological studies alleged no evidence to support the thesis that capital punishment deterred crime. That capital punishment deterred crime, they said, was a largely intuitive and anecdotal argument. More recently, these studies have been judged to be flawed scientifically. Specifically, it is impossible to control all the variables in such studies.

However, more current argument has dealt with the difficulty of applying capital punishment in an even handed manner. During the past decades in the United States, minorities have been put to death for crimes out of proportion to their numbers in the population. Such figures do not of themselves prove discrimination since there are many possible causes. However all should agree that such findings should give cause to reflect. Further, the application of justice in the western world finds it better that a guilty man go free than that an innocent man be put to death. It is undeniable that some possibility exists that innocent people have been put to death. Some would argue that the difficulty in proving some guilty should preclude use of the death penalty. Such an argument however arises partially from a skepticism toward any possibility of certain human knowledge whatever in contemporary society. Certainly a state has an obligation in distributive justice to ascertain with moral certainty guilt of a party before punishing with death. That such moral certitude can be reached is a clear epistemological possibility. Philosophically, we may conclude that capital punishment is theoretically justifiable, but should be used with extreme caution because of difficulty in applying it with justice.

Recently, in theological circles a "seamless garment" argument has arisen. Mankind should be pro-life in all regards. Thus to be anti-abortion, but to be pro-capital punishment would be a contradiction. The analogy between these two actions limps somewhat. In the first, we are dealing with an innocent life. In the second, with criminal activity. Nevertheless attention should be given to the argument, especially in view of the people who hold it. The "seamless garment" argument has had recent papal approval. Indeed, the pope himself has used it with regard to the assassination attempt on his own life.

CHAPTER 7

Professional Ethics

Growth in specialization during the past century has given rise to a need for application of ethics to various fields. Out of this situation have come medical and business ethics. To a professional, ethics can designate an ethos, the way things are done in a particular profession, the ambience or situation in such a profession. In this context, morality refers to moral principle and its application. Evidently this contemporary distinction reaches back to Hegel. To those who hold such a distinction, ethics understood in this sense would have nothing to do with philosophy. As used in this work, the science of ethics deals with moral principle. Ethics for various professions is an application of principles drawn from general and special ethics to particular circumstances. As Aristotle noted, the most difficult part of ethics is to apply general principles to particular situations. In contemporary professions, this dilemma has become unparalleled. The difficulty arises principally from the unchangeable nature of ethical principles and the constant change in the practice of the professions. Ethics deals with being and professions deal with becoming. Justice for example deals with giving others their due. What that obligation entails in particular professions can be difficult to determine and changes from age to age. In professions and business, advances in knowledge, changes in practice, and fluctuations in human affairs continue apace. The nature of ethical problems in professions demands knowledge in particular professions and businesses, on the one hand, and moral philosophy on the other. Hence, specialized ethics must arise from practitioners of the professions themselves, in consultation with moral philosophers. A pertinent example for contemporary society is the advance in computers. Nevertheless, ethicists should lay down general principles which find application in specialized fields and can *mutatis mutandis* be applied to others.

JUDGES

A judge is an official legitimated by public authority to speak about the law and render decisions or opinions, either in civil or criminal processes. He is sometimes called an arbiter. There are judges of fact and judges of law.

A judge must possess knowledge, jurisdiction, and integrity. A judge must have the requisite knowledge concerning the laws which pertain to cases which belong in his court. If he does not have such knowledge, he is morally bound to obtain it. A judge who knowing his own ignorance causes harm to others because of his lack of knowledge is bound to reparation. When he commits an error, he is bound to advise those whose interests are involved.

A judge must have jurisdiction over the cases which he hears. If he does not have the requisite jurisdiction, his decision or opinion is invalid. He does damage to the judge whose power he has usurped and to the matter itself over which he has falsely claimed jurisdiction. In recent times, jurisdiction of American courts has been discussed. Many experts claim courts to have overstepped their jurisdictions.

A judge must possess integrity. He should serve all under his jurisdiction with justice without regard to persons, without hate or love, and without accepting special pleas or gifts. He may not demand payment from litigants as a stipend for his judicial role or for rendering an opinion. To receive such gifts violates both legal and commutative justice. In the latter case, he demands payment for something which he owes to the litigants on other grounds. If he receives such gifts, he is morally bound to return them. A judge may also not accept gifts offered by kindness unless they are of little worth. Such a practice is prohibited by natural law. The acceptance of such gifts exposes the judge to danger of rendering an unjust opinion. But if he receives such gifts, he is not morally bound to return them. Small gifts are not thought to affect a judge's judgement.

A judge is morally bound to render a just decision in an expeditious manner. By his office a judge is obliged to take due diligence in rendering a prudent judgement. He should not protract a case so that damage arises to either party. If damage arises due to his fault, the judge is morally bound to restitution to the damaged party. Legal justice demands that a judge follow due process. A judge is bound to the laws in place, as long as and isofar as they are just. A judge offends against commutative justice when he does not render justice in civil matters. In such cases he is bound to restitution. But he is not bound to restitution if he frees someone from a pecuniary obligation unjustly since he offends only against legal justice. A judge may not offer favorable advice to one of the parties. Such advice is the role of the lawyer. The judge is bound to render judgement only according to what has been alleged and proved.

A judge must render a judicial opinion according to both his knowledge of the law and what has been alleged and proved. The judge is a public person and must act according to public knowledge. For a judge to let a man free who has been juridically acquitted, but whom from private knowledge he knows to be guilty, is not an offense against justice. In fact he would offend against justice were he to act otherwise. In case of an innocent man who has been found guilty, the situation changes. In the first place, the judge is obliged by charity to use all means at his disposal to free an innocent man from undergoing punishment. By charity human beings are bound to avert grave injustice to their neighbors. In rare cases, the judge can not save the innocent man in this manner. Here there is a conflict between individual rights. In matters of property, rights of society to right order may override an individual's right to property. In cases of imprisonment or capital punishment, opinions differ. But it ought to be proved that it is not intrinsically evil to condemn an innocent man even if he is legitimately proved guilty.

A certainly just sentence of a judge obliges in conscience. This is true even for a punishment of a penal law, since a penal law by definition obliges to the sanction. A sentence of a judge which defines a strict right imposes a duty to restitution, for example a judgement over a will. A certainly unjust decision produces no obligation in conscience. This is true in every case, whether the judge is in good faith or bad, whether the injustice arises over the matter itself or in the judicial process. If one is deprived of goods and no other remedy is in sight, occult compensation is justified. One who in good faith finds himself in possession of goods not his own because of an unjust judicial decision is bound to restitution, but is not bound to pay expenses since he is in good faith.

In cases of doubt, a decision of a judge is presumed to be just and obliges in the external and internal fora. However, in criminal cases, the position of the accused is to be preferred, that is in cases of doubt he should be set free since punishment must arise from a crime certainly committed. In civil cases, the possessor in good faith may keep the object until the right of the other is proved. When no one possesses the object, the case should be decided in favor of the more probable owner. If the probability is equal, the judge ought to pursue an amicable settlement; lacking that, the judge has the right to decide for whom he pleases. Nothing prohibits a judge from dividing a divisible thing between litigants, whether there is equal or unequal probability. The judge may not accept money or gifts to make a judgement in favor of one of the litigants,

A civil law that contravenes natural law does not bind. It is immoral to render a decision from such a law. A judge is bound to give up his office rather than render a decision according to such a civil law. Further, a judge may not punish an innocent person to avoid grave personal damage to himself. A judge can not impose even a light punishment on an innocent person from a certainly unjust law, unless the permission of the innocent party is given or may be presumed.

A judge who renders an unjust decision from grave fault on his part, either from malice or from ignorance, must revoke his decision, even with grave inconvenience to himself. If he can not, he must repair damage done. If he has rendered a bad decision because of error or forgetfulness, the judge is bound to revoke his decision without grave inconvenience to himself. If he is unable to do so, he is bound to nothing. A judge who does not revoke an unjust decision when he is able to do so is bound to restitution. If a judge imposes a punishment greater than is just, he offends against commutative justice and is bound to restitution. A punishment is unjust when it goes beyond the limits of the law. But it is also thought to be unjust if the punishment is within the limits of the law, but, when circumstances are considered, exceeds the custom of the court. If a judge frees a person unjustly from paying a debt, the judge is not bound to restitution, since the obligation does not arise until the decision of the judge has been rendered.

PLAINTIFFS AND GOVERNMENT ATTORNEYS

A plaintiff is one who calls another into judicial process in a civil matter. An accuser is one who brings a case in a criminal matter. Each has an obligation to prove his case. The manner in which these processes are brought about differs according to time and place. Today, criminal processes are ordinarily brought about by the prosecutor, district attorney, or government attorney. Public authority has given them the office of accusation of crimes. From commutative justice, these public officials are bound to bring accusations for which their offices have been created, even with grave inconvenience to themselves. They should use prudent judgement in prosecuting these cases. If they do not do so, they are bound to restitution to the community or property owners for damages and in certain cases should return their salary. A private person is bound even with grave inconvenience to himself to report cases to the proper authorities when grave damage to the common good has or will come about. He has an obligation from charity to report cases to avert or repair damage done to an innocent third party. Obligations from charity do not oblige with grave inconvenience to oneself. At times civil law prescribes such accusations. To report such crimes, it must have been certainly committed. If the crime is only highly likely, it must be reported in those terms. It is morally permissible to report hidden crimes which bring about damage to the common good or innocent third parties.

THE ACCUSED

An accused is the one against whom a case is brought. In civil cases, he is the one from whom a debt is demanded. In criminal cases, he is the one accused of a crime. In criminal cases, the right of society to punish crimes collides with the accused's right to a good reputation. In meting out punishment, the common good collides with the individual's right to life and freedom.

In criminal cases, an accused is under no obligation to admit a crime committed. But he must not lie in responding to judicial questions. Nevertheless, denying a crime which has been committed is a broad mental reservation. Roman law demanded admission of crime except in cases of capital punishment, life imprisonment, or confiscation of goods. One is obliged to a superior commanding unless he commands something impossible. But modern civil law has tended in the opposite direction. A judge may only ask the accused if he wishes to respond to the charges. The accused is morally allowed to manifest hidden crimes of his accusers or witnesses to bring their testimony into question if and only if it is necessary to his purpose. One is not bound to preserve another's reputation with grave inconvenience to himself. But if it is not necessary or useless to his defense, he may not do so. This restriction binds under justice and charity. From charity he is held not to manifest hidden crimes of others if greater damage to them would come about than to him. It is never licit for the accused, not even if he is innocent, to calumniate his accusers. This is true even if he might undergo capital punishment or there is no other way to avoid a guilty verdict.

An innocent person or he who has received an unjust sentence may be compared to the one who suffers unjust aggression and may defend himself as such. He is obliged to avoid scandal. He can flee, resist, and threaten or use weapons to do so. He should not injure those who are carrying out the law.

A guilty person should obey the ministers of justice, may not positively resist, and must undergo the punishment. He may attempt to flee the punishment but may not resist. Before the sentence, a guilty accused person may attempt to flee. After the sentence, but while still detained, he may attempt to flee. After the judicial sentence, the guilty person is bound in conscience to undergo the punishment. He may not flee prison. If the punishment is excessive, he is morally allowed to flee. One who is morally allowed to flee may deceive his detainers, but must not use force or injure them. He may not bribe those detaining him. An innocent person may bribe those who detain him if he forewarns them that he is innocent. One who justly flees is not bound to reparation to the damages which the guards suffer, especially if others are also fleeing. He is using his right and only permits the damage.

In civil cases, the accused is not bound to begin a legal process. But if his debt is certain, he is morally bound in conscience to satisfy the debt, even if he has been absolved from payment by judicial judgement. Whether he is bound to pay expenses incurred if he owes the debt, though he has been absolved, depends upon whether he has used unjust means or not. But whether or not he has used unjust means, if he has been absolved because of a defect in proving the case, not because of unjust means, he is not bound to pay expenses.

LAWYERS

A lawyer is one who takes up defense of a judicial case of a second party. A lawyer can also protect the cause of one initiating a judicial process. With regard to knowledge and due diligence, a lawyer's moral obligations are the same as those of a judge. If he brings harm to his client because of ignorance or lack of due care, he is bound to restitution unless the client retained him fully cognizant of the situation.

In civil cases, a lawyer must not defend a case which he knows to be certainly unjust. He can take cases which are doubtful, even those whose probability is less. Often cases which appear less probable at the beginning become more probable during the course of a judicial process. A lawyer who during a judicial process becomes certain that his client's case is unjust is morally bound to exit the case. Otherwise, he brings injury to an innocent party. If he continues the case at the insistence of his client, he is bound to restitution. A lawyer is bound to use only just means to defend his client. He may hide those matters which impede his case since he does not deceive, but merely permits the deception. A lawyer who succeeds by unjust means, for example by bringing forth false or abrogated laws, by producing false witnesses, or by producing false documents is bound to repair damage done. This is true whether he does so on his own initiative or that of his client. Out of charity he may advise the other party concerning circumstances which could help his case, but of which the other party is ignorant or has neglected. He is not bound by justice to do so. In criminal cases, he may defend someone whom he certainly knows to be guilty, but he may not use fraud, deception, or other immoral means. An accused is not held to punishment unless and until convicted. Therefore, a lawyer may defend rights of the client, that is he may impede either proof of a case or certain demonstration of a crime. A lawyer may not use false documents. Even if his client's guilt is doubtful, in using false documents he offends against justice and truthfulness. If his client's right is certain and he substitutes for documents which have been lost, he offends against veracity, but not against justice.

A lawyer is bound to examine his client concerning the case and to advise him concerning the injustice, the certitude, or the probability of he case. The lawyer is duty-bound to declare the state of a case if the situation demands it or if the situation notably changes, lest there be undue costs. If the lawyer omits this advise with grave culpability, he is bound to restitution for any harm which a client has incurred. If a lawyer fails to warn his client that a case is doubtful and a client would not have prosecuted a case had he known, a lawyer is held to restitution. A lawyer is held to at least ordinary industry not only that he win the case, but that he do so promptly. If harm arises to the client because of negligence, the lawyer is bound to restitution. A lawyer may not help his client's opponent by communicating depositions of witness or by other acts. He may not manifest his client's secrets.

A lawyer may receive payment for his work, but he may not demand exorbitant fees. There is a serious problem in contemporary society concerning the propriety of applying business billing practices to the legal professions. If such fees are taxed by the state, a lawyer himself, not a client, is bound to pay taxes on the stipend. Such tax laws may however be penal laws. Such taxes may be considered in establishing a fee. Only if tax laws were to bind in commutative justice must the lawyer pay restitution. From charity, a lawyer is bound to take some cases of the poor free of charge, *pro bono.* To those in extreme necessity, he is seriously bound even with grave inconvenience to himself, to those in serious difficulty, he is seriously bound to help, but not with grave inconvenience to himself, and to those who are in ordinary need, he is bound to help if he can conveniently do so. To fulfill this obligation, it is sufficient that he spend some of his free time. To refuse to serve those who ask is an offense against charity if the lawyer foresees that grave harm will come to them because of his refusal.

WITNESSES

A witness is a suitable person who is chosen to build faith in a case. Civil law determines who can be a witness. A witness must know the facts about which he testifies. Ordinarily, a witness is thought to know only those matters which he has perceived by his senses. In civil and often in criminal cases, a witness may be obliged to take an oath to speak only the truth and the whole truth. A witness is not morally bound to testify unless he is asked by a legitimate judge who has jurisdiction.

No moral obligation exists to offer testimony voluntarily except in two cases: (1) from legal justice one is bound to testify in case of grave danger to the state, even with grave inconvenience to the witness himself; (2) from charity a witness is bound to testify to avert grave harm to another without grave inconvenience to himself. When a situation concerns merely punishment, no one is bound to offer testimony voluntarily since no punishment or lesser punishments bring about grave harm to the state. A witness who knows that another has committed a crime is not morally bound to produce a culprit in order to free an innocent party. The malefactor is not an unjust cause of condemnation of the innocent. When a witness is officially asked by legitimate authority to testify, he is ordinarily morally bound to do so. This obligation is grave, but not in cases of light matter.

A witness is seriously morally bound by legal justice to respond to questions according to his conscience unless he is legitimately excused. A witness who presents false testimony offends against the virtue of veracity by lying, against the virtue of religion, if he has taken an oath, and against commutative justice, if he brings damage to another. Lying differs from hiding the truth. He who hides what he knows to be true does bring positive harm to another, but only impedes an investigation. In such a case, a witness does not offend against commutative justice, unless he is bound to testify by office or contract. If a witness is the cause of a guilty man going free or a debtor not paying a just debt, neither the judge nor the witness is held to restitution.

A witness is validly excused from moral obligation to testify in the following cases. (1) A confessor may not testify from knowledge he has received in the confessional (there is no case in which this does not bind). (2) He who possesses knowledge by natural or entrusted secrecy has an obligation not to testify except in cases in which the obligation of secrecy no longer binds. (3) He who reasonably fears grave harm to himself unless harm to the state or an individual which would follow from his denial to testify would be notably more significant is not obliged to testify. (4) No one is bound to testify against his relatives unless to avoid grave public harm. Such testimony is regarded as grave inconvenience. (5) He who came to the knowledge through immoral means, for example by reading others' mail or through force or fraud, is excused from testimony. (6) He who is not certain concerning his testimony, for example knowledge received from an unworthy source, is not bound to testify. (7) He who knows that the accused has not acted against his conscience, for example has used the principles concerning occult compensation, can but need not testify. The judge is thought to be inquiring concerning the existence of a crime. In civil cases which concern juridical guilt, the witness ought to testify even if he knows that the accused is in good conscience. (8) A sole witness need not testify. The accused should not be condemned on the authority of one witness, unless other testimony or other indications proving guilt are present. In all cases where a witness has cause to hide the truth, he may say that "he does not know." Such statements are broad mental reservations.

One who has given false testimony is bound to revoke it. If he has given materially false or erroneous testimony, if a revocation is useful to another, and if one could recall the testimony without grave harm to himself, he should revoke his testimony. One who has knowingly and willingly given false testimony should revoke his testimony when it is useful to another and he can do so without graver harm coming to himself than has arisen to the accused because of his false testimony. If both his life and the life of the accused are endangered, a witness is bound to revoke his testimony. In addition, a witness giving false testimony is bound to restitution under three conditions: (1) he was the efficacious cause of harm to the accused by reason of his false testimony; (2) he gave false testimony knowingly; or (3) he gave false testimony in good faith but has not revoked it when he could have done so, and the revocation would have been useful to the accused.

MEDICAL ETHICS

During the past century biological research has progressed more than in the previous history of mankind, One can hardly read a newspaper without noting some advance in genetic research or other biological theory. Medicine has been influenced by such research and the practice of medicine has changed enormously. Surgical interventions which once were mere dreams are today common medical practice. Organ or joint replacement is an often recommended operation. Even a visit to the family doctor has changed so that blood analysis has become the common basis for medical recommendations. The advances in research and medical practice has lead to greater expectations for healthcare among the population of the western world. Who should receive what treatment has become a common debate. As a result of these expectations and the attendant costs, payment for medical care has become a customary political theme. Ethical considerations concerning medical matters have become more necessary and difficult than previously. Unfortunately, no social consensus exists over ethical system and the principles following from such systems. Over matters such as stem-cell research and *in vitro* fertilization, social utilitarianism or a natural law ethics can come to entirely different ethical conclusions. Often ethical committees in hospitals over policy and help to be recommended to families in individual cases become hamstrung over the variance of ethical view. At times, this situation has led to replacement of ethical principle with legal considerations. Further, specialized knowledge in science and medical practice has made moral judgement by ethicists more difficult. Consultation between specialists has become necessary to render an ethical opinion or judgement.

For all these reasons and many more which will go unmentioned, derivation of general moral principle for contemporary medical personnel is rendered difficult. The above situation makes it imperative to apply conventional moral principle to a vastly altered situation. Some ethical considerations concerning healthcare have already been given to patient and professional alike. Specific ethical considerations over medical procedures and contemporary techniques and research must be left to specialists. Nevertheless, general ethical principles and their applications can help doctor, nurse, and other healthcare personnel alike.

Moral obligations to knowledge necessary for practice of their professions and to due diligence is the same for medical personnel as for judges and lawyers. Obligations to help the poor *pro bono* are likewise similar to those of lawyers. A physician who is not paid a stipend for his care is morally bound to care for a patient from charity, but not from justice. A physician commits a grave moral offense if he refuses to help a seriously sick person when no other physician is present and he may do so without serious inconvenience to himself. A physician who agrees to care for a patient is held by commutative justice by tacit agreement to help the infirm by the better and more certain methods, if he can. He may not desert the patient, even if a patient has a contagious disease, unless someone else can be found to care for the patient. He is bound to help a patient during the night unless he is certain that no harm will come to the patient by delay. He is also morally bound to help a patient during times of epidemic and contagious disease.

A physician is morally obliged to use the remedy which he believes safer. He must prefer a certain treatment over a doubtful one. If none is certain, he is morally bound to use the more probable since he must treat a patient in the better manner. If the case is desperate and only a doubtful remedy is at hand which can be helpful and can do no harm, the physician can and must use it since he is morally bound to help a patient in the best way he can. If a case of a sick person is desperate and only a doubtful means is at hand which could cure the illness, but might lead to death, the physician may use the remedy, especially if he believes the possibility of help is probable. In such cases, he should seek consent of the patient. When a patient's situation is grave, a physician may offer treatments which are painful or cause ancillary damage, even if such medications are useless in some cases. He must seek the permission of the patient if possible. That being impossible, the permission of close relatives should be sought. The physician should avoid great expense. If the patient is disturbed that no treatment is being prescribed, prescriptiom of medication can be useful and consent of the patient may be presumed.

It is never morally allowable to use an experimental treatment with grave danger to health or death, not even with consent of the patient. It is *in se* evil to expose another's life to danger. Human beings do not have dominion over their own lives. According to the second principle of the double effect, it is immoral to do evil so that good can come about. Therefore, it is immoral to expose oneself to danger of death to help future generations. It is especially odious to use the poor or infants as subjects for experimental treatments. A patient may expose himself to grave danger to his life to remove notable or dangerous inconvenience. Of course, a patient may expose himself to light harm if such harm can easily be repaired. It is immoral to participate in immoral operations such as direct abortion, sterilization, and craniotomy. One may not use drugs to the extent that it injures health or brings death. A physician may not give medical advice which directly opposes the virtue of chastity.

The natural law dictates that a physician advise a patient when the patient is in proximate danger of death, if such advice is necessary to avoiding grave harm to the patient. Only thus may a dying person put his affairs in order. A physician may fulfill this obligation himself or through another. If others can not or will not perform this function, or if a patient will not believe them, a physician must perform this task himself. If a physician is morally certain that a patient's temporal affairs are in order, he is excused from this duty. Physicians are held to professional secrecy concerning matters which they learn from a patient in the course of treatment.

A physician is held to avoid useless expenses. This is true even if the patient is not paying himself, but through a third party, for example government or health insurance. A physician may not bring in specialists when they are unnecessary. He may not multiply visits without necessity or demand exorbitant fees or appointments. He should not protract the care of a patient beyond what is appropriate, or prescribe useless or superfluous medicines. A physician may not demand more than the commonly accepted fee. A physician who agrees to participate in treating common infirmities implicitly agrees to this fee. Like the just price, the range of ordinary physician's fee is determined by local conditions. When a physician or surgeon performs extraordinary services which demand expert knowledge, and agreement with a patient over the fee has not been reached prior to the operation, the physician may not demand whatever fee he pleases. He must charge the fee to which the patient has implicitly agreed. A patient has implicitly agreed to a fee reached according to the difficulty of the procedure and the degree of labor. This fee should be proportional to fees which other learned professionals charge for their services from persons of the same financial means in a given area. The same ethical principles concerning fee payment apply *mutatis mutandis* to third-party payment for medical care. A serious question over the appropriateness of applying business principles to the medical profession, both on the part of professionals and third party payers, exists today. When professions become businesses and acquisition of money is placed ahead of or on a par with patient or client care, professions as professions become degraded.

READINGS

1. John Paul II, *Fides et Ratio* 1–7
   a. http://w2.vatican.va/content/john-paul-ii/en/encyclicals/documents/hf_jp-ii_enc_14091998_fides-et-ratio.html
2. Augustine of Hippo, *De ordine* II,v,16; II,9,27; *De beata uita* IV,35; ; *De uera religione* XXIV,45.
3. Anselm of Canterbury, *Proslogion* 2–4
4. Thomas Aquinas, Excerpts from *Summa contra Gentiles* I. (Readings on faith and reason).
5. Plato, *Republic* VII; *Symposium* 203a–2011b.
   a. https://www.gutenberg.org/files/1600/1600-h/1600-h.htm
6. Augustine of Hippo, *De libero arbitrio* I,vi, 14- xi, 21–22.
7. Thomas Aquinas, *Summa theologiae* I, q.79, art.14; q. 82, art. 1–2; q. 83, art. 1; I–II, art.1; art. 3; art. 5; art. 8.
8. Thomas Aquinas, *De Veritate*, quest. 17 Conscience, art. 1–5; quest. 22,art.5; quest. 24, art. 1.
9. Thomas Aquinas, Treatise on Law, *Summa theologiae* II–I, quest. 90–94
10. Thomas Aquinas, *Summa Theologiae* II–I, quest. 1–5.
11. E. Gilson, *The Christian Philosophy of Thomas Aquinas*, pp. 251–256.
12. V. Bourke, *Ethics*, chapter 3. (Excerpts)
13. G. Grisez, *Moral Philosophy*. (on human acts)
14. Aristotle, *Nichomachean Ethics* I,II,X. (Only the parts on happiness)
15. Søren Kierkegaard, *Leap of Faith*,
16. A MacIntyre, *Beyond Virtue* (excerpts)

Cases—Midterm

DIRECTIONS: Please tear out the following pages and turn in answers to the cases as you normally would.

1. A man is driving a car which knows to have faulty tires. He is driving fairly fast when one of the tires blows out. Unable to control the vehicle, he swerves off the road and injures a pedestrian seriously. Is the driver responsible for this injury? Why?

2. An engineer is directing the construction of a bridge when the contractor, his ultimate boss, decides to cheat on the specifications for the bridge and to use single strength spans, instead of the double strength ones called for in the plans. Before the actual time of construction, the contractor is temporarily called away and the engineer is placed in charge. He realizes that the blueprint (which calls for the double strength spans) should be followed, but also realizes that he will lose his job if he does not follow the orders of the contractor. He is fifty years old, has worked all his life with this company, and would pay dearly if he left it. He has two daughters and a son in or near university age. The engineer decides to use the single strength spans. How would you judge his responsibility for this act?

3. Wade Boggs, a famous baseball player, returns home one night after a rough road trip to find his wife in bed with her lover. In a fit of anger, Mr. Boggs takes his hunting rifle from the closet, kills the lover, and injures his wife. How would you judge his responsibility and why?

4. An officer is pursuing a known, though not convicted, drug dealer through the streets of Philadelphia. At a crucial point in the chase, the officer opens fire on the dealer as the only means at his disposal to stop him. On a nearby porch, two young children are playing bridge. Two stray bullets from the officer's gun hit the children, killing one and maiming the other. How would you go about judging the morality of the officer's actions?

5. Mary Ann VanDeweghe has just passed her driving test. She is driving quite carefully on the icy road, but for the first time. She hits a patch of ice and jams on the brakes to avoid hitting a pedestrian. Unfortunately, she does not know that jamming on the brakes on ice is worse than useless. She hits the pedestrian and he injures his right hand severely so that he is unable to deal cards anymore (he is a dealer at the Atlantic City Casinos). How responsible is Mary Ann and why?

6. Mary Ann, after having learned her lesson from this driving experience, must drive her father to his doctor's appointment. The roads are icy again. She now knows that she should not slam on the brakes on ice, but should pump them patiently. Clarence Jass, a star basketball player at a local university, has just, gotten out of. ethics class. He steps off the curb, and Mary Ann, as a reflex action, slams on the brakes, but skids on the ice and runs into Clarence. He sustains an injury which will preclude his playing on the team that year and the school thus may lose their annual NCAA bid. What is Mary Ann's responsibility in this case and why?

7. John Brecht attends a party for his friend Ted. Quite frankly, John has difficulty holding his alcohol and can not have more than one normal-sized drink. Jim, trying to be a good host, is spiking the drinks, but John does not know it. He becomes drunk after his usual one drink, gets into his car, and is involved in an accident. Whom would you hold responsible and why?

8. Dr. Martin Kramer examined John Murphy and found that he was in need of medicine for his pancreas. John was poor and could not afford the medicine, so Dr. Kramer gave John some samples which were given him by

a pharmaceutical salesman. As it turned out, the medicine was mislabeled and it aggravated John's condition. What responsibility does Dr. Kramer have?

9. Peter Weglarski started drinking at the age of fifteen and is now a heavy drinker, if not an alcoholic. When he is sober, he treats his wife and family well; however, when he has been drinking, he often beats them. Due to his drinking, he has trouble keeping a steady job. Finally, Peter comes to his senses and decides to give up drinking. He tries quite hard, but finds it impossible not to have a drink once in a while. Occasionally, he reverts to his old habits, though he returns to his sober ways and regrets his activities while drinking. What is his responsibility for his actions under the influence of alcohol and why?

10. A major world power has problems with its citizens being terrorized at foreign airports. This major power has attempted to work with its allies and through other diplomatic channels to end the terrorism, but to no avail. As a last resort, the major power bombs the training area of the terrorists, hoping to end the terrorist activities. During the attack, innocent civilians are killed or injured. The major power knows that this is likely to happen. How would you judge the morality of this act?

11. The neighbor of a small country has had a major nuclear incident near its borders. As a result, this small nation has become aware of environmental pollution and has taken means to protect its atmosphere. One of the means is to prohibit importation of automobiles that do not meet its emission control standards. This nation requires use of platinum in its catalytic converters. A larger industrial nation refuses to use platinum, claiming that the metal is only available through South Africa and that purchase of platinum from that source indirectly supports apartheid. The larger nations puts pressure on the smaller one to import their automobiles despite their poorer converters and even threatens to block the entry of the smaller nation into the Common Market, an entry which is vital for the smaller nation's economic well-being. How would you evaluate the morality of these actions.

12. Why are children not held responsible for actions for which their parents would be held fully responsible? For what are children responsible?

13. A child is born blind and crippled. The physician gives the child poison to remove the heavy burden of raising such a child from the parents and to prevent the child from suffering greatly. How would you evaluate the morality of such an act?

14. A sailor in charge of a lifeboat has a full boatload of passengers. He knows that an attempt to take any more passengers into the lifeboat would endanger the lives of those already on the boat. He deliberately rows away from several people in the freezing water of the North Atlantic. How would you evaluate the morality of his actions?

15. The Thetis submarine was trapped six kilometers under the freezing water of the North Atlantic. Seven of the sailors, including Captain O'Hara, asked that they be allowed to serve as buoys to guide the rescuers to the sunken British submarine. If a person opened the outer hatch before drowning, his body with the notation of the exact position of the submarine would float to the surface and guide the rescue attempt. Captain O'Hara was the first to go and he got through. The next three were drowned before they reached the outside hatch. How would you evaluate this case?

16. Two people are trapped in the debris of a hotel, destroyed by a tornado. One finds that, if he pushes up on the beam pinning him down, he can struggle free. However, in moving the beam, he would bring half of the ceiling crashing down on his companion (who would have difficulty escaping in any event) thereby killing him. How would you evaluate this act?

17. A large hotel is on fire. All means of escape are cut off and the fire is raging. A number of people jump from the windows with the practical certainty that they are jumping to their death. How would you judge their responsibility for their actions? If responsible, how would you judge the morality of the actions?

18. A pregnant woman suffers from a serious ailment which directly threatens her life. The ailment is not caused by the pregnancy, though it is aggravated by it. The physician Knows of only one medicine which will cure her ailment and avert her death. The medicine will result in the death of the unborn child. How would you advise the physician?

19. Ann, the mother of five small children, is badly burned in an oilstove explosion and brought to the hospital. The physicians find that she is pregnant with twins. They tell Ann (1) that she could not stand the strain of childbirth in her weakened condition; (2) that the babies will not be normal; (3) that the babies may be born dead. Their birth may even cause her own death. The physicians advise her to have the babies taken from her. She has five children at home. How would you judge this advice?

20. An officer flying a plane sees, through an opening in the clouds, an enemy aircraft carrier on its way to attack the fleet. His position is such that he can not launch a missile effectively against the carrier. He deliberately dives out of the clouds and rams the carrier for the purpose of putting it out of commission. He succeeds, but is killed instantly. Assuming that this war is justified, how would you judge his actions?

21. How would you judge the morality of the World War II Kamikazi pilots?

22. A cruiseship is sailing the Greek islands. In the hold, an automobile breaks loose from its moorings and crashes through the side of the ship. Water rushes in and threatens to sink the ship. The captain orders the bulkheads in that part of the ship secured, although he knows that a number of the crew will be drowned. How would you judge this case?

23. During World War II, the Westbahnhof in Vienna was the central train route east and west for supplies for the German troops. When it became feasible in 1944, the allies bombed that train station, though it was in the heart of Vienna. The Barmherzige Schwestern had a hospital in the area; the general vicinity was residential. Due to the inaccuracy of bombing techniques at that time, it was virtually certain that many non-combatants would be killed. How would you judge the morality of this bombing?

24. During World War II, the allies saturation bombed the German city of Dresden. It is famous only for its porcelain. The purpose of the bombing was to frighten the German populace into surrender, thereby saving many allied (and perhaps German) lives. How would you judge the morality of this act?

25. How would you judge the morality of the bombing of Hiroshima and Nagasaki?

26. How would you judge the morality of terrorist bombing?

www.ingramcontent.com/pod-product-compliance
Ingram Content Group UK Ltd.
Pitfield, Milton Keynes, MK11 3LW, UK
UKHW051508290926
15471UKWH00008B/1494

9 781524 922870